Ordinary People and Ex...

Many people come to analysis appearing quite "ordinary" on the surface. However, once below that surface, we often come into contact with something quite unexpected: "extra-ordinary protections" created to keep at bay any awareness of deeply traumatic happenings occurring at some point in life.

Judith Mitrani investigates the development and the function of these protections, allowing the reader to witness the evolution of the process of transformation, wherein defensiveness steadily mutates into communication. She lucidly and artfully weaves detailed clinical observations with a variety of analytic concepts, and her original notions – including "unmentalized experience" and its expression in enactments; "adhesive pseudo-object relations" and the ways in which this contrasts and compares with normal and narcissistic object relations – provide valuable tools for understanding the infantile transference/countertransference and for the refinement of our technique with primitive mental states.

Ordinary People and Extra-Ordinary Protections will prove stimulating and accessible in its style and substance to a broad analytic readership, from the serious student of psychoanalysis to the most seasoned professional.

Judith L. Mitrani is a Training and Supervising Analyst at both The Psychoanalytic Center of California and the Los Angeles Institute and Society for Psychoanalytic Studies. She is the author of *A Framework for the Imaginary: Clinical Explorations in Primitive States of Being*, and the co-editor (with Dr. Theodore Mitrani) of the book *Encounters with Autistic States: A Memorial Tribute to Frances Tustin*, and numerous published papers.

THE NEW LIBRARY OF PSYCHOANALYSIS

The New Library of Psychoanalysis was launched in 1987 in association with the Institute of Psycho-Analysis, London. Its purpose is to facilitate a greater and more widespread appreciation of what psychoanalysis is really about and to provide a forum for increasing mutual understanding between psychoanalysts and those working in other disciplines such as history, linguistics, literature, medicine, philosophy, psychology and the social sciences. It is intended that the titles selected for publication in the series should deepen and develop psycho-analytic thinking and technique, contribute to psychoanalysis from outside, or contribute to other disciplines from a psychoanalytical perspective.

The Institute, together with the British Psycho-Analytical Society, runs a low-fee psychoanalytic clinic, organises lectures and scientific events concerned with psychoanalysis and publishes the *International Journal of Psycho-Analysis*. It also runs the only UK training course in psychoanalysis which leads to member-ship of the International Psychoanalytical Association – the body which preserves internationally agreed standards of training, of professional entry, and of professional ethics and practice for psychoanalysis as initiated and developed by Sigmund Freud. Distinguished members of the Institute have included Michael Balint, Wilfred Bion, Ronald Fairbairn, Anna Freud, Ernest Jones, Melanie Klein, John Rickman and Donald Winnicott.

Volumes 1–11 in the series were prepared under the general editorship of David Tuckett. Volumes 12–39 appeared under the general editorship of Elizabeth Bott Spillius. Subsequent volumes are under the general editorship of Susan Budd. Ronald Britton, Eglé Laufer, Donald Campbell, Michael Parsons, Rosine Jozef Perelberg, David Taylor and Stephen Grosz have acted as associate editors for various periods.

ALSO IN THIS SERIES

THE NEW LIBRARY OF PSYCHOANALYSIS
40

Ordinary People and Extra-Ordinary Protections

A POST-KLEINIAN APPROACH TO THE TREATMENT OF PRIMITIVE MENTAL STATES

JUDITH L. MITRANI

BRUNNER-ROUTLEDGE
ALERE FLAMMAM
Taylor & Francis Group

First published 2001
by Brunner-Routledge
27 Church Road, Hove, East Sussex BN3 2FA

Simultaneously published in the USA and Canada
by Taylor & Francis Inc.
325 Chestnut Street, Philadelphia PA 19106

Brunner-Routledge is an imprint of the Taylor & Francis Group

© 2001 Judith L. Mitrani

Typeset in Bembo by Keystroke, Jacaranda Lodge, Wolverhampton
Printed and bound in Great Britain by TJ International Ltd, Padstow,
Cornwall

British Library Cataloguing in Publication Data
A catalogue record for this book is available from the British Library

Library of Congress Cataloging in Publication Data
Mitrani, Judith L.
Ordinary people and extraordinary protections : a post-Kleinian approach to
the treatment of primitive mental states / Judith L. Mitrani.
p.   cm. — (New library of psychoanalysis ; 40)
Includes bibliographical references and index.
1. Psychoanalysis. I. Title. II. Series.
BF173 .M57 2001
150.19′5—dc21   00-062804

ISBN 0–415–24164–2 (hbk)
ISBN 0–415–24165–0 (pbk)

Contents

Foreword

As we begin a new century and millennium, we are able to discern significant trends appearing in the geopolitics of psychoanalysis around the world. In England and the United States, in particular, we find the following significant developments: the Kleinian school seems now to be predominant in England, and its proponents, now third-generation Kleinians, often called "contemporary" or "post-Kleinians," seem to have extended and modified Klein's ideas while blending them with some of the concepts of Bion, principally his idea of the "container and the contained," which represents the contemporary Kleinian entry into intersubjectivity. What continues to be missing from the contemporary Kleinian oeuvre are integrations with the vast body of work of Fairbairn, Winnicott, Tustin, Bowlby, and other contributors from the Independent School.

Meanwhile, in the United States, first Relationism, Self Psychology (arguably an offspring of the Independent School), and then varying indigenous schools of Intersubjectivity all came on the scene to compete with a weary and aging Ego Psychology. In the midst of this "catastrophic change" there began slowly to develop an interest and then formal training in object relations, Klein, and Bion, chiefly on the West coast. What is of interest geopolitically in this last case is that many of these new "Kleinians" became steeped not only in Bion but also in Winnicott and Tustin, thereby forging integrative bridges between these bodies of work that had not yet been achieved in London.

The recent prolific contributions of Dr. Judith Mitrani belong in this new Americanized integration of Klein, Bion, Bick, and Meltzer on one hand, and Winnicott and Tustin in particular, on the other. Out of that amalgam emerges a significantly new view of very early object relations. In her writings Dr. Mitrani shows a crisp, articulate, and versatile grasp of the extraordinary measures those who have had early misadventures with objects resort to in order to survive. The very title of her work bespeaks the close attention she pays to the unique aspects that lie hidden in the ordinary analysand that psychoanalysis allows to surface and be actualized, as well as the extraordinary measures of defense which I just mentioned. All of this is formatted in her own unique conceptions of inter-subjectivity, the current lingua franca of psychoanalytic thinking and practice on both sides of the Atlantic about what is thought to go on and what really goes on between analysand and analyst. In other words, intersubjectivity, especially when viewed through the lens of the container and the contained, becomes the current way of understanding the mutuality of transference and countertransference. Much of Dr. Mitrani's present work clusters around this interchange.

Dr. Mitrani's views on intersubjectivity clearly fall within the views of the Bion-inspired contemporary Kleinians who regard the analyst's counter-subjectivity as an invaluable psychoanalytic instrument in understanding the analysand but not one to be shared with them. She beautifully reveals how she works with her counter-subjectivity, especially in Chapter 5.

One of the subjects she explicates is that of adhesive identification. The concept was originally coined by Esther Bick and then elaborated upon by Donald Meltzer, both of whom had apparently found its presence in autistic children and then applied it also to normal development. What was unique about this new idea was that it challenged the Kleinian notion that the paranoid-schizoid position was inchoate. Bick and Meltzer, as well as Winnicott and some classical analysts, argued that an inchoate infantile state exists which can be characterized by non-integration, and it is associated with an autosensual orientation to the container-object especially oriented in terms of a skin-to-skin experience so that the infant can develop its own sense of a skin boundary frontier and thereby be able to differentiate inside from outside.

Thus, adhesive identification would be the route whereby the infant apposes its own skin to mother's skin, experiences the interaction and the differentiation, enhances its experience of its own autosensuality, and identifies with these adhesive moments of contact. Once the infant has developed this autosensual format, then inside can be differentiated from outside and psyche can be differentiated from soma. Now is the time for projective identification and introjective identification to come online and the rest of the paranoid-schizoid defenses to appear, including disintegration as opposed to its antecedent, unintegration.

Other contributors, such as Didier Anzieu, Jacques Lacan, and Thomas Ogden, have speculated about the phenomenology of this inchoate autosensual position. It has also been characterized as the percept- or sensation-dominated stage. Dr. Mitrani's views of it are unique in their own right. Utmostly, she emphasizes that we may all too frequently encounter these "extra-ordinary" defenses clinically as "adhesive pseudo-object relations" and misunderstand them as narcissistic resistances rather than as last-ditch defenses against catastrophic anxiety and/or nameless dread. She defines this form of pseudo-object relations as ". . . an asymbolic aberration of normal development, rooted in traumatic experiences of extreme privation occurring *in utero* and/or in early infancy. This way of 'being' pre-maturely interrupts the necessary development of and trust in a 'rhythm of safety' . . . between mother and infant, resulting in a crippling of the emerging elemental state of subjectivity and the gradual development of true objectivity." She is articulate in describing the survival function of Bick's "second skin" phenomenon as a desperate coping technique.

The concept of adhesive identification generally and the second skin particularly is associated with another theme that Dr. Mitrani has focused on, that of "unmentalized experience." For instance the second skin, one example of which is motoric hyperactivity, will be invoked by the subject in order to prevent the inexorable pulsion toward mentalization or comprehension, either in infancy or in psychoanalysis, if the consequences of realizing the truth of it would augur disaster. Thus, unmentalized experience would designate both the raw proto-thoughts which have to be thought about to become true thoughts and feelings (corresponding to Bion's beta elements or noumena) and the archaic defenses against their becoming realized. In its more sophisticated form it is something like a pathological organization or psychic retreat.

Dr. Mitrani's view of introjective and projective processes also deserves mention. In her poignant depiction of the allegory of the "Flying Dutchman" in Chapter 4, she expands on Bion's idea of "reverie" and "container/contained" to suggest that not only must the analysand be permitted to project into the analyst; the analyst must correspondingly introject those aspects of the analysand's internal world that are relevant at the moment. Ultimately, if all goes well, the analysand will be able to introject the successful experience of being absorbed (contained) without retribution for his/her projections.

There are many additional themes that Dr. Mitrani elegantly depicts and expands upon, such as Bion's "reverence and awe," Winnicott's "fear of breakdown," Tustin's "autistic maneuvers," Steiner's "analyst- and patient-centred interpretations," and others which I can only mention here so as to whet the reader's appetite for an unusual feast of reading.

James S. Grotstein

Acknowledgements

First, I would like to thank all those colleagues and friends who have, over a period of many years, provided me with the encouragement and support essential to the writing of this book. As an editor, Dr. Susan Budd went far beyond the call of duty with her dedication, generosity, kindness, and her sensitive comments. She most certainly has played a vital role in bringing my work to press. As always, my husband and colleague, Dr. Theodore Mitrani, helped me to focus and refine the expression of my ideas, and his keen observations are embedded in and lend clarity to every chapter of this book. Finally, I wish to express my gratitude to my patients, students and supervisees whose material appears on these pages, as well as all those others who participated actively in the evolution and clarification of my thinking.

Permissions

The author would like to thank the following for permission to quote extracts from their work:

Sigmund Freud © Copyrights, The Institute of Psycho-Analysis and The Hogarth Press for permission to quote from THE STANDARD EDITION OF THE COMPLETE PSYCHOLOGICAL WORKS OF SIGMUND FREUD translated and edited by James Strachey.

From THE PROPHET by Kahlil Gibran. Copyright © 1923 by Kahlil Gibran and renewed 1951 by Administrators C T A of Kahlil Gibran Estate and Mary G Gibran. Reprinted by permission of Alfred A Knopf, a Division of Random House Inc.

ALL THIS USELESS BEAUTY (COSTELLO)
© 1992 Sideways Songs administered by PLANGENT VISIONS MUSIC LIMITED.

For the extract from *Celestial Navigations* by Anne Tyler. Published by Knopf (Berkeley paperback edition). Reprinted by the permission of Russell & Volkening as agents for the author. Copyright © 1974 by Anne Tyler.

For extracts from "Las Pas" and "Palme" by Paul Valéry as published in (1969 paperback edition) *The Penguin Book of French Verse – 4: The Twentieth Century*, introduced and edited by Anthony Hartley. Copyright © Editions GALLIMARD.

Introduction

Yes we are psychoanalysts, and of course you may join us, but
you know, we're just barmy people treating barmy people!
Frances Tustin (1984)

This book is about ordinary people – analysts and patients – who share a common
humanity consisting of strength and frailty, triumph and failure, joy and tragedy,
agony and ecstasy. We've each suffered and avoided experience, behaved with
both dignity and hubris, been courageous and cowardly, stupid and wise. We have,
at times, been lost and have also had the good fortune to be found, we've been
seen as well as overlooked, often dropped and sometimes up-lifted.

Perhaps it is our capacity for what Tustin called "ordinary being" – rather
than an illusion of omnipotence – that psychoanalysis may help us to develop.
At its best, psychoanalysis encourages us to turn toward human beings. It enables
us to process our sensory experience in relationships with other people, by the
evolution of expressive activities, and by percepts and concepts that enable us to
live in the ordinary world.

Many people come to analysis appearing quite ordinary on the surface. They
are often depressed or anxious, discontented with their lives, their relationships,
or their work. However, when we scratch that surface we often find something
quite unexpected: extra-ordinary protections that keep at bay the awareness of
extra-ordinary happenings occurring at some point in life when the awareness
of such happenings would have been overwhelming, even life-threatening.
Survival is a part of human nature and our instincts (however misguided) are
directed toward this elemental goal, perhaps spurred on by a preconception of
some thing or some one to live for.

While writing and re-writing this book, I have had the opportunity to give
considerable thought to my basic philosophy of human nature, to the particular
way I work, and to whom and what have influenced that philosophy and therefore
my way of working in analysis. Although I am American, my early training was

1

rooted in Great Britain. As a beginning student, studying psychology at the University of California, I was introduced to the work of Melanie Klein by a professor of literature who sought to help students to construct the basis for a deeper understanding of the dark writings of Tolstoy, Dostoyevsky, Mary Shelley, Keats, Plath, Sexton and others.

My first analysis, although perhaps classical by London standards, was anything but dogmatic and gave me the leeway to know what I thought. A similarly rigorous yet unorthodox graduate education allowed me to extend my reading of the work of Klein, Bion, Bick, and Winnicott as a major aspect of my Master's and doctoral studies, while my early work with patients and supervisors helped me to learn from my experiences. During this period I was also introduced first to the work of Frances Tustin and eventually to Mrs. Tustin herself. Her subsequent mentorship inspired and fostered an intensive period of dissertation writing, which in turn afforded me the time to integrate my academic and clinical work and to begin to formulate my ideas about what I call "unmentalized experience."

A subsequent personal and eventful meeting with Donald Meltzer, regarding the notions set forth in my dissertation, encouraged me to greatly expand and deepen my clinical experience. I proceeded to take on a considerable number of seriously troubled patients from whom I learned much, and I grew rich in experience early on in my analytic training within a small independent institute founded by a group of analysts most of whom had been analyzed or supervised by Bion in Los Angeles. Eventually I embarked on a second analysis with a former analysand of Dr. Bion's. Far from being indoctrinated by this "Kleinian" analyst, I was further encouraged by her to find and to have my own mind, to articulate and publish my own thoughts. Throughout these pages I will attempt to make these thoughts and their evolution as explicit as I possibly can.

However, as tempting as it might be for the reader to mistake this book for a guide to analytic practice, it is solely intended as an example of *how one analyst works*, for whatever that is worth! Furthermore, the themes that run through these chapters have developed (not unlike Kleinian theory itself) out of the immediate clinical experience and are frequently presented in that context. The struggle to understand and to give meaning to experience is engaged in by analyst and analysand, and each bit of understanding, each interpretation is unique to that clinical moment. As Bion once said:

No one can tell you more than you know yourself. With different people, different situations arise; even with the same person – today isn't the same as yesterday . . . analysis is not static. Analytic theories are quite useful for about three sessions – you know nothing about the patient and therefore have to fall back on theory. After that the answers are on the couch or in the chair, and in what you hear and see for yourself.

(1975, pp. 8–9)

Perhaps some of what is written here may serve to help other therapists to get beyond the first "three sessions," to encourage them to look and listen, and to provide some inspiration to develop and to use their own language to communicate what they "see and hear" to their own patients and their colleagues. Additionally, I hope to underscore our ordinary-ness: "We are just barmy people treating barmy people."

Chapter 1 focuses on the value of detecting and further fostering the emergence of the earliest infantile aspects of the patient from the beginning of the treatment through direct and rigorous interpretation of the transference. This way of setting the "framework" for the analytic work places the emphasis on what Bion called "being" analysis rather than explaining "about" analysis, and offers the patient an early sense of being followed rather than being led, of being under-stood by the analyst rather than having to under-stand the analyst. Throughout the clinical material presented I touch upon some defensive maneuvers that patients often employ against an awareness of the transference and of psychic reality, including the phantasies of splitting, projection, and displacement as well as some more primitive autosensual forms of defense that come under the heading of what Esther Bick called "adhesive identification" (1968).

In Chapter 2, I outline the evolution of Bick's (1968) theory of adhesive identification, which provided the foundation for Tustin's understanding of the extra-ordinary proto-mental protections employed not only by autistic children but by "ordinary" adults seen in analytic practice. I conclude this chapter with the introduction of what I have termed *adhesive pseudo-object-relations*, comparing and contrasting this new model with normal/narcissistic object relations. Although this chapter is largely theoretical, in Chapter 3 I go on to demonstrate some of the most common ways in which various sensation-dominated delusions manifest themselves in the clinical setting, that is, in the patient's attitude, in psychosomatic symptoms, and in various forms of enactment. Additionally I attempt to underscore the ways in which the analyst comes to provide a containing object: a thoughtful and feeling substitute for these most primitive defensive organizations.

The remainder of the chapters examine numerous aspects of the therapeutic process, demonstrating how the analysand may or may not develop a mind for thinking rather than evading thoughts through adhesive and projective maneuvers, and I focus in on some of the features in the setting, in the analyst and/or in the analysand that may contribute to or obstruct such development. In these chapters I also address several technical issues as they arise from within the clinical situations presented.

In Chapter 4, I present a longitudinal cross-section of the work with Hendrick, whom I have briefly introduced in Chapter 3, to demonstrate the impact of the maternal state of mind upon ordinary development in the face of severe trauma and loss, and the mitigating influence of the analytic relationship in severe borderline pathology in mid-life. In Chapter 5, some of the vicissitudes of maternal development are further explored through a detailed examination of the analysis of Chloe, a young woman struggling to learn what she is about before, during and after becoming a mother.

In Chapter 6, I further focus in on one aspect of the function of the containing object: that which concerns the experience of ecstasy. Additional material from Chloe's analysis – and from the analysis of Carla (a patient first introduced in Chapter 3) as well as other patients – is used here to demonstrate this under-explored aspect of ordinary human suffering and the analytic process. In Chapter 7, I report on the cascading breakdown – in both analyst and analysand – experienced during the analysis in the face of extreme emotional turbulence, and the difficulties inherent in over-riding the takeover of the defensive organization.

In Chapter 8, I present a discussion of the use of the infantile counter-transference and the difficulties in overcoming the analyst's resistance to learning and growing beyond theory. Finally, in Chapter 9, a few concluding thoughts, regarding the technical implications of several key concepts that have informed my work, are highlighted and elaborated upon.

Transference interpretation and the emergence of infantile dependency in ordinary people[1]

> To say that all communications are seen as communications about the patient's phantasy as well as current external life is equivalent to saying that all communications contain something relevant to the transference situation.
>
> Hanna Segal (1981, p. 8)

This chapter will focus on beginnings: the beginning of analytic thinking about the transference; the beginning of an analytic treatment; and the beginning of the individual as it is expressed in the transference in the first session. In his early writings, Freud emphasized the centrality of the transference in analytic work (1912; 1913; 1914; 1917). He discovered that *the work of analysis revolves around and depends upon the handling of the transference,* and was convinced that the war against mental illness would be won or lost on the "battlefield of the transference" (1912, p. 108).

Following Freud's lead, Melanie Klein and her exponents developed a rigorous technical stance based upon an understanding of the ubiquitousness of internal unconscious fantasy life (Isaacs 1952) and its externalization in both the negative and positive transferences (e.g. Rosenfeld 1947). Kleinian tradition thus emphasized the importance of paying careful attention to transference elements implicit in both verbal and non-verbal modes of expression and to their interpretation in the here-and-now of the analytic hour right from the first moment of contact. Klein (1952b) also proposed that the *transference situation* encompasses whole constellations of past experiences, emotions, defenses, and object relations.

For many years transference was understood in terms of direct references to the analyst in the patient's material. My conception of transference as rooted in the earliest stages of development and in deep layers of the unconscious is much wider and entails a technique by which from the whole material presented the *unconscious elements* of the transference are deduced.

(Klein 1952b, p. 55)

Klein helped us to become more mindful of the fact that the patient

turns away from the analyst as he attempted to turn away from his primal objects; he tries to split the relations to him, keeping [the analyst] either as a good or bad figure; he deflects some of the feelings and anxieties experienced towards the analyst onto other people in his current life, and this is part of "acting out".

(Klein 1952b, pp. 55–6)

This technique of seeking out and interpretively addressing each indirect reference to the relationship with the analyst serves to acknowledge, to make contact with, and to begin to mitigate the early infantile splits in the ego, allowing the analyst to commence an analytic process with patients who had once been thought of as "unanalyzable." Additionally, it is a matter of observable fact that by gathering up these widely disbursed or deeply buried aspects of the transference, and by drawing them directly into the therapeutic connection, we may be able to lessen the burden upon the patient's day-to-day life and his relationships outside the treatment.

Although explicit opposition to the Kleinian approach in London (King and R. Steiner 1991) inevitably spread throughout the mainstream of American ego psychology, it may be of interest to note that, in the last few decades, some analysts (e.g. Gill 1979) supported and even extended the idea that all communications from the patient contain an element of transference, which must be interpreted in the immediacy of the therapeutic situation from the beginning of the treatment. Gill also emphasized the importance of the analysis of a specialized form of resistance – that resistance which is directed toward the *awareness of the transference* – in order to encourage the expansion of the transference. Additionally, Gill argued that the major work of analysis lies in

examining the relation between the transference and the actuality of the analytic situation from which it takes its point of departure and the new experience which the analysis of the transference inevitably includes; and that while genetic transference interpretations play a role . . . genetic material is likely to appear spontaneously and with relative ease after the resistances have been overcome in the transference in the here and now.

(1979, p. 287)

In his writings, Gill made the point that transference interpretation – like extratransferential interpretation and any other behaviour of the analyst – in its turn affects the transference, which then needs to be re-examined if there is to be a minimum of unanalyzed transference.

Joseph's (1989) technique, with its attention to the minute shifts in the transference, seems to demonstrate this way of working. Joseph takes into account the "acting-in" potential inherent in the analyst's interpretations as well as in her manifest behavior, which may at times (but not always) respond to the patient's nudging the analyst to collude with the patient's unconscious need for and subsequent attempts to maintain psychic equilibrium, which runs counter to his conscious desire for psychic change.

Of course Bion's (1959; 1962b) model of the container and the contained and of projective identification as the earliest form of pre-symbolic communication between mother and infant has led to the recognition that such "acting" in the transference is related to the baby's most elemental fears about dependency. When these fears of the "infant" in the child or adult are understood by the analyst, and that understanding is interpretively communicated to the patient, the process of psychic change can begin.

Experience has shown that the setting for psychoanalytic treatment – with its frequency, regularity, and the use of the couch – may further facilitate this process of psychic change. However it has often been called to my attention, particularly by psychotherapists and analysts-in-training, that little has been written about the "introduction" of this setting. As a rule rather than as an exception the majority of today's patients are ordinary people who come to us seeking psychotherapy on a once- or perhaps twice-weekly basis, whether or not they are aware that they have been referred to a psychoanalyst. In fact, relatively few prospective patients know anything about psychoanalysis, let alone that it is traditionally conducted four or five times per week with the patient reclining on a couch and the analyst seated out of sight behind him.

In light of this situation, some have suggested that we need to *educate* patients *about* psychoanalysis to get them to go along with the programme. In fact, in certain circles and in many psychoanalytic training institutes, "instruction" is a recommended practice for candidates wishing to "convert" psychotherapy cases into analytic "control" or training cases. However, others have found that by listening to patients' needs, desires, and fears for and about closeness and dependency, and by interpreting these in the transference, we may be able to give patients a first-hand *experience of analysis*; that is, a sampling of our capacity to closely hold them both firmly and tenderly in mind. In this manner we may demonstrate our willingness to welcome and our ability to tolerate the emergence of the infantile aspects of the patient that are perhaps those most in need of contact and understanding, and by doing so we may relieve the patient of his inclination to "hold on" to us with his eyes as well as the compulsion to stoically toughen-up between what he feels must be infrequent and tenuous encounters with an extra-ordinary, unknown and unknowable stranger.

I am indeed emphasizing the need for "learning from experience" (Bion 1962a) which must take place right from the beginning of the analytic work if there is to be a viable process in which the patient can truly be expected to grow. Just as the infant in the act of discovering the world can move forward out of his own sense of agency only when he feels safely held in the attention and gaze of the mother who follows him wherever he goes, so the patient on his way to discovering his internal workings must feel free to explore his mind without suffering the paralyzing fear of becoming lost in the act of compliantly following the analyst's lead. As Winnicott (1948) suggested, in analysis:

> The important thing is that the analyst is not depressed and *the patient finds himself* because the analyst is not needing the patient to be good or clean or compliant and is not even needing to be able to teach the patient anything.
>
> (p. 94, my italics)

For the analysand, knowing about psychoanalysis must never supersede experiencing and "being" psychoanalysis (Bion 1962a), just as the analyst's desire to teach analysis must not be allowed to supplant his analytic function.

Perhaps through the clinical vignettes presented in this chapter, I may be able to demonstrate how some ordinary patients commence to experience their needs and/or desires; how they come to feel free to ask (directly or indirectly) for additional hours; and how they may begin to *organically* wend their way to the couch, rather than be guided there *didactically* by the analyst.

Anthony

The first patient I wish to discuss is Anthony, a single man in his early thirties who was referred for therapy by a colleague. During the course of initial consultations, which took place on a Monday and Thursday of the same week, Anthony sat in a chair and quite calmly and matter-of-factly presented a very well-organized history of his "very ordinary" early childhood, education, and career, as well as a description of his relationships to date. Nearly emotionless, Anthony ended each of the interviews right where he had begun: with a simple statement that he wanted to see a therapist because there was something that did not feel quite right.

Anthony seemed deeply unhappy and alone in spite of what *appeared* to be an uneventful childhood and college experience, and some satisfactory if not intimate or close relationships with both male and female friends. I sensed that there was some aspect of Anthony's experience that we had not yet arrived at in these interviews, something that he was helpless to know or to tell me about.

This feeling was especially strong in me at moments when there would be a pause in his otherwise smooth narrative. During these pauses, Anthony seemed to focus his gaze on my couch, positioned to the left of me against the wall opposite from the chair in which he sat. He said he felt "oddly comfortable" with me and wanted to make another appointment for the following week, although he did not know what we might accomplish.

In our next meeting, the patient reported the following dream in which:

He is sitting in a room, watching over a baby lying in a crib. He senses there is something wrong and begins to feel anxious. Then he notices that the sides of the crib have either been left down or are missing altogether. Only the two ends are there. He also notices that the baby's head is unsupported and it seems uncomfortable to him. He thinks that the baby needs a pillow or a cushion, but wonders at the same time if very little babies can suffocate with a cushion.

He looks across the room from where he sits and sees a pillow on a couch. However he feels suddenly unable to move in order to reach it. His arms and legs are weak and unsteady and he knows he needs help, perhaps to pull up the sides of the crib so that the baby won't fall out.

A woman sits in a black leather chair, not far from him. He has some thoughts that she might be able to help, but he is unsure that she would want to. He thinks in the dream, "she would need to carry me over to put the sides up, but what if she doesn't want to? Or perhaps she can't." He feels hesitant at first to ask the woman for help. Finally he calls out, but she can't hear him and he wakes up frustrated, crying.

After a pause Anthony said that he didn't have any idea what the dream meant. As if in his defense, he quickly added that he didn't have much experience with babies. Glancing away, he mentioned that the black chair in the dream was something like the one in which I sat. Then he paused and looked directly at my couch. Suddenly he blurted out "You know, that's an odd piece of furniture! It looks rather like a cot, not like a couch at all." He said that he had noticed that there were no cushions at the back, only at one end. "Do people *really* lay down on those things?"

I offered that it seemed to me that there might be a baby-he, like the baby in the dream, who needs watching over: a little-one who suddenly appeared after our meetings last week and whom he felt he had been left by me to care for all by himself over the weekend. I added that I thought that perhaps he'd been worrying that this baby-he was in danger of falling, with only the ends of the week in place. Anthony seemed surprised and interested in what I was saying to him, so I continued, wondering aloud if he might be expressing a wish to ask for my help to secure the baby-him with two more hours per week as a way of supporting his mind and giving him both comfort and a feeling of safety. However, perhaps he was also expressing a concern that I *could* not or *would* not

9

be able to "carry" him, and was also somewhat concerned that so much contact between us, like a cushion, would feel dangerously suffocating for him.

Anthony responded sheepishly, confirming that he had indeed been wondering if anyone ever came to see me more often than twice per week. Then he had the thought that he might not be able to afford to come more frequently. I probably wouldn't agree to adjust my fee to accommodate him. He had also wondered, many times during our sessions in the previous week, if he could lie down on the couch and what it would feel like if he did. However this had seemed too scary even to ask about it.

After a few moments, Anthony said that he had just remembered something that he'd long forgotten. To my surprise his eyes welled-up with tears. He told me that, as a baby, he had been adopted. When he was in his early teens his adopted parents had explained to him that his "real" parents had been too young to keep him. Thus, they had "given him up" at birth. He said that he now wondered why he had not thought much about it over the years until now.

I told Anthony that perhaps the missing parents of his birth were like the sides of the crib that were missing. I thought he was telling me that we needed all four sides – four hours per week on the "cot" with the pillow – so that he might feel safe with and comforted by me while he gave some thought to these childhood losses, even though it was clear that we would need to be mindful of a baby-he who could be in danger of being overwhelmed both by such close contact with me and also by his feelings about what he may have missed long ago and was more recently experiencing missing.

One might see, in this example, how a dream presented in the very beginning of the treatment can readily be taken up in the transference; how this works to mobilize additional unconscious material while establishing a close connection between analyst and patient, thus affording the patient an experience of the analyst's willingness to contend with a burden the patient has felt unable to bear on his own. One can also observe how anxiety-ridden issues of frequency of sessions, fees, and the use of the couch might be heard in the patient's material and addressed early on in the work.

Now of course, it is not always the case that a desire for greater frequency of hours or a curiosity about the couch will develop this early in the treatment. Other patients work up to this more gradually, as trust in the analyst's ability grows more slowly. I will now give an example of such a case brought to me for supervision by a colleague.

Cora

Cora was in the process of undergoing intensive fertility treatments, including artificial insemination, when she began analytic therapy twice weekly. Within a few weeks Cora's material began to speak to a desire for "more frequent treatments, which were needed to facilitate conception." The analyst told the patient that she thought that she was also speaking about a felt-need for more frequent meetings, in order that the analytic couple might be able to conceive of a baby-Cora who wished to be brought to life in the mind of a mother-analyst. The patient was very moved by this interpretation and the frequency of sessions was subsequently increased to three per week.

During the next several months of the treatment, there was evidence in the patient's associations that she experienced herself and her analyst as "growing more and more compatible with each other." The material also spoke in a round-about way to Cora's sense that her analyst was becoming "more receptive and able to conceive" of her. Indeed the analyst felt, during this time, that she could better understand and could now begin to formulate and to transmit, in a timely way, some rudimentary understanding of her patient's most primitive fears.

However, each week, over the four-day break, the patient would become seriously depressed and hopeless and the material presented during these times seemed to throw up images of a baby being dropped, aborted, or drained away in a bloody flow. Cora communicated her sense of a womb that was not ade-quately constructed to sustain an embryo that would consequently be "sloughed off soon after conception." Complaints that the fertility treatments were wasted, the money spent on these flushed down the toilet, and the feeling that her fertility doctor was not available when needed, led Cora's therapist to interpret these communications as expressions of the disillusionment with the analyst suffered by the patient during the too-long four-day weekends, and her experience of the bloody battles which she would engage in with her analyst on Mondays when she returned in an enraged state after the break.

Although it was clear that Cora was incapable of sustaining the experience of contact with herself over the breaks and that during the sessions she often wasted time by arriving late, this line of interpretation (in which the therapist adopted the patient's vertex,[2] taking responsibility rather than augmenting her already harsh super-ego) seemed to open the way for the patient, while feeling less persecuted, to be more direct with her therapist about her discontents. Cora's increasing sense of being understood, and the experience of someone who could tolerate that which she could not, seemed to be connected with her request for an additional hour.

While still sitting up in a chair, Cora now began to bring dreams of a baby needing to be held in her mother's lap and in her arms close to the breast; of an infant with a heavy head, too little to sit up; of fearsome predators attacking from behind; and of a father who fondles her and a mother who comes at her in a jealous rage with a knife, while she lies prone and helpless in her bed. Taking up these dreams in the transference as an expression of Cora's wish to be close to her therapist, her desire to lie on the couch, as well as her fear of being vulnerable if she does so, eventually enabled the patient to use the couch. The subsequent deepening of the transference relationship in all its many positive and negative forms was further facilitated, and within a short time the patient requested a fifth hour.

Finally, I would like to give an example of those patients who quite frequently become aware of their desire for more contact with the analyst early on, just as Anthony did, but who feel financially unable to increase their hours. Some might think of this as an early resistance to or attack upon the treatment, ignoring the fiscal realities. At the other end of the spectrum, some might focus on the latter, without giving a thought to the former.

However, I would like to address a different problem: that of the resistance that resides in the analyst. At times, the analyst may unwittingly avoid addressing such material, especially that aspect of the patient's material that speaks to the need and/or the desire for more contact. When I have pointed this out to those whom I supervise, they often speak to a concern that, by interpreting their patients' desire or need for more frequent contact, they might only be tantalizing them. Although this is certainly a rational point of view and a valid concern, we have often discovered that – at the core of this argument – there may be a quite understandable reluctance to *becoming the tantalizing object* who knows what the baby needs and withholds it, *or to becoming the infantile part of the patient* who is always at risk of being dismissed, minimized, or rejected out of hand.

The following example may demonstrate the importance of "telling it like it is" with respect to our patients' internal psychic reality, regardless of the external reality of their situation, since an enormous amount of work can and must often be done to remove adjunct obstructions to increased contact, interwoven into and bound up with an external fiscal reality. In the process of this kind of analytic work, perceived or realistic financial impediments may also be ameliorated, as was the case in the analysis of a patient whom I call Lily.

Lily

A 28-year-old graduate student, Lily entered therapy on a once-weekly basis, referred by a clinic. However it soon became apparent, in the material presented in the first few hours of the treatment, that the chronic depression of which the patient complained was characterized in part by a hopelessness about the prospect of ever achieving a close and caring relationship. The contemporary version of what I took to be an early hopelessness, experienced in her primary connections, was expressed in terms of her relationship with a man with whom she had been intimate for a number of years.

She had hoped, almost from the beginning, that their affair would lead to marriage and "having a baby." We soon came to understand that this also expressed a deeply unconscious longing for such closeness with me: a steady, analytic marriage and the formation of an analytic couple capable of conceiving of and bringing to life a baby-Lily who could then develop and grow into a creative individual.

However, just as Lily's boyfriend had shied away from serious considerations of marriage and children and saw her "only once a week because of financial deficiencies," Lily unconsciously feared that I too might refuse to commit to a true coupleship and to participate with her in parenting the baby-her. My interpretation of Lily's need, and her fear that this need would never be met when she felt she had so little to offer me, seemed to diminish her sense of helplessness, and within weeks she was able to see her way clear to obtain a second part-time job in order to pay for an additional hour each week, which she had felt encouraged to ask for.

At this juncture, I was seeing Lily on Monday and Tuesday of each week, when she began to speak with some frequency about her parents who provided partial support for her while she pursued her graduate studies. Lily also let me know that, although she was in almost daily contact with her parents, she actively avoided and therefore had little to do with her younger sister, Rose.

Rose had been born when Lily was just 16 months old and had a lengthy history (since before adolescence) of psychotic depression and bulimarexia, with multiple suicidal attempts that had resulted in hospitalizations of varied duration. I heard and therefore took up this material as also pertaining to Lily's sense that I was only partially supporting her, referring to the two hours per week, and her feeling that this situation left unhelped a very ill sister-aspect of her that was left out and untouched in the treatment, as well as her conviction that it was I who wished to avoid contact with that deeply troubled part of her Self.

Although at first Lily had only briefly referred to her sister Rose and the intense nature of the competition between them, her dreams at this time, as well as some memories unearthed by or alluded to in the analysis of the transference, now began to aid us in fleshing out some of the complexities of this connection with Rose and its numerous unconscious internal counterparts as these were enacted in our connection. For example, during one Monday hour Lily was telling me about a growing sense that her boyfriend did not like babies. This troubled her as it seemed just one more piece of evidence in support of her fear that she would never have the baby she so wanted.

I pointed out to her that she might be in despair due to the suspicion that had grown in her, during the breach in our contact these past five days, that I did not like that baby-her and the awareness of how unwanted she had felt by me. After a pause she made no direct reference to what I had said, however she recalled that she had never had a baby-doll when she was a child. Apparently she had even been afraid to ask her parents for one.

This thought reminded Lily that she had not been allowed to see her baby-sister until Rose was old enough to walk, and she had taken this to mean that her parents were fearful that she might harm the new baby in some way. We came to understand that she had been feeling that it was dangerous for her to come directly into contact with a helpless, needy, baby-part of herself and that she had been keeping this baby-self out of sight and out of mind for protection. However, it seemed that, in spite of this, there was also some part of her that wanted to have contact with this baby-doll-sister aspect of herself, but was afraid to ask for it, just as she was afraid to ask for more contact with me.

Lily went on to say that she had been grocery shopping over the weekend when she saw a woman. From behind, this woman looked so thin and emaciated that Lily thought to herself that she must be very ill. Once the woman turned around, Lily recognized her sister. However she was so taken aback by Rose's frail condition that she had hidden herself from view until Rose left the store. Lily's report of this incident led us to better appreciate how persecuted she felt by any in-sight into the state of that baby-self, starved and neglected over the years and even more immediately over the long interruption in our contact. She became aware of how she continues to hide from this aspect of herself, which only serves to perpetuate her terrible sense of guilt.

In the Tuesday session, Lily reported a dream in which:

Hundreds of little mice were running loose in a diner or market in which she worked. She was ordered by her "boss" to destroy the mice with a broom. At the counter a customer was playing a game of tiddlywinks. She was angry that this customer just wanted to talk, but would not help her to eradicate the mice. She was able to kill one mouse, but the other mice had escaped.

It soon became apparent that, at least on one level, Lily was quite cross with me for not helping her to kill-off her mousy, run-away, infantile feelings of hunger and dependency, which a very bossy part of her orders her to destroy. She felt my desire to talk with her about these feelings was like some wasteful and idle "game" I wanted her to play with me, but that I would do nothing to help her with her task of killing-off those vulnerable aspects of herself.

In the hours to follow it became more and more clear that Rose also had come to represent a psychotic, out-of-control and suicidal part of Lily that she was both terrified to associate with and painfully ashamed of; an envious, greedy usurper who threatened to take away, or more accurately, to take over her creative capacities; as well as a stunted or as-yet-undeveloped part of her that was always holding her back. In the transference, I soon became all of these things for Lily. During this period, she often feared she would destroy me with her hatred; that I would take away some good experience which she'd had in school; that she would be made to feel ashamed if someone found out that she was in treatment; or that I was holding her back in her progress in the analysis due to my incompetence.

Associated with the latter was a maternal transference in which Lily experienced herself either as a "smart baby" who had to take care of the mother-me, educating and organizing me as well as picking up after me in my mindless incompetence, or as a "stupid, ugly, messy baby," unwanted, abandoned, and neglected by the mother-me. In this way, when I was felt to be dependent upon her, Lily seemed able to fend off anxieties related to envy of her caretaking object, and when she could feel that I had drained away all of her resources, she was able to diminish the pain of gratitude.

At times, I was also experienced either as a diabetic father-analyst "in a state of self-inflicted coma," unconscious, mindless, and speechless (especially during my silences); or as a cruel, heartless, erratic and incomprehensible father-analyst (when she experienced my interpretations as abusive and meaningless). Lily's profound reluctance to overtly expose her hostile feelings toward me seemed also to stem from some early experience with her father, who appeared to be quite authoritarian as well as physically abusive with her. Apparently, on one occasion Lily *had* struck back at her father during a particularly cruel incident in which he had pushed her to the floor and kicked her. However, her attempts at defending herself on that occasion served only to arouse further violence on Father's part. It seemed that, during this period in the analysis, Lily's silences functioned as a passive means of protecting herself from those interpretations felt to be violently attacking of her and which she dared not actively deflect.

Soon it appeared that Lily's initial inability to be direct with me about her needs and wants and also feelings of rage in the face of the inevitable frustrations inherent in the analytic setting and the limits of the relationship was related to a well-remembered prohibition by her mother against "drinking directly from the milk carton." Lily's oblique style of reporting material and responding to inter-pretations appeared to correspond to the "bent straw in the glass" from which she recalled being made to drink her milk as a child.

During this period, Lily would often report that whenever she called home to speak to her mother, Father always answered the phone. Thus she had to pass by him to get to her mother. This pattern surfaced as a current-day representation of Lily's elemental sense of a circuitous contact with her mother, which nearly always had to be screened by the father, proceeding only with his consent. It was clear that her experience of me as unavailable echoed an early one in which the mother was compelled to put the needs of the father, as well as those of the new baby-sister Rose, ahead of the still-dependent little Lily.

Here I believe it is important to point out that, although the triadic situation is a fact of life, one which the baby-in-the-patient must eventually be able to face and contend with creatively in the course of healthy growth, yet another fact of life or perhaps a fact of infantile psychic reality exists: the fact of the baby's absolute need (at least in the beginning of life) to have an experience of at-one-ment with the mother as a "subjective object" (Winnicott 1958) or "background object of primary identification" (Grotstein 1980);[3] this is in order to ensure that the baby's psychological birth will not turn into a psychological catastrophe (Tustin 1981). This level of provision necessitates that the mother be (at least for some time) in a state of "maternal preoccupation" with her baby, almost to the exclusion of her own as well as the father's needs.

It is my belief, based upon clinical observation, that this essential occurrence forms the basis for the development of the baby's capacity for "having a mind" of its own, unadulterated by a prematurely-impinging concern with the mind of another or others that might otherwise impose upon it. Such an imposition may become the template for the baby's and later the adult's tendency towards what Bion (1959) called "attacks on linking," a hardened cynicism with regard to the existence of and trust in a containing object, and the compensatory development of many other organized barriers to intrapsychic and interpersonal relatedness.

Fortunately, in spite of the existence of such barriers to our connection, around the anniversary of the first year of the treatment Lily began to bring material related to themes of containment. For example, she reported seeing a "baby-bag snow-suit for sale in an L.L. Bean catalogue" that approximated her "dream of being safe and warm." However, she also imagined that there might be a feeling of claustrophobia or some constriction of movement associated with wearing this suit, as "there did not seem to be space for the hands and feet to move about freely" (that is, "it did not appear to have adequate articulation"). Just the same, it did seem to Lily to offer safety and warmth.

Soon Lily was able to express not only her angry feelings toward me, but also the sense that I could tolerate the unbearable excitement that she had been unable to contend with regarding some very positive developments occurring at that time in her life. She seemed to become increasingly able to differentiate the me whom she experienced in the transference from the me she experienced as a new object who could be trusted to articulate and to contain, rather than to distort or restrict her experience and her development.

Lily's growing sense of being held in a caring and safe ambience in the analysis led to an increasing awareness of her dependency upon me. In turn her increased longing for more closeness with me brought her nearer to those feelings of emptiness and loneliness and of having nothing inside during my absences. This empty feeling was at first dealt with by filling up her schedule, especially letting things pile up until the weekend so that she had to work around the clock to complete her school and work assignments. Although this served as an efficient way of warding off the terrifying feelings of falling to pieces, placing enormous pressure on her like the constricting baby-bag snow-suit that seemed to act as a second skin (Bick 1968) that would hold her together, a now-exhausted Lily, feeling even nearer collapse, began to binge on food that helped her to feel full inside.

At this time, a delusional jealousy emerged toward the baby-Lily who could depend upon me, as well as toward the adult-Lily who was engaged in a creative intercourse with me in the analysis. This jealousy seemed to be located in that part of her that felt consistently left out, ignored, and having to fend for and feed itself: a part of her that was so angry that she often refused my help and availability.

This refusal frequently took the form of the sort of stony silence that appeared to afford Lily a sensation of being "hard and mean" rather than soft, vulnerable, helpless, needy and defenseless.

Another aspect of Lily's history now surfaced unexpectedly, presenting a complicated technical dilemma. Although she had attempted to keep it from me, on returning from a longer than usual weekend the patient let slip that she had been having problems in one area of her studies. Preoccupied with her examination and exhausted from cramming all night, she had an automobile accident. When I suggested that she had felt it necessary to shield me from what she called "the bad news," after a few moments she asked if she had ever told me that her parents had not allowed her to either ride a bicycle because she might fall or cross the street by herself as she might be hit by a passing car. Consequently, when she would arrive at her street after school, she had to wait across from the house, calling for Mother to come and escort her home.

Often Mother failed to hear her, sometimes for a long period of time. What made matters worse was that she not only felt left calling-out for help, unheard and unattended to, but she was also prohibited from helping herself. Lily felt that she had not been allowed to fall – or perhaps to fail – in the normal ways children do, so that she could have an experience of being picked up or of being capable of picking herself up when she did fall. Thus, falling – stunted in its early infantile form, untransformed by experience – remained a terrifying threat to her, and she seemed to have inherited her parents' fears on top of her own. Lily thought that her parents – and myself in the transference – *needed her to be safe for them, in order that they might be shielded* from re-experiencing their own dangerous childhood traumas.

In part, this experience of hers – that her parents needed her to protect them from an awareness of their own early experiences – appeared to be at the core of her identity and was indeed her *raison d'être*, so much so that she seemed compelled to forfeit her own needs, including her need for more analytic hours, in favor of obligations and duties toward others. At the same time, it seemed that such rigidly-adhered-to commitments functioned as a secure and reliable structure, omnipotently created (Symington 1985), within which Lily could feel relatively safe from an overwhelmingly intense fear that "the world would otherwise come to an end." Without this preoccupation with the needs and desires of others she was faced with an empty space to be filled with "who-knows-what."

The "who-knows-what" possibilities of life and of our connection were unbearably frightening for Lily and she now experienced my silences as "the dangerous unknown." Many times I felt compelled to say something before I even had the time to realize what I thought was happening with her. It seemed that she merely needed to hear my voice in order to allay her fears that I had deserted her. Perhaps in part this was an expression of her need to have me fill up the spaces between us at times when she felt she might otherwise float away off the face of the earth into nothingness. My "familiar voice" was felt to hold her together at such times, regardless of the content of my interpretations (Mitrani 1992). My understanding of this, coming just prior to a holiday break, seemed relieving to Lily and led to her admission that she hated to be aware that I was so important to her, since this awareness left her feeling "unglued" in my absence.

This period of the analysis seemed to free Lily to think more and more clearly about her own needs, and also to increase her sense of herself as a valuable person, one who deserved more than she had previously allowed herself. Subsequently she was able to seek and to find more appropriate and profitable employment. With a dramatic increase in her income as well as her self-esteem, she was able to ask me for two additional hours.

Conclusion

Such experiences, as I have attempted to convey in this chapter, have convinced me that careful analytic listening and consistent interpretation of the ordinary patient's experience in the here-and-now of the hour facilitate the emergence of the infantile transference, bringing it out into the open while at the same time mobilizing and mitigating certain anxieties and those protections constructed to deal with them.

Furthermore I have come to believe that – especially with new patients, in the beginning – if we can refrain from early genetic interpretations that tend to leave the patient feeling pushed away, or intrapsychic interpretation that may inflame the primitive super-ego, we may be able to demonstrate our willingness to offer ourselves as an object that can take responsibility for those unwanted, unbearable and therefore intolerable aspects of self and experience. In doing so, we may provide for the patient a new experience of a reliable and broad-minded presence, leading to the development of an optimal analytic setting while at the same time contributing to the build-up of an internal containing object. In other words, when the infant-in-the-patient can find a place in the mind of the analyst, one that is free of persecutory tendencies, then psychic development that had been previously derailed or perverted can once more be set in train, and learning from experience can proceed, obviating the necessity for educating the patient.

2

Extra-ordinary protections: the evolution of the theory of adhesive identification

> Models are ephemeral and differ from theories in this respect; I have no compunction in discarding a model as soon as it has served or failed to serve my purpose. If a model proves useful on a number of different occasions the time has come to consider its transformation into a theory.
>
> W.R. Bion, *Learning From Experience*

The previous chapter emphasized the effectiveness of beginning the therapeutic process by detecting and interpreting the infantile transference in the here-and-now. I have demonstrated how our patients' fluctuating experience of the analyst may be deduced from reports of the ordinary present-day events outside the analysis, as well as from those remembrances of the past that may arise spontaneously in the initial moments, days, and weeks of the treatment.

Additionally, defensive maneuvers that patients often employ against an awareness of the transference and of psychic reality, including the phantasies of splitting, projection, and displacement as well as some more primitive auto-sensual forms of defense, have also been highlighted in the course of the clinical discussion. In this chapter, I will focus in on the latter in more detail through a review of the evolution of theory primarily stemming from the work of Esther Bick, Donald Winnicott, Donald Meltzer, Frances Tustin and others. In Chapter 3, I will go on to present further clinical examples of the appearance of these extra-ordinary protections in the ordinary people whom we see in ongoing psychoanalytic practice.

The concept of adhesive identification

In her few published papers, Bick (1964; 1968; 1986) delineated a primitive mode of defense – *adhesive identification* – that developmentally precedes those outlined in Klein's (1946) theory of projective identification. Bick's model subsequently provoked many analytic workers to revise their thinking and inspired them to begin charting an additional dimension of object-relating that had previously been overlooked: a dimension in which the centrality of the process of "getting inside" the object is subordinated to the primacy of "being in contact with" the object. This process is thought to be extraordinarily archaic and appears always to be linked with an object of psychic reality equivalent to the skin (Etchegoyen 1991).

Bick (1968) described certain behaviors that caught her attention time and again in those infants which she and her colleagues and students observed. Meticulous research led her to hypothesize that very young babies may initially lack the psychic boundaries sufficiently capable of holding together their mental and emotional contents, as yet indistinguishable or undifferentiated from their bodily contents.

In her succinct way, Bick proposed the notion of a *psychic skin*, which ideally serves to passively bind together experiences (or parts of the nascent self) on their way toward integration into an increasingly cohesive sense of self. She described this psychic skin as a projection of or corresponding to the bodily skin, and she proposed that it was "dependent initially on the introjection of an *external object*, experienced as capable of fulfilling this function" (Bick 1968, p. 484).

The external object that Bick referred to might be thought of as a *complex undifferentiated object composed of experiences of continuous interaction between a physically and emotionally holding and mentally containing mother, and the surface of the infant's body as a sensory organ.* Perhaps Freud (1923) was alluding to this phenomenon when he proposed that "the ego is first and foremost a bodily ego; it is not merely a surface entity, but is itself the projection of a surface" (p. 26).

Bick (1968) further hypothesized that "identification with this [psychic skin] function of the object supersedes the unintegrated state and gives rise to the [ph]antasy of internal and external space" (p. 484). She maintained that this phantasy of space forms the essential basis for the *normal adaptive splitting and projection* necessary to the processes of idealization and separation described by Klein. However, she forewarned that "until the containing function has been introjected, the concept of a space within the self cannot arise . . . [and] construction of an [internal containing] object . . . [will be] impaired" (p. 484).

Along with her description of the primal tendency of the infant to relate to objects in a two-dimensional way, that is, prior to the development of a sense of internal space, Bick made a crucial distinction between *unintegration* as a helpless, passive state of maximal dependency, and the active *defensive* maneuvers of splitting, with "disintegration" as a hyperbolic form of the latter. She associated unintegration with the earliest catastrophic anxieties, while correlating disintegration with later persecutory and depressive anxieties. Along these lines, she stated that:

> The need for a containing object would seem in the infantile unintegrated state to produce a frantic search for an object – a light, a voice, a smell, or other *sensual* object – which can hold the attention and thereby be experienced, momentarily at least, as holding the parts of the personality together.
>
> (p. 484)

She further specified that:

> The optimal object is the nipple in the mouth, together with the holding and talking and familiar smelling mother . . . experienced concretely as a skin. Disturbance in the primal skin function can lead to development of a "second skin" formation through which dependence on the object is replaced by a pseudo-independence.
>
> (p. 484)

In a later clarification of the subject, Bick (1986) noted that these "secondary skin devices may arise in collaboration with peculiarities of the maternal care such as muscular or vocal methods" (p. 292). Stated another way, the psychic skin substitute may be patterned after *perceived sensual characteristics of the mother* or other primary caretakers. Bick also suggested that such primeval defenses may come under the heading of "second skin formations" and are originally *non-mental phenomena* constructed to protect the very young infant against what she described as

> the catastrophic anxiety of falling-into-space, and the dead-end [which] haunts every demand for change and which engenders a deep conservatism and a demand for sameness, stability and support from the outside world.
>
> (p. 299)

Clinical/observational evidence

Bick (1968) provided us with many excellent clinical examples to illustrate her ideas. For example, she vividly described one infant who was moved to develop a pre-mature muscular type of second skin in compliance with the needs of an insecure mother. She deduced that this mother had need of some early proof of her infant's vitality and later, out of the necessity of her situation, pushed her baby towards pseudo-independence.

21

Bick also wrote about her treatment of a schizophrenic 3-year-old who spoke of herself as a "sack of potatoes," in constant peril of spilling out due to the holes that she picked in her sack; and an adult patient who oscillated between an experience of herself as a "sack of apples" in which she felt easily bruised and threatened with catastrophe, and as an aggressive, tyrannical, and stubborn "hippopotamus." Impressively, one 5-year-old patient conveyed the sense of how precariously she felt held together, insisting that her clothes be firmly fastened and her shoes tightly laced during the absence of her therapist. Here I will add an example from my experience of observing an infant whom I call Mathew.

Mathew

During one observation hour, upon being undressed for his bath 6-week-old Mathew began to show signs of distress while his clothes were removed as he lay on the changing table, his mother's attention being diverted momentarily to the observer. His response to this gap in maternal attention — as well as the concomitant loss of sensation of his mother's close and affectionate handling and the clothing which contained his body, all perhaps felt as a part of his physical as well as psychic skin — was to rigidify his muscles by arching his spine, clenching his fists and toes and drawing these together in rhythmic movements as if to hold himself together, thus attenuating his distress.

These actions were relinquished as soon as he was once again held in his mother's arms and as she slipped him into the warm, soothing bath water, which seemed to provide a continuous sensual experience of contact both with the warm waters of the bath and with his mother's constant and attentive gaze and touch. As he was lifted from the bath and dried, Mathew once again appeared to grow increasingly distressed at the loss of these comforting sensations. The signs of his anguish escalated markedly, as Mother's undivided attention was withdrawn while she resumed her conversation with the observer.

Becoming more and more agitated, Mathew seemed to search his environs with worried eyes, until he was finally able to focus and fix his gaze on the mirror to the side of the counter on which he lay. Once again he gradually began to quieten down, as if he were now feeling held securely within his own image in the glass. However, when abruptly turned away from this holding mirror-image by his mother, Mathew let out with a shriek, which was accompanied by a burst of tears, sudden urination, and a stream of wind from both mouth and bottom. It seemed the baby had felt torn away from that holding image in the mirror, and that this tearing feeling had undermined the integrity of his tenuous experience of being held safely together. The tear in this illusory "skin" seemed to precipitate a spilling out from his eyes and penis and a diffusing or evaporating through both his mouth and his anus, as if these orifices had become equated with that tear, threatening his survival.

The survival-function of the second skin

In a further expansion of Bick's concept of the second skin, Joan Symington (1985) highlighted the *survival-function* of such omnipotent protections. She explicitly described one such defensive maneuver as a tightening or constricting of the smooth muscles of certain internal organs, that provide the baby with a sensation of a continuous skin, without gaps through which the self risks spilling out into space.

Symington's many examples from psychoanalytic infant observation, as well as her experiences with adult patients in the analytic setting, gave credibility to her conclusions that:

> The primitive fear of the state of disintegration underlies the fear of being dependent; that to experience infantile feelings of helplessness brings back echoes of that very early unheld precariousness, and this in turn motivates the patient to hold himself together . . . at first a desperate survival measure . . . gradually . . . built into the character . . . the basis on which other omnipotent defense mechanisms are superimposed.
>
> (p. 486)

Symington emphasized that these catastrophic unintegration anxieties are likely to be present at times in the *majority* of ordinary people and she warned that while holding themselves together through the use of these primitive methods, patients will likely *appear to be in opposition to the analytic relationship*. I would submit that elective mutism, "blocking," stubbornness, immutable rage, falling asleep, intellectualizing, "forced speech," superficiality, zoning-out on the analyst's voice, appropriating the analyst's interpretations, reading books about analysis, flitting from one subject to another, and other such behaviors *might mistakenly be interpreted as a turning away from the analyst and as intentionally destructive to the analytic process* while these may in fact be motivated by a will to survive the analysis rather than to destroy the analyst or her work. This shift of focus may provide a new vertex for understanding the complexities of some negative therapeutic reactions.

Anzieu's "Skin Ego"

Anzieu's (1989) work in France, stemming from a non-Kleinian orientation, complemented Bick's and Symington's in several ways. He referred to the psychic skin as a "Skin Ego" and described this as an "envelope"

> which emits and receives signals in interaction with the environment; it "vibrates" in resonance with it; it is animated and alive inside, clear and

luminous. The autistic child has a notion – doubtless genetically pre-programmed – of such an envelope, but for want of concrete experiences to bring it into being, the envelope remains empty, dark, inanimate, dumb. Autistic envelopes thus provide a proof *a contrario* of the structure and functions of the Skin Ego.

(p. 230)

He pointed out that the significance of the surface of the body and its representation in the mental sphere is absent from Klein's original formulations, which is,

Surprising in that one of the essential elements of that theory, the opposition of introjection (on the model of feeding) and projection (on the model of excretion) pre-supposes the setting up of a boundary differentiating outside from inside.

(p. 37)

Here I would like to clarify that, although Klein's theory may have failed to take into consideration the function of the somatic skin and its psychic representation, what Anzieu described as the autistic child's "genetically pre-programmed" expectation does indeed correspond to Bion's notion of an innate "pre-conception" of the good breast as a mentally and emotionally containing as well as a nourishing object.

Furthermore, Bion coined the term "nameless dread" to denote the severe consequences of the failure of the environment not only to provide the "realization" of what has been "pre-conceived" by the baby, but also by adding insult to injury by stripping its sense impressions of any and all rudimentary meaning analogous to the psychic-skin. Unfortunately, like many classical analysts and ego-psychologists who take a good-enough infancy for granted, many classical Kleinians often take for granted the development of the "container" as well as "the contained" from the moment of birth or even *in utero*. However, such crucial developments *cannot* be taken for granted, as these are dependent upon both innate and environmental factors, an issue that will be discussed further on in this chapter.

Anzieu (1989) thought that certain reservations regarding Kleinian technique might be understood in this context, as what he referred to as an "interpretative bombardment" can often be felt to strip the ego of its protective envelope. Ironically Mrs. Klein considered that, by itself, defense analysis constitutes poor technique. Even so, many Kleinians do often fall into a pattern of analysis in which the deepest anxiety – that which motivates the construction and mobilization of defensive structures – is left unaddressed and therefore uncontained, in Bion's sense of the term.

This concern was also expressed by Symington (1985) who warned that interpreting the defense and its destructiveness – without acknowledging the patient's fear of catastrophe and his conviction that he must hold himself together – risks leaving him feeling uncontained and misunderstood, and often results in silent hurt and increased defensiveness. I have come to suspect that the increased defensiveness to which Symington referred may frequently be expressed in an *attitude of extreme compliance* that, while simulating improvement, merely signals the development of a new and more subtle version of the second skin; one that is patterned on the personality and theories of the analyst and is therefore "acceptable" to him. Once this transformation in the second skin is achieved it becomes scotomatized in the mind of the analyst and is therefore no longer accessible to interpretation.

Winnicott's contributions

Winnicott's work on the subject of unintegration (1949) as well as the importance of the skin in early object relations (1960) actually predated Bick's publications. He pointed out that a part of the development taking place in what he termed the "holding phase of infancy" is the establishment of the baby's psychosomatic existence; a primary integration which he had earlier referred to as the "indwelling of the psyche in the soma" (1949). He noted that in the course of normal development:

> There comes into existence what might be called a limiting membrane, which to some extent (in health) is equated with the surface of the skin, and has a position between the infant's "me" and his "not-me." So the infant comes to have an inside and an outside, and a body-scheme. In this way meaning comes to the function of intake and output; moreover, it gradually becomes meaningful to postulate a personal or inner psychic reality for the infant . . . the beginning of a mind as something distinct from the psyche. Here the work on primitive fantasy, with whose richness and complexity we are familiar through the teachings of Melanie Klein, becomes applicable and appropriate.
>
> (Winnicott 1960, p. 45)

In his theory of mental development, Winnicott proposed that in the event of a deficiency in "good-enough mothering," the infant is likely to be subjected to sudden and/or chronic *awareness of disconnection*, leading to unthinkable anxieties associated with the *felt* state of unintegration. The anxieties to which Winnicott (1962) referred were enumerated by him as the fear of going to pieces, of falling forever, of having no relationship to the body, and of having no orientation in space.

Winnicott also noted that such unthinkable anxieties arise out of the primary state of unintegration, experienced in the absence of maternal ego-support. He further stated that these are anxieties that result from privation, characterized by a failure of holding in the stage of absolute dependence, and are thus to be differentiated from those of disintegration or fragmentation, which stem from an active production of chaos related to the more sophisticated omnipotent defenses associated with *deprivation*, activated *only after* some measure of ego integration has taken place.

It may be important to note that the capacity to experience unintegration as relaxation – what Winnicott (1958) referred to as the "capacity to be alone" – also occurs *only after* the child has had the opportunity, through "good-enough mothering" and the "experience of being alone in the presence of the object," to build up a belief in a benign environment. Without this experience, the baby may fall into a void of meaninglessness, and his otherwise normal state of unintegration may become a *feeling of disintegration*.

This "feeling of disintegration" (Winnicott 1948, p. 99) must be differentiated from *disintegration as a defensive phantasy*. Severe disruptions in the baby's sense of his own "continuity of being" may produce an "over activity of mental function-ing" (Winnicott 1962, p. 61), a precocious development of omnipotent phantasies of a defensive nature produced "to take over and organize the caring for the psyche-soma; whereas in health it is the function of the environment to do this" (Winnicott 1962, p. 61).

The usurpation of environmental functions by the "mind" may lead to confusional states, second skin adaptations, and the development of mental functioning as a thing in itself. Winnicott (1949) coined the term "pathological mind-psyche" for this phenomenon and thought that this structure is perceived as an enemy to the "true" self and must therefore be localized in the head for purposes of control.

I have introduced Winnicott's ideas here not only because they are often neglected in the context of what are often thought to be post-Kleinian notions, but also because they add a much-needed elaboration to the concept of uninte-gration and its concomitant anxieties, serving to flesh out Bick's concept of the second skin by articulating its mental component. It is also my understanding that Winnicott's pathological mind-psyche is a pseudo-mental apparatus that develops in the event that the environment fails to support the integration of psyche and soma. I believe that this pathogenetic state – in which intellectual functioning is employed as a protective barrier – may be one and the same as that observed and described by Meltzer as a mental apparatus that falls apart in the process of what he understood as unintegration.

Meltzer's theoretical and technical contributions

Unlike Winnicott, Meltzer (Meltzer *et al.* 1975) understood unintegration to be a *passive defense* against anxiety. He used the term "dismantling" in relation to unintegration and described this as a splitting of the sensory apparatus, and consequently of the experience of the object, into its sensory components resulting in the obliteration of what Bion called "common sense."

Meltzer also employed Bion's term "reversal of alpha function," assuming that the mental apparatus and the thoughts processed and/or generated by it are stripped of meaning that had previously been established. Viewing unintegration in this light, Meltzer seemed to suggest that pathological psychogenic autism is related to a passive type of *destructive regression* and the collapse of *previously developed mental structures*.

In contrast to Meltzer's use of the term, Winnicott, Bick, and Tustin used "unintegration" to designate a *natural state of being* in infancy: one that existed prior to the mother's application of her capacities to sort out the baby's nascent sensory experiences in her own feelings, thoughts and behaviors, thereby lending support to the baby's innate tendency toward the integration of such experiences. For them, unintegration was understood as *a state of being*, which is only experienced by the baby as a dangerous disintegration *if and when* maternal containment becomes inaccessible before the baby has the chance to develop a stable psychic skin.

I would suggest that, when viewed in this context, *unintegration may be seen as a normal primary state that is only experienced, felt, feared and therefore evaded when needed environmental supports are absent*. In this model normal unintegration is conceptualized as a feeling-state rather than a pathological-development occurring at the expense of normal mental and emotional growth. Here it follows that the baby, while chronically deficient in the experience of a suitable skin-object, may *out of necessity* organize his primary sensory experiences, without benefit of meaning, into an impenetrable second skin. This second skin thus provides a tentative if illusory form of integration that is false! The resultant pseudo-mental-maturity, not unlike what Winnicott described as a pathological-mind-psyche, may also be akin to what Bion and later Meltzer referred to as a "Beta-screen."

Meltzer (1975) further concurred with Bick's notion of adhesive identification (as a primitive narcissistic state, preceding that subsumed under the paranoid-schizoid position) in a paper that enriched the findings that he and his co-workers had reported in the classic *Explorations in Autism* (Meltzer *et al.* 1975). Thus, he substantially contributed to the area of psychoanalytic technique with such elemental states in adults as well as in children. He wrote about how he and his colleagues at the Tavistock Clinic began to notice that interpretations along the lines of projective identification didn't seem to carry any weight in certain situations. We were in trouble with certain kinds of patients and saw that something else was going on that certainly was connected with identification processes; it was certainly connected with narcissism, but it seemed to have quite a different phenomenology from what we gathered together under the rubric of projective identification . . . something that had to do with states of catastrophic anxiety in certain infants whose mothers seemed somehow unable to contain them. When these infants got anxious, their mothers got anxious too and then the infant got more anxious and a spiral of anxiety tended to develop . . . which ended with the infant going into some sort of . . . disorganized state.

(p. 295)

Meltzer also recalled how Bick observed that some adults were also subject to similar states. Apparently it was she who noticed that:

Suddenly they wouldn't be able to do anything. They would have to sit down and shake. It wasn't that they were anxious in the ordinary sense . . . they just felt muddled, paralyzed and confused and couldn't do anything. They just had to sit down or lie down until it went away. The material of the analysis at these times and the dreams began to throw up an image of something . . . not held together, not contained . . . these people all had disturbances related to the skin or their experience of the skin . . . that they weren't properly held together by a good skin, but that they had other ways of holding themselves together . . . with their intelligent thinking and talking . . . with explanations . . . [or] muscularly.

(p. 296)

Meltzer reported that a similar phenomenon was observed in autistic children. At certain stages these children

functioned as if there were no spaces, there were only surfaces, two dimensions. Things were not solid, only surfaces that they might lean up against, or that they might feel, smell, touch . . . get a sensation from . . . they didn't seem to hold things well . . . words went right through them. Their responses [to interpretation] seemed so delayed often that one felt that all that had been left behind of what you had said was a kind of musical disturbance that they eventually reacted to or reacted against.

(p. 299)

Most useful is the distinction which Meltzer explicitly made with regard to the course of the treatment with such patients. Along these lines he clarified that what was previously thought to be associated with motivation – the problem of negative therapeutic reactions related to envy, masochism, jealousy, and unconscious guilt – could now be seen as a manifestation of a structural defect.

> [These patients] do just fall to pieces occasionally, and one has to be very patient with particular countertransference problems that have to do with being able to contain the patient . . . the chief manifestation of this is the ability to worry about the patient . . . these seem to be patients who need to be worried about, although they are not the kind of patients who clamor for it . . . one cannot expect such patients to move very fast . . . they have to develop an internal object that can really hold something, that doesn't have a leak in it and they are very slow to develop this because they have a leak and they can't hold anything very well themselves . . . one just has to wait for something to accumulate [like rust or corrosion] . . . one just can't plug up the hole.
>
> (p. 306)

It would seem that a skin object or "alpha membrane" (Meltzer 1978, p. 79) must be incorporated very early on in mental development in order to allow for a space within the self to develop in a timely way, so that the mechanism of projective identification as the primary method of non-verbal communication between the mother and infant can function without impediment. Indeed, the work of Mauro Mancia (1981) supports the notion of a potential for this early development of a psychic skin *in utero*.

Evidence for the pre-natal development of the psychic skin

In his paper on the proto-mental life of the fetus, Mancia (1981) integrated empirical data from cutting-edge embryological and peri-natal research regarding the motor functions, the sensory abilities, and the appearance of REM or active sleep in the fetus (which can be observed between 28–30 weeks of gestation) with the work of Bick (1968) and Bion (1962a, b). Mancia hypothesized that:

> Active sleep constitutes a "biological framework" within which the sensory experiences coming through the maternal container are transformed by the fetus into "internal representations." Such an operation would constitute the beginning of a protomental activity in evolution which would build itself around a nucleus of an instinctual nature transmitted genetically from the parents.
>
> (1981, p. 355)

Mancia seems here to suggest that the pre-natal psychic nucleus, which is based upon phantasy elements transmitted by the extrauterine objects through

29

the intrauterine boundary, may contribute to what Bion (1962a, b) referred to as the baby's "pre-conceptions." He also discussed the role of REM sleep in the pre-natal development of

> the psychological function of the [psychic] "skin" which . . . may be able to contain the self of the child and to protect it from disintegrating under the pressure of impulses which come into play at the moment of birth.
>
> (p. 355)

Furthermore, Mancia (1981) posited that the pre-natal foundation of the "psychic skin" favors the inception of the "container–contained" relationship, indispensable for the development of an apparatus for "feeling" and "thinking" (Bion 1962b). His fascinating conjectures, based mainly upon non-psychoanalytic data, broaden this perspective as well as deepening our understanding of the impact of the earliest experiences upon psychological development of the individual.

Most significant are Mancia's reports of findings, in observation of both the fetus and some prematurely born infants, that the disruption of the maternal environment (whether physical or emotional) results in a reduction of active (REM) sleep and an increase in motor activity, which he interpreted as an indication of the evacuation of "Beta elements" rather than the transformation into "Alpha elements" that would theoretically coincide with REM sleep.

As I have previously established in this chapter, the *potential* for the development of the foundations of the psychic-skin, and therefore the containing inner space, exists in and perhaps coincides with perceived qualities of the womb. However, the realization of this potential cannot be taken for granted. Certainly the dilemma of the autistic child is the most stunning example of the failure of the early inception of a containing object.

The work of Frances Tustin

Tustin's work with autistic and psychotic children had its roots in and branched outward from Bick's and Meltzer's ideas on adhesive identification. Until her death in 1994, she devoted her attention to developing an understanding of the elemental world of these atypical children. Her pioneer efforts enabled psycho-analytic child therapists to proceed where the work with such patients had previously been stopped. With the elaboration of her models of autistic objects (1980) and the autistic shapes (1984), she forged a key with which many were able to gain entry into the once-forbidden and foreboding area of their patients' earliest experiences.

Among her many original achievements, Tustin (1972) described a state of normal "flowing-over-at-oneness" (not altogether unlike Winnicott's (1945) "illusion" and Balint's (1968) "harmonious interpenetrating mix–up") as the forerunner of "normal projective identification as a means of communication." The latter assumes some tolerance of what she called "flickering state of awareness" of bodily separateness between mother and infant. She explained that normally:

> In spite of the caesura of birth, there is not an absolutely abrupt transition from the sensations associated with being inside the womb to being outside of it. Tactile sensations of being in a "watery medium" (Bion's term), appear to linger on and to be carried over into the child's earliest experience of the outside world.
>
> (1981, p. 183)

Here Tustin cited Rolland's (1930) term "oceanic feeling" as apposite to the description of the pre-, peri-, and post-natal experiences of the infant.[4] Like Mahler *et al.* (1975), Tustin distinguished between physical and psychological birth, the latter occurring gradually after the time in which:

> Within the sane and healthy sheltering, but not entangling, of the post-natal womb, psychological integrations take place, just as bodily integrations took place within the physical womb of the mother's body.
>
> (1981, p. 185)

Tustin stated that in the event of a "premature psychological birth," which she targeted as the root cause for infantile psychosis and autism, the inadequately prepared infant experiences too great a gap between itself and the now suddenly-separate mother and defensively withdraws into its own disconnected sensual experiences. These sensual experiences, which had once linked mother and infant, now become autosensual: totally under the omnipotent control of the baby who then becomes cut-off from the experience of human contact with the primary object. The "black hole with the nasty prick" (Tustin 1981, p. 91) – John's experience of the sudden wrenching away of the nipple from the mouth it was felt to be a part of – represents the "nameless dread" (Bion's term) of "premature twoness" (1981, p. 91) that must be defended against through the use of autosensual "hard" or "soft" objects (both animate and inanimate, undifferentiated from one another).

These extra-ordinary auto-generated protections are rallied by the baby in an effort to fill the intolerable gap between the self and the (m)other. This gap – felt as a "black hole" that threatens to suck the spilling self and all life into it – is covered over through the use of various sensation-dominated delusions. Tustin suggested that in these instances the holding and containing functions of the mother were inadequate "for that particular infant" (Tustin 1981, p. 93).

31

This means that instead of normally-timed differentiation and integration, explosive disintegration or paralyzed unintegration is the order of the day.

(1981, p. 193)

The blocking of awareness of reality that Tustin observed in encapsulated autistic children and the distortion of reality observed in confusional autistic children (1992a) may be linked to certain psychosomatic or somapsychotic maneuvers. Tustin's schema of autosensual defenses may also be applicable to yet another form of primitive existence: that which is prevalent in the perversions.

Tustin (1986a) discovered that, in the absence of a containing presence, chronically "unintegrated children" (p. 127) quell their unbearable terrors of falling or spilling away forever by creating sensations of adhering to the surfaces of hard things. She observed how these sensations afford the child an immediate if ephemeral experience of bodily continuity, safety, and survival, when the child becomes *equated* with the surface of the hard object. In its extreme form and used to excess, the child becomes addicted to this mode of survival.

Tustin (1992b) preferred the term "adhesive equation" to Bick's original term "adhesive identification." She clarified that autistic children are chronically stuck to their mothers in such a way that there can be no space between them in which the development of a true object relationship can take place. She further noted that autistic children, in contrast to schizophrenic-type or symbiotically psychotic children, *cannot identify*. Along these lines, Tustin emphatically underscored the point that *without an awareness of space there can be no relationship, and without relationship the process of identification cannot be set in motion*. It might be said that adhesive equation (or "adhesive identity" as Bick later called it) serves to establish a *sensation of existence* rather than a *sense of self and object as separate living entities*.

In *adhesive equation* the "subject" feels *the same* as the "object" with no space between them, while in *adhesive identification* the "subject" feels *similar to* the "object" and there *is* space between them.

(Tustin 1992b, personal communication)

Tustin (1986a) also cited Eugenio Gaddini's (1969) "imitative fusion" as yet another model for the apprehension of this phenomenon. She reiterated that:

It is important to realize that, since the child's body seems fused with "autistic objects," these have scarcely reached the status of an "object" in the usual sense of the term . . . [and these also] need to be differentiated from Winnicott's "transitional objects" which . . . can facilitate ongoing psychological development.

(p. 128)

Gaddini (1969) conceptualized this phantasy of fusion as "an attempt to gain a vicarious identity, magically acquired through [fusional] imitation" (p. 478), an idea that resonates with Bick's description of the second skin as the resultant of an act of "mimicry."

It might be important to note that even before Gaddini, Helene Deutsch (1942) described the "as-if personality" as one existing in a state of "imitative identification." Deutsch noticed that certain patients behaved "as-if" they themselves *were* their loved objects. Tustin came to understand this as a "delusory state of fusion" rather than a special case of identification.

Tustin distinguished autistic objects (1980) from inanimate or animate objects, in that autistic objects are *not related to as objects in the ordinary sense*. Instead, these are *used for the tactile sensations which they engender* upon the surface of the skin of the subject. In like manner, she differentiated autistic shapes (Tustin 1984) from objective shapes – such as a square or a circle – in that these are idiosyncratic, endogenous swirls of sensation produced upon the surface of the skin, or upon internal surfaces with the aid of bodily substances or malleable and impressable objects. Such distinctions between ordinary shapes and objects and extra-ordinary ones – first based upon Tustin's observations with autistic children – have been extended to include numerous other behaviors observable in ordinary adults and children, behaviors that may be conceived of as *sensation-dominated delusions*. I will attempt to demonstrate a variety of these sensation-dominated delusions in Chapter 3.

I believe that it is important to make note that the key word here is "sensation." Such sensations as are provided by the autistic use of objects may not only be tactile in nature, but may be visual, auditory, olfactory or gustatory sensations as well. These are delusory in that they either function to distract one's atten- tion away from feelings of anxiety – providing an illusion of safety, strength, and impermeability – or they may have a numbing or tranquilizing effect upon the individual, which serves to block out some terrifying and unbearable awareness. These so-called delusions may be understood as serving to accom- modate very early indigestible experiences, protecting the individual from the return of potentially unbearable feelings of the catastrophic loss of and painful longing for the primary caretaker that threaten him with a sense of non-being that could lead to a state of panic or what Bion (1992) referred to as a *sub-thalamic terror*.

Tustin was perhaps most widely appreciated for her evocative descriptions of some of the most elemental human terrors alive and active in each of us, as well as those specialized protective forms that ordinary people create in order to survive. Among these she noted the sensations of mutilation, of spilling and falling, of dissolving and evaporating (Tustin 1986a), which characterize what she called the intolerable terrors of two-ness. She then traced the problem of psychogenic autism to the troubled nature of the earliest relationship between mother and nursling.

Tustin gradually came to understand that the mothers of many severely disturbed children, as well as those of our more neurotic patients, seem to have unwittingly reacted towards their babies as if they were parts of their own bodies, and thus fell short of being able to provide a satisfying and reliable nursing experience and a rhythm of safety (1986b) that might have subsequently been internalized, this perhaps due to their own feelings of inadequacy, loneliness, and depression. She observed that these well-meaning mothers compensated for this lack in their capacity to be mindful of their babies by over-protecting them, perhaps out of an unconscious wish to bring them – and their own infant selves with which their babies were equated – back to a state of fetal bliss within their own bodies, while at the same time filling in the "black hole" of their own sense of being overwhelmed: their own sense of inadequacy, emptiness, and loneliness. However, such over-protection left their infants extremely vulnerable in times of felt absence.

It is noteworthy that unlike others working in that difficult field of research – while acknowledging the importance of the environment as well as the innate disposition of the baby – Tustin did not find it necessary to blame or vilify these mothers. Instead she pointed out the fact of their preoccupation with their own struggles to survive while feeling unsupported, unsure of themselves, or depressed and helpless before and after the birth of their babies. Unfortunately, these feelings are more common in new mothers than we like to think, as many are geographically or emotionally cut-off from the close and affectionate support of their families, especially their own mothers, sisters, aunts, or grandmothers. Sometimes their husbands are themselves preoccupied, for example with the responsibilities of providing for an expanding family, especially when they find they are, at least temporarily, solely responsible for earning the family's living, or upon becoming first-time fathers.

Tustin suggested that when a mother is impaired in her ability to feel for and think about her baby, that baby becomes tied to and overly reliant upon the mother's *bodily presence*. At such times, separation and closeness are achieved concretely, rather than symbolically. There is no psychic distance or symbolic closeness and any strong emotion is felt in terms of physical sensation rather than sentiment. Subsequently, these mothers can be felt to be both too close and too far away. They are unable to make sense out of their infants' non-verbal communications. Such children are then at grave risk, since their own capacity to give the rudiments of meaning to what they experience is under-developed, and they are pushed to action rather than thinking as a form of containment.

Tustin helped us to understand how autism acts as a protective shell (1990) – made up of these "sensation-dominated delusions" – that serves to block out the unbearable agony of awareness of two-ness, and the threat that such an awareness represents to a sense of personal continuity and integrity. She used the term "delusion" not in the common psychiatric sense, which implies some degree of symbolic process, fantasy, and thought, but in a very concrete sense. She accurately intuited that these delusions are the thing-in-itself, not to be confused with a representation. She also demonstrated how this protective shell constitutes a barrier to the potentially healing effects of the relationship with the therapist (1986a).

In this regard, Tustin's teachings truly made a significant difference in the outcome of many psychoanalytic treatments. Since the publication of her findings, mainstream psychoanalysts of various orientations have taken up and extended her work in an attempt to expand our relatively meagre understanding of certain phenomena that impede emotional and intellectual development in many patients formerly thought – unfortunately and usually in retrospect – to be unanalyzable. I believe that such phenomena may often be found at the root of severe or even unresolvable impasse in the work with some patients and what we might think of as interminable analyses with many others.

Tustin's contributions not only added a new dimension to the work with atypical psychotic children, but also led to the realization that *ordinary people* may be haunted by similar kinds of primal happenings and that they may resort to the same *extra-ordinary protections* against the awareness of these happenings. Her acute observational skills have led to a more well-informed analysis of autosensual pathology in neurotic, borderline, and psychotic adult patients, and her realizations have been applied by workers from various analytic orientations to problems ranging from drug addiction to eating disorders and from panic disorders to psychosomatic illness, as well as those problems encountered by quite ordinary people who may seek help at some time during their lives with difficulties in the area of creative work and intimate relationships. The developments stemming from Tustin's seminal work are steadily increasing in number. I will here mention only a few published in the last two decades.

Some developments stemming from Tustin's work

The implications and applications of Tustin's ideas on the apprehension and treatment of autism to the psychoanalysis of ordinary adults and children have expanded throughout the global analytic community. For example, in London, Sidney Klein (1980) described patients who – despite the appearance of progress in analysis, and even a subjective sense of some gains made – feel that they have not been touched in some essential way. He observed some encapsulating force that seemed to cut the patient off from himself, as well as from the analyst, and he posited that, walled off in some isolated area of mind – and therefore unavailable to conscious thought – are intense and unbearable fears of "pain, and death, disintegration or breakdown," (p. 400) fears that are related to troubled separation experiences originating in early infancy.

Another British analyst, Innes-Smith (1987) eloquently discussed the hyperbolic use of "sensation objects" as a factor in the etiology of adult psychopathology, and emphasized the importance of attending to those early states of mind in which dyadic communication is achieved on a non-verbal level, and those moments in analysis when such states predominate.

In Chile, Gomberoff and his study group (1990) focused in on certain aspects of the therapeutic interaction wherein there develops a collusive tendency in the analytic couple to transform the analysis – particularly some aspects of verbal language – into an autistic object whose function it is to ward off anxiety over two-ness for both analyst and patient.

In Buenos Aires, David Rosenfeld (1992; 1997) found that the concept of autistic encapsulation may be applicable in the treatment of survivors of the Holocaust who have used autistic mechanisms as a way of preserving positive childhood memories and identity. Tustin also influenced his work with patients ranging from drug addicts to psychosomatizers and hypochondriacal organ transplant recipients. He developed a sophisticated classificatory nomenclature and demonstrated the centrality of sensation-dominated disturbances, discussing the occurrence of autistic pockets concealed within the larger more obvious syndromes of established pathologies.

In Rome, Maiello (1995) explored one particular aspect of pre-natal experience, presenting convincing clinical material that suggests that the sound of the mother's voice *in utero*, alternating with silence, may give the child a proto-experience of presence and absence, which not only gives rise to primitive defensive reactions, but may also be said to form the basis of a pre-natal sensual-object. Maiello concluded that this "sound-object" is connected with a preconception of the breast and may be one of the many precursors of the post-natal maternal inner object. However, she also pointed the way to further comprehending how, when this process goes awry, the pre-natal sensual object can be misused after birth and may constitute an impediment to the development of symbolic thought and true object-relatedness.

Isca Wittenberg – a contemporary of Tustin's who, along with others in Meltzer's group at the Tavistock, wrote about her own explorations in autism (Meltzer *et al.* 1975) – later hypothesized (Wittenberg 1997) that there are individuals who adopt autistic defenses as a barrier to falling into a state of despair and hopelessness, which dates from an infantile experience of a mother who is depressed and unable to deal with her own or her baby's fears of death and dying. She identified a pattern wherein babies who are born highly sensitive and intelligent, and with a great lust for life and beauty, are often overwhelmed with depressive anxiety when their preconception of a lively, responsive, and caring object (that is, the mindful breast) fails to materialize. While holding themselves responsible for this disturbance in the mother, they attempt to protect her omnipotently. However, the failure of such attempts triggers a shift from trust in the ordinary human object to a "hard-object" that is often manifested in some obsessional activity used as an escape from the terror of hopelessness and death.

In France, Lechevalier (1997) hypothesized a mode of adhesiveness occurring at the point of first contact with one or both depressed parents. She demonstrated how some undigested horror or grief in the parent, transmitted non-verbally and deprived of meaning for the baby, creates a nameless dread against which the adhesiveness defends.

Inspired by Tustin, American author Thomas Ogden (1989) developed the concept of an *autistic-contiguous position* – with its own form of object-relatedness, set of anxieties and defenses against these persisting throughout life and appearing throughout the analytic process – running parallel to and in dynamic relation with Klein's paranoid-schizoid and depressive positions. He suggested that this more primitive position is an integral part of *normal development* through which a distinctive mode of experience is generated.

Adhesive pseudo-object-relations

My own ideas diverge from those of Ogden in several ways. While Ogden described the nature of the infant's autistic-contiguous object relationships as a pre-symbolic dialectic between continuity and edgedness, between bounded-ness and at-one-ment with a subjective-object, I have outlined the development of an enduring mode of *adhesive pseudo-object-relations* (Mitrani 1994a and 1995a) as an *asymbolic aberration* of normal development, rooted in traumatic experiences of extreme privation occurring *in utero* and/or in early infancy. This way of "being" prematurely interrupts the necessary development of and trust in a "rhythm of safety" (Tustin 1986b) between mother and infant, resulting in a crippling of the emerging elemental state of subjectivity and the gradual development of true objectivity.

Such a mode of pseudo-relating may exist, on something similar to what Grotstein referred to as a "dual track" (1986), alongside normal and narcissistic object relations.[5] However, in its encapsulated, enduring and rigidified form, *adhesive pseudo-object-relations* are nearly always *pathologically defensive and static.* Thus, they are additionally pathogenetic and obstructive to the ongoing develop-ment of normal object-relatedness. This formulation is consonant with Tustin's autistic phenomena, whether these be present in autism proper or as a part of autistic states in ordinary individuals, which are always pathological. In her final paper she stated unequivocally:

> I have come to see that autism is a protective reaction that develops to deal with the stress associated with a traumatic disruption of an *abnormal*, perpetuated state of adhesive unity with the mother – *autism being a reaction that is specific to trauma.* It is a two-stage illness. First, there is a perpetuation of dual unity, and then the traumatic disruption of this and the stress that it arouses.
>
> (Tustin 1994a, p. 14, emphasis in original)

In other words, whereas normal pre-symbolic autosensuality – as described by Tustin (1984) – is the seed which, when cultivated and nurtured within the context of human relationship, germinates, sprouts, and grows into object relations proper, I suggest that should experiences of a sensory nature be left unprocessed by a thinking and feeling object, symbolic meaning may fail to evolve out of the rudiments of the existential experience inherent in sensory contiguity and rhythmnicity, and that these untransformed and unmentalized experiences (Mitrani 1993b; 1995b)[6] may become rigidified and hypertrophied as fortified protections against the awareness of those primeval experiential states of terror related to bodily and emotional separateness.

I will here attempt to operationalize and add clarity to the term *adhesive pseudo-object-relations* by comparing and contrasting it with normal/narcissistic object relations. First, in normal/narcissistic object relations, objects are perceived either in terms of their "parts" – that is, as synonymous with a part of the mother's body or with some singular aspect of maternal functioning – or as a whole. Such objects are also recognized by the subject as animate, as possessing life, and therefore as able to move about as a result of their own or another's act of volition. Objects in normal/narcissistic object relations are *actual* objects; by this I mean that these are *not only objects apparent to the observer, but those which are actually experienced by the subject as human beings with separate existences*.

In contrast to this, in an adhesive state of pseudo-relating, objects are *not* experienced as humanly animate, lively entities, existing in a space of their own, but rather as inanimate "things" which are to be absorbed, exploited, manipulated, or avoided by the subject in a desperate attempt to gain a sensation of existence, safety, and impermeability. Objects in this latter sense of the word are *only apparent to an observer*. I wish to stress this point, drawing a distinction between what we as analysts might observe and what is actually experienced by the patient.

Second, in a normal/narcissistic state, some degree of awareness of separateness and/or differentiation of the subject from the object exists and is tolerated to a greater or lesser extent. By contrast, in adhesive states, normal "flickering states of awareness" of otherness (Tustin 1981) are unable to be tolerated. Consequently self and object remain largely undifferentiated. They are one-and-the-same and the resulting pseudo-relationship with the object is mainly experienced by the subject on a sensuous level. In such a state, objects are not related to *per se* but are instead "utilized" for the tactile sensations which they engender upon the surface of the skin and/or the mucous membranes of the subject. These sensations serve either to distract the subject's attention away from anxiety – providing an illusion of safety, strength, and impermeability – or they may have a numbing or tranquilizing effect upon the subject, which serves to block out some terrifying and unbearable awareness.

Third, while normal/narcissistic object relations prevail, anxieties defended against by the subject are either paranoid-schizoid, manic, or depressive in nature:

anxieties which have been well defined by Melanie Klein. In contrast, those anxieties evaded through autosensual/adhesive maneuvers may more accurately be conceptualized as *states of raw and unmitigated panic*, equated with the elemental fear of falling forever, of discontinuity of being, of nothingness, dissolution, and evaporation – of being a no–body–nowhere – anxieties described in the work of Winnicott and Tustin.

In the former, the individual engages in complex defensive phantasies of splitting, projective identification, and manic denial to defend against the pain and despair of envy and the awareness of helpless dependence upon the object. In the latter, the individual employs adhesive equation and the blocking-out of painful and life-threatening awareness through autosensuous actions, which protect the self from the terrifying sensations of falling, spilling, dissolving, evaporating, and diffusing without hope of recovery.

Fourth, in normal/narcissistic object relations, the ego oscillates either between a state of *increasing integration* and a state of *non-defensive regression to unintegration* on the one hand, or between a state of *integration* and a state of *defensive dis-integration* on the other. However, in adhesive pseudo–object–relations the ego exists and operates predominantly in an unmitigated state of *passive primary unintegration*.

Fifth, the nature of thinking in normal/narcissistic states is either abstract or concrete, and may be either realistic or omnipotent in nature. However, in adhesive states there is little actual mentation. What appears to the observer as "thinking" remains on the level of a reflexo-physiological reaction. Here, what Tustin referred to as "innate forms" prevail in the absence of symboliza-tion, phantasy, and imagination, since the experience of "transitional space" is inexistent.

Sixth, while the normal/narcissistic individual reacts to separation and loss with either expressions of neediness or a tight-fisted control of need through the use of tyranny and seduction, the adhesive individual reacts with either total obliviousness or complete collapse. The awareness of dependency in the normal/narcissistic individual is either experienced as the need for and the act of reliance upon an object that is separate from the subject, or it is defended against through pseudo–independence. However, in the adhesive individual, dependency assumes the form of a thin and tenacious clinging to the surface of an as-yet undifferentiated object, felt to be part of and contiguous with the subject. This is really an *appendancy* (T. Mitrani 1992) rather than an experience of dependency.

Finally, when defenses against the awareness of separation and loss break down in the normal/narcissistic relationship, there is an experience of a threat to the subject's sense of omnipotence, culminating in feelings of rejection. In contrast, when omnipotence fails in the adhesive pseudo–object–relationship, this failure is felt as a totally catastrophic collapse or as a dreadful sensation of being ripped-off and thrown away.

In a sense, the latter is an experience of total and irreversible dejection. It is not an experience of the loss of the object or even the presence of the absence. Instead it is an experience of the presence of what Kristeva (1982) termed "the abject." She suggested that the "abject" – *a jettisoned object* – retains only one quality of the object it once was – that of being opposed to or separate from the subject. In other words, whereas the object – in its opposition to the subject – stimulates the desire for meaning, which paradoxically creates a link between subject and object, the *abject* – having been radically excluded and its existence denied – can only draw the subject toward "the place where meaning collapses" (pp. 1–2). This place of collapse aptly describes the subjective experience of space in this state of existence. You will recall that Tustin's autistic patient John (1992a) called this the "black hole with the nasty prick." Grotstein (1990) further characterized this "black hole" experience as an "awesome force of powerlessness, of defect, of nothingness, of 'zero-ness' expressed, not just as a static emptiness but as an implosive, centripetal pull into the void" (p. 257).

In the next chapter, I will present detailed material from several cases of ordinary people in analysis who exhibit the extra-ordinary protective features that I have discussed, while demonstrating the detection of the use of autistic shapes and autistic objects and their therapeutic handling in the analytic setting. I trust that these vignettes will also serve to further emphasize the survival function of these and other sensation-dominated delusions.

3

Ordinary people and extra-ordinary protections

> As therapists our task is to help our patients toward humanness when so much of the time the ordinariness of being human is not available to them.
>
> Frances Tustin

Before going on to the clinical illustrations, I would like to underscore some important technical points that seem essential to the analysis of such ordinary patients. These technical considerations are derived both from my own observations in the practice of analysis and from my ten years of consultation with Tustin, who was able to draw much wisdom from her years of observing the mothers of the autistic children whom she treated.

Going forward

After some time working with autistic children and their mothers, Tustin deduced that a vicious cycle had been set in train when these infants were felt to reject their mothers' efforts to bond with them. In other words, when the autistic child was felt to be unresponsive to its mother's overtures, the mother seemed unable to bear the insult to her self-esteem. Such mothers, while lacking sufficient internal or external support to pursue their withdrawn babies, would themselves withdraw in despair, action which only served to compound the problem.

By the time Tustin (1986c) first spoke with me about this cycle I had already encountered similar situations with patients with whom I had been working. For instance, I might offer an interpretation to a patient and he would either withdraw into silence or would reject outright whatever I had to say. At times I was frequently left with an overwhelming sense that what I had said was not good-enough. Of course, it is often the case that we may mis-understand or not understand well-enough, or in a timely manner, what the patient is trying to communicate. However, sometimes we might mistakenly take this to mean that it is we who are not good-enough.

This state of affairs can be demoralizing for any therapist, often leading to withdrawal from the patient. Such acts of withdrawal are at cross-purposes with our attempts to think and to seek out some better understanding. Withdrawal impedes further discovery of what has gone amiss and leads to an arrest of our capacity to find a way to acknowledge this to the patient so that he might feel relieved that we really wish to help, not just to be correct or to know it all.

When Tustin (1987) recommended that – in times like these – we must always push ourselves to go forward, she did not mean that we should push ourselves onto the patient by insisting that we are right. She felt it essential not to permit our need for approbation to get in the way of the work of analysis. Tustin encouraged us to take great care to avoid the temptation to retreat into our own protective shells, sometimes represented by our theories.

In this regard, Tustin appreciated that it was of paramount importance for therapists to be properly supported, just as she emphasized the importance of support for the new mother, which is necessary to insure that she will not lose heart, so that she might be able to be helped to breast the initial rejection of a sensitive or difficult baby. Tustin offered herself as a source of support to her students and colleagues while encouraging us to find additional sources of sustenance and gratification outside our work, so that we might not need to receive a sense of fulfillment from our patients. In fact she felt that this was one of the most important functions of supervision.

Of course it goes without saying that managing our own wounds is only one of the many technical demands encountered while working with autistic states. In addition, it is important to keep in mind that each of our patients has come up against situations, usually in early infancy or even before – at birth or perhaps *in utero* – that they were not psychically equipped to deal with at the time. Consequently, these "happenings" become walled off from conscious awareness, much as a grain of irritating sand inside an oyster becomes encrusted in a pearl. A hard encapsulation takes place, constituting a state of mind wherein the patient may become nearly impermeable to contact. While in this state of mind patients are difficult to reach and the obstacles we encounter are enormous, if by no means insurmountable.

For example, we might easily be lured to analyze the pearl or the shell, the false-self (Winnicott), the "persona" (Jung), or the "fake ego" as Tustin sometimes liked to call it. Thus we may never get down to the part of the patient that most needs contact. Or we might recognize that the shell is just that – a shell – and we may resort to defense analysis, trying to pry the shell open in order to get at the heart of the matter. Unfortunately, both these tactics often lead to further fortification of the defense in such a way that we can even be fooled into thinking that we have succeeded, when really we have just helped the patient to create a new coat of armour: one that complies with our ideals or our preconceived notions and theories.

Perhaps it is only when we have allowed some experience to envelop us and to percolate throughout our system and when we have mustered the full capacity of our imagination to circumnavigate these experiences, that we may be able to envision the predicament of the infant or even the fetus in the patient. Finally, it is only when we are able to articulate this vision, with genuine and spontaneous feeling emerging from this process of emotional and mental digestion, that we may gain access to those tender aspects of the patient that lie walled-off in an irritated state beneath their protective crust.

Undoubtedly we are most helpful when we are able to convey both our awareness of the specific agony as it is enacted in the transference of the moment and our earnest respect for the way in which the patient has dealt with such agony. With time, if we are able to offer something fresh and new while allowing the patient to choose when to relinquish his old and reliable method of survival, we may be able to make some headway toward reaching and relieving that part of the patient that most needs relief. Of course, this requires that we be patient, forthcoming, and able to withstand the sense of personal helplessness that comes with not knowing where it comes from, where it will all lead, or even if our efforts will lead anywhere at all.

Quite frequently, in those ordinary adults seen in today's practice of analysis, a degree of mental growth has indeed taken place by circumventing an area of amputated development that has been callused over or encapsulated. As one patient put it: "I have this hole – an empty spot deep inside me – maybe I'm just afraid to find that nothing is there." This patient, whom I call Hendrick – an overtly angry and bullying man – seemed to cover over these holes with a "chip on his shoulder." Eventually we came to understand this "chip" or callused cynical attitude and tough bullying behavior, as a "chip off the old block," which referred to his feelings about his father. One day, this patient lamented, "He protected me, but he just didn't seem to know what to do with me when I couldn't throw the ball right. He thought I was a sissy – I threw the ball like a girl."

Eventually Hendrick and I were able to understand that he was also attempting to communicate something about his growing awareness that, like his father, he could only protect the soft, tender part of his experience by covering it over with a hard "daddy-chip" when he was frightened of and did not know how to help or handle the baby-him with the soft spot on his head, the soft skin that could be easily bruised, and the tender loving feelings he had for the mother-me in the transference, which were always at risk of being belittled and depreciated.

As this patient (whom I will discuss further on in this chapter as well as in Chapter 4) demonstrates, ordinary people who find their way to analysis struggle courageously to give verbal expression to those primitive states in which development has been impaired. Their symptoms and actions can often be seen as valiant if perverse attempts to give expression to their bodily experiences and to communicate their deepest terrors so that we may lend meaning to them through our interpretive work.

Many of our patients are moved to communicate their states of dis-ease as these are brought into and re-experienced in the analytic relationship, often provoked by the innumerable separations engendered in the analytic frame, at the end of the analytic hour, the analytic week, and around holiday breaks, as demonstrated in the following clinical vignettes. Although I will focus here on the difficulties encountered in the work with these individuals, it might be important to preface these accounts by mentioning that each of these treatments was successful in the estimation of both the patients and myself and resulted not only in transfor-mations in the therapeutic relationship, but also in long-lasting and far-reaching inter-personal and professional gains outside the analysis.

Hope

Hope, a woman in her early thirties, was referred for analysis after many years of conventional non-analytic therapies. This is, at least in the USA, the norm rather than the exception to the rule for those patients who cross the threshold of analysis. Having recently lost her father after nursing him through a painful illness, Hope had moved to Los Angeles to be closer to her elderly mother, whom she also saw as needy and frail. She attributed her own depression to a recent abortion, and complained of her relationship with the father of the aborted baby, a man she described as unprepared for the responsibilities of marriage and children.

As Hope was predisposed to experience almost all those around her as needy and dependent upon her, it seemed at first glance that there was ample evidence that much of her suffering was a result of a profound intolerance towards a needy and frail baby-part of herself and the tendency to handle this painful aspect of her experience through excessive splitting and projective identification. However, the handling of this constellation over time, as it appeared in the relationship with me, seemed to result in only a limited measure of relief, and it soon became apparent that there was something else going on. We were soon to discover that Hope had hidden away, in an autistic enclave, a very dependent, sick, and dying baby-part of herself and that this encapsulation was interfering with her relationships as well as her work.

Relevant to the material that I will present, I will give a bit of Hope's history. Her mother had been severely depressed after the death of her own mother and, just six weeks after the birth of the patient, Mother's milk suddenly dried up. Around this same time, it seems that Father dropped the baby-Hope while holding her in his arms, and her lip was painfully split open in the fall, the scar remaining into adulthood.

In this session, the first of the week, which took place in the third year of the analysis, Hope began with a long silence characteristic of her re-entry on Monday after the three-day break. During this silence, lasting several minutes, I had the unsettling sensation of falling, as if my chair were being progressively lowered into the floor beneath me. When finally I broke the silence by asking Hope if she could tell me what she had been going through, she began by telling me that over the weekend her boyfriend had gone out with friends, and that she had awakened in the middle of the night to find that she was still alone in their bed. She said that she could not fall asleep, as she was hurt and angry at the boyfriend, and fearful about being alone, thinking she heard noises outside as if someone were trying to break in.

While immobilized by her fear of intruders, she told me that she had lain very still looking up at the ceiling, concentrating upon one single spot. She felt physically that she was being lifted up into a soft, pink cloud as she spread her tongue between her teeth, filling her mouth from corner to corner and touching her lips. She reported how soothing the sensation was of uniting with this soft pink cloud, and how she had soon drifted off to sleep. In fact, she said she had been doing that same thing – trying to get back there – when I interrupted her silence.

Hope then went on to tell me that, on the previous morning, she had made love with her boyfriend. She spoke of how delicious this had been until all of a sudden he had jumped out of bed to prepare for work, leaving her feeling as if her heart had been "torn out of her chest." I said that I wondered if perhaps she was also letting me know how it felt to be deeply touched and fed by me throughout the last analytic week, only to feel me wrenched painfully away from her on the weekend, as if a vital part of her had been torn away, or as if I had dropped her, just as she may have felt her mother's nipple torn out of her mouth, leaving a terrible wound in its place.

As Hope's hand went to her mouth and she began to weep, I told her that she also seemed to be communicating something about how she experienced me on Monday – transformed into a dangerous predator-intruder – and how my betrayal of her trust had almost paralyzed her capacity to allow me to help her with these feelings of being dropped and wounded.

It might be seen that, by *filling the space between us with these soft sensations of her own tongue in her mouth*, Hope could give herself the continuous comfort which I failed to offer. However, this also seemed to stop up the analytic work, interfering with the kind of healing which comes through interaction with a caring human being.

Hope later went on in that session to say that she had often taken refuge in the pink cloud as a child, feeling its suffocating sweetness, getting lost in the pinkness of it all, as if this "pink" were the soft, wet, and full sensation of her own tongue in her mouth. This feeling filled her mind at times when she felt unbearably disappointed, empty and alone.

Tustin reminds us that we must be able to bear these terrifyingly lonely states of dissolution for our patients for quite some time, so that we may be better equipped to weave, out of the threads of our own experience, a blanket of understanding which may eventually serve to adequately hold and warm them, if we are to expect them to relinquish the self-soothing protections they have come to rely upon so heavily.

Hendrick

In contrast to Hope, who used *soft sensation shapes* engendered by her own tongue to protect against unbearable sensations of falling and emptiness, Hendrick, a professional man in his forties, seemed to rely more upon the *hard autistic objects* that Tustin tells us about. As I will be reporting extensively on Hendrick's analysis in Chapter 4, at this point I will confine my discussion of this analysand to just one aspect of his treatment, which demonstrates his use of hard objects.

Hendrick's mother had a history of clinical depression which pre-dated his birth. One of Hendrick's unique characteristics was manifested in his lack of verbal expression for feelings such as sadness, anger, or even pleasurable excitement. These emotional states were instead expressed in terms of substances, movements, and physical sensations in various parts of his or others' bodies. For example, he spoke of his tears as moisture without reference to feeling sad; of his nostrils twitching without the notion of anxiety; of his feet moving, without the experience of sexual arousal; and I struggled to de-code this idiosyncratic mode of expression for well over a year.

Hendrick seemed to feel ever at risk of having his feelings spilled out through what he referred to as "the hole in his body" or "the hole in his head," which were equated with the deep emotional wounds that impacted both his physical and intellectual functioning. His longing for me over the weekend was not felt, but was instead heard as a barking dog that startled him, hurtling him out of bed onto the floor, gasping for air. He threatened to kill the dog if only he could find him. I imagined that he was communicating about feeling caged up by an uncaring owner who left him out alone to whine and howl. I took his murderous threat to be an expression of an almost-suicidal despair and a preference for death by his own hand over the feelings of spilling and falling uncontrollably when left by an uncaring mother-analyst over the long weekend break.

Hendrick often spoke of his compulsive masturbation as a means of stopping the twitching nostrils and the wiggling feet in a soothing rhythmic way, and he used earplugs to keep himself from spilling frightened out of bed. Often in the sessions he would present an impermeable hostility towards me or a stone wall of silence, or he would bite his fingers mercilessly in a desperate attempt to ward off contact with the more vulnerable soft center of his experience.

By the beginning of the third year of his analysis, Hendrick had revealed much of surprise to both of us. For example, murderous jealousy and paralyzing guilt experienced towards a child patient that he had encountered in the waiting room led to the unearthing of long-buried memories (which will be discussed in detail in Chapter 4).

Such memories came in spurts. Often I felt certain that these surprise revelations – these moments from his history – had leaked out, like some vital substance from deep within an inner capsule, when the emotional contact between us was such that he could be certain that I would retain and contain for him, in my mind, this precious if painful overflow. Then, just as quickly, these would be sealed off during subsequent weekend or holiday breaks in the treatment, leaving us to contend with many mysterious gaps in his experience.

In the twenty-ninth month of the analysis, Hendrick was able to tell me more about the nature of this deeply hidden reservoir, in which those painfully traumatic or unbearably pleasurable early experiences were stored for safekeeping, albeit out of reach of his conscious awareness and the analytic process. One Monday Hendrick returned from a horseback-packing trip to the mountains, where he had gained some sense of his own progress. He felt proud to tell me that he had ridden a horse up and down many miles of narrow switchback trails without the fear of tumbling to his death. Unlike times past, this time he had faith that his mount had been along these same trails before. She seemed sure-footed and confident. He felt that perhaps his lifelong fear of heights had finally been overcome and was quite pleased and encouraged by this accomplishment, which he connected with the work of the analysis.

This was Hendrick's first open and direct acknowledgement of being in any way helped by the analysis. He spoke of how gratifying it was for him to tell his colleagues at work about his weekend, and noted how this differed from his usual sense that he had nothing going on in his personal life to share with others. He had previously felt so dead and empty, especially after a weekend away.

In the Tuesday hour Hendrick was quite sullen and sarcastic, spending a good portion of the session in a familiar and impenetrable mute silence. I found myself falling into a state of despair, feeling him lost to me – unreachable and almost dead – followed by a conviction that he was punishing me for some heinous crime that I had unwittingly committed. When asked about his silence, he would simply reply, "I'm empty."

On Wednesday, we came to understand that he had felt lost and alone at the end of the Monday hour, as I became transformed first into a deadly, depressed mother who was leaving him alone, spilling over with excitement, and then, on Tuesday, into a mean, withholding and envious mother who had taken from him all that of which he was proud. It seemed his impermeable muteness was employed primarily as a primitive survival tactic to stem the flow of dissolution-ment into nothingness, and secondarily, as a means of preserving his good objects from attack.

47

I had the feeling that we had somewhat mitigated his disillusionment with me in the Wednesday hour when I found Hendrick in the waiting room on Thursday, socks and shoes off, stretched like a hammock between the two benches that he referred to as "love seats." "I wouldn't have thought I could do this," he exclaimed as he collected up his belongings and came into my consulting room. "But it wasn't as uncomfortable as I thought," he added, referring to his new position. As he lay on the couch, I said that I thought he was telling me something of how he had felt after the Wednesday hour: that the two of us had somehow been linked together, connected in a comfortable if awkward way between the sessions, and that he was now feeling it unnecessary to hide his tender-parts from me.

Seemingly touched by my remarks, Hendrick soon recalled how he had felt on Monday with Sarah, his supervisor, when she seemed to reach out to him in a personal way by asking how his holiday had been. He said, "I was afraid – no one wants to get into that shit – my loneliness. I guess I felt that she was like my mother. I did call my mother over the weekend and I finally asked her about Kathleen [referring to the dead baby-sister he had resurrected in his memory some months before in the analysis]. But she seemed too busy to bother with me. She sounded superficial and preoccupied with others, and I was so disappointed." Then he paused and said, "I guess I just felt that I had nothing personal to share with Sarah."

When I observed how curious it was that, with Sarah, he had felt empty and seemed to have forgotten his experience of the weekend trip of which he had been so proud, just as he had felt empty with me in the Tuesday hour, he fell suddenly silent. When he finally spoke again, it was only to utter the words, "Four worn-out tires."

I had come to know such utterances as Hendrick's attempt to share with me various images as they flashed across his mind. These flashes of his experiences seemed often to startle him and rarely could he comment on them in the moment. However, this time he seemed physically to struggle in his prone position, as if to move his experience from his body into his mind. Finally he was able to speak: "I'm wondering if they have inner tubes or not."

I replied that it appeared that it might be important to know. "Yes," he said, and further explained, "An inner tube is for protection. In case of blow-out, it would be less dangerous." Suddenly I thought to say, "I think these four worn-out tires are the analysis, felt perhaps like the mother-me on the weekend, when you experience me as too worn-out to get excited about you and your progress, or too preoccupied with my other children to help you bear your dreadful losses, fears, and loneliness. This must feel to you like some kind of dangerous blow-out – like going mad or exploding to pieces, or leaking out everywhere."

His enthusiastic nodding in response to what I had offered encouraged me to add that I thought the inner tube in his mind was his way of protecting himself from the threat of losing everything. "Perhaps you keep all these personal experiences sealed up in this tube for safety. But it's so tightly sealed that you

48

become cut-off from the very things you feel you need in order to have a relationship with me, as with Sarah, which is like forgetting, and leaves you feeling empty inside."

For Hendrick, the skin, or "four worn-out tires," representing the experience of the four analytic hours during the break (the "blow-out"), required fortification, at least for some time, by the "inner" tube or the encapsulation of experience during felt absence and loss. However, in his muteness, he was indeed sealed off from his experiences – both past and present – and future contact was in jeopardy as well.

As Tustin recommended, going forward in an imaginative way, rather than giving in to our despair, distinguishes the analyst from figures in the patient's past, those who perhaps could not tolerate the narcissistic wounds or the feelings of abject loneliness which patients like Hendrick often engender in us for a very long time.

Like autistic objects and shapes, psychosomatic presentations also seem to be effective substitutes for unconscious phantasies. However these must not be confused with mentational processes. Rather these are what Tustin (1987) called "innate forms." She defined these as innate biological predispositions with psychic overtones. In psychosomatic patients, as with autistic patients, these forms have remained un-transformed by reciprocal interactions with an attentive thinking mother, and thus they find expression in physical illness where the symptom may act as a bodily container or a second skin (Bick 1968), functioning as depositories for unmentalized experiences (Mitrani 1993b; 1995b) that ensure survival, but which further block development and transformation.

Carla

Not unlike Hendrick, my patient Carla (who was asthmatic) seemed to rely upon a hard, impermeable object to protect her from spilling out uncontrollably. However, rather than being expressed in an attitude – like Hendrick's "chip" – Carla's hard object took the form of a hard mucous plug in her bronchial tubes. Having lost her mother to complications of asthma at a very early age, just shortly after they had been abandoned by her father, Carla presented herself mostly as a tough, streetwise chick, whose toughness served as a second skin equated with the tight leather clothing she often wore, and which we eventually traced to her image of the father's erect member representing a paternal protective function that she could provide for herself in her father's absence.

In the second year of her analysis a fragile baby-part of Carla began to emerge. In one session, Carla began to cry like never before, a cry that penetrated me to a depth that seemed to correspond to the stratum from which it emanated. This stratum appeared to be far beneath either the level of her father's abandonment or her mother's death, perhaps somewhere in her deepest and earliest experience of infancy. When I said as much, she replied, "I feel like something terrible wants out of me. I can't let myself breathe. I don't want it to come out. I'm afraid I'll never stop crying." She seemed to be saying that she would spill out and be gone, unable to collect herself at the end of the hour as she experienced once again the loss of her tentative sense of security. I will re-introduce Carla in Chapter 6 in an attempt to convey more about the specifics of what I learned of her early infantile experience as it was revealed in the transference and countertransference.

Many patients, like Carla, while lacking the mental structure necessary to catch the unbearable overflow of their painful experiences, take refuge within certain areas of their own body just as they had once been protected deep inside the recesses of the body of the mother. Others substitute the delusion of being at-one-with the body of the analyst. Such was the case for Robert, a 34-year-old man who had been referred for analysis after a series of hospitalizations following the suicidal death of his mother.

Robert

Robert's psychiatric history and his obvious lack of a sense of continuity were extreme to the degree that he needed, at least for a time, to be seen six times per week. Even so, he suffered extreme despair and anxiety between the analytic hours and during the Sunday break.

In the seventh month of the analysis, Robert was reminded of the events surrounding his actual birth. While living in a third-world country, no doctor had been available when his mother commenced labor, and thus the delivery was performed by his inexperienced and impatient father, resulting in trauma for both mother and infant. The grief, rage, and terror of this event were soon to be re-experienced by my patient with me in the transference, provoked by my moving office.

From a quiet, dark brown paneled room – which he described as "humming" and in which we had spent the first few months of the treatment – Robert suddenly found himself in what he felt to be a too-bright environment, with light-colored walls and carpeting. This catastrophe was felt in a thoroughly sensation-dominated way, as though the sounds, sights, and textures were painful impingements uncontrollably entering his body in unmitigated form, leading to an experience of actual physical pain.

Robert often cried out from such painful assaults, and could not open his eyes for many months while on the couch in my new office. Every sound precipitated a bodily start, and he longed for the feel of the wooded wall next to the couch in my old consulting room, which he had often stroked as a soothing presence in times of extreme distress, just as he had stroked and been stroked by his mother in her bed throughout childhood and early adolescence, to soothe both of them in their seemingly shared and undifferentiated depression.

Similar to the autistic patients described by Tustin, Robert had had an unduly close physical relationship with his mother, one which had fostered false hopes that his body was one with an ever-present immortal being, and as such would never come to an end. When Robert's mother died, he was forced to become aware of his bodily separateness from her. She had jumped from a ten-story window to her death, but he was left falling forever – out of windows, out of spaces and absences.

Unable to cope with such terrors, Robert was tenaciously insistent that I be the reincarnation of this immortal mother, and he attempted to maneuver me in ways which would give credence to this belief, since he felt certain that his life depended upon a sense of physical continuity with me. The loss of my old consulting room, as the womb-mother, re-evoked in him the earliest experiences of being barbarically torn from his mother's body at birth, and the later versions of this event, which were numerous, all leading to the mother's suicide as the final straw that toppled what he called his "house of cards."

In the following session, occurring midway between our move to my new office and the Spring break, Robert demonstrated one of the numerous ways in which he attempted to reinstate some sense of safety by reconstituting a concrete delusion of bodily continuity with me. In this session, Robert began by telling me about a woman who had just had a spontaneous abortion, and about how sad he felt when she appeared to him like a wounded animal. Then he told me how desperate was his need to take photographs of various scenes that had come into view during the day in order to bring these to my attention in palpable form.

I acknowledged Robert's unspeakable frustration over the awareness of his separateness from me between the hours, and his desire to have me know what he had experienced; how having to tell me about these experiences only made all the more harsh the cruel fact of our separateness, adding to his frustration, his woundedness and grief.

Robert then told me about having come upon a shop that sold large statuary, displayed in great numbers in front of it. He described the atmosphere of the day as gray and gloomy, the same color as the plaster from which the statues were made. He said that although the figures were of varying styles, shapes, and sizes, some replicating ancient works of art, others more contemporary, arranged with some in the foreground and others behind, he could envision in his mind's eye the composition of a black and white photograph in which all distinction between background and foreground, old and new, large and small, would be lost. As there was no sun, there would be no shadow and all would appear as one. Time would be compressed, spaces would be obliterated, as would any difference between these otherwise varied objects.

I said that he seemed to be telling me about a state of pristine at-one-ment that could be frozen in time with the click of his camera shutter, providing the concrete proof of this blissful state of affairs. I also called his attention to the urgency of such proof at night and on Sundays, when the separation between us became unbearable to him. His response was to tell me that the pronoun "I" was the thing he hated most in all the world. The solution Robert proposed to what he called "the problem of this analysis which made [him] be an 'I'" was the fantasy of placing his camera on a tripod in my room, setting it for a thirty-minute exposure, which would blur the two of us into a state of one-ness with no space between and no distinction of sex, age, or position in the room or in the relationship. The resultant photograph would serve as tangible proof of this perfect state, an amulet without which he would feel ever at risk.

Such delusions permeated the analysis of this young man, and he often yearned for the safe if constricting enclosure of the hospital and the four-point restraints he had known many times prior to the beginning of our work together. Perhaps the unthinkable, uncontrollable over-spill of emotions that threatened Robert with dissolution is what we call madness, and the straitjacket or four-point restraints were, like the autistic shell, a defense against this madness. However, like the locked ward of a mental hospital, such delusions disallowed, at least for some time, the establishment of caring connections with the therapist – the "gentle straitjacket" to which Tustin (1986b) referred.

At a much later point in his analysis, after such connections were allowed to develop, Robert began to bring photographs he had taken – this time in vivid color and clearly three-dimensional – of ancient structures gently and loosely shrouded and surrounded by supportive scaffolding, all in the process of restoration. This restoration eventually resulted in the rebuilding of Robert's career as a photographer of some note, his marriage and the birth of a son.

Vickie

Like Robert's concrete fantasies, obsessional thinking and fluid speech are often used by some patients to hold themselves together in a self-made womb during times of extreme distress. Unfortunately, this form of "second skin" may thus go unnoticed and therefore unabated in the process of our psychoanalytic therapies that rely heavily on words and thought to convey meaning, as I will here demonstrate in the case of a patient whom I call Vickie.

Vickie had been raised by a severely disturbed mother who, as the patient was told, closed the door to her newborn infant's room when she cried because she did not know how to mother her. In brief, Vickie seemed to re-experience in the transference a time in early infancy when, while lying in her crib, she had attempted to make meaning of her mother's failure to attend to her.

I often had the impression of a baby who must have been continually obsessing about whether she had cried too loud or perhaps not cried loudly enough. Maybe the pitch of her cry was too high or maybe too low. Maybe she should continue to cry out or perhaps she should stop at once, and, if so, for how long? Vickie seemed to wonder was Mother ill or asleep, or had she finally left forever? Was Mother dead or was it she who did not exist?

I had a sense that this patient had been unable to really be a baby-at-one-with-her-mother, and so was pushed to develop a pseudo-mind in service of avoiding a dreadful experience of perishing, as well as a rather precocious concern for her caretaking object. She would then become terrified when, in this avoidant state, she could no longer feel her own body.

Initially my interventions with Vickie ran the expected gamut: transference interpretations addressing the weekend breaks, the holidays and the endings of sessions, and the experiences of abandonment along with the anxieties and defenses against these anxieties provoked by painful separations. However, although Vickie's material was quite communicative of this type of experience as it has been discussed in the mainstream of Kleinian literature, it became apparent that *her ruminations were not really thoughts connected to experiences, but rather an agglomeration of words that provided a cocoon of sensation within which she could wrap her precarious self for protection.* She seemed also to use those interpretations of mine that addressed the content of her associations as additional stuff for the construction and maintenance of that cocoon. Consequently I was often left feeling that we were *going nowhere together.*

Indeed I was puzzled by this pattern for some time, but when I was finally able to understand that this was exactly the point – that we were to be *prevented from going anywhere* – and when I was finally able to communicate to her my sense of her perpetual activity of *spinning me, and my words as well as her own, into a safe and impenetrable cocoon* within which she might be able to protect her self and me from some catastrophic experience of *being gone* – she had the following association.

Tearfully Vickie recalled that she had once been told by a family member that on the day she was brought home from the hospital she was left wrapped up in a blanket in the middle of her mother's bed, where no one was permitted to enter or to pick her up in order to offer her comfort when she cried. It appeared that Vickie's naive if well-meaning mother believed that this treatment would help to "toughen up her baby" and would diminish her dependency upon her caretakers.

With such patients it may be said that *if we attend only to the text rather than the texture of their communications,* we run the risk of colluding with their attempts to "toughen-up" and to protect themselves against the heartfelt awareness of these early experiences, while failing to help them to contain these. Such toughening leaves little room for the emergence and development of a genuine "felt-self" which, in Vickie's case, had became more and more compressed and out of reach of feeling.

Literary afterthoughts

Before concluding this chapter, I wish to add that I believe that Tustin not only helped us with her insights to open ourselves up to fresh perspectives on our patients' communications, but she also encouraged us to turn to the poets and artists who might further help us to develop an even greater understanding of the experience of breakdown, which most of our patients fear and which some may have already encountered (Winnicott 1974).

For example, in her novel – *Celestial Navigations* – Anne Tyler (1974) described one character who, like Vickie, lived in a fragile yet impermeable world created as a variation on a design by his mother. Tyler depicted the constant terror which threatened to overwhelm her protagonist should he emerge from his self-made fortress. I believe she described Jeremy's experience of the "black hole" in a most sensitive way when she wrote the following:

These are some of the things that Jeremy Pauling dreaded: using the telephone, answering the doorbell, opening mail, leaving his house, making purchases. Also wearing new clothes, standing in open spaces, meeting the eyes of a stranger, eating in the presence of others, turning on electrical appliances. Some days, he awoke to find the weather sunny and his health adequate, and his work progressing beautifully; yet there would be a nagging hole of uneasiness deep inside him, some flaw in the center of his well-being, steadily corroding around the edges and widening until he could not manage to lift his head from the pillow. Then he would have to go over every possibility. Was it something he had to do? Somewhere to go? Someone to see? Until the answer came: Oh yes! Today he had to call the Gas Company about the oven. A two-minute chore, nothing to worry about. He knew that. HE KNEW. Yet he lay on his bed feeling flattened and defeated, and it seemed to him that life was a series of hurdles that he had been tripping over for decades, with the end nowhere in sight. On the Fourth of July, in a magazine article about famous Americans, he read that a man could develop character by doing one thing he disliked every day of his life. Did that mean that all these hurdles might have some value? Jeremy copied the quotation on an index card and tacked it to the window sill beside his bed. It was his hope that the card would remove half of every pain by pointing out its purpose, like a mother telling her child, "This is good for you. Believe me." But in fact, all it did was depress him, for it made him conscious of the number of times each day he had to steel himself for something. Why, nine-tenths of his life consisted of doing things he disliked! Even getting up in the morning! He had already overcome a dread before he was even dressed! If that quotation was right, shouldn't he have the strongest character imaginable? Yet he didn't. He had become aware lately that other people seemed to possess an inner core of hardness that they took for granted. They hardly seemed to notice it was there; they had come by it naturally. Jeremy had been born without it.

(pp. 76–7)

Tyler also communicated something of the nature of Jeremy's survival tactics, what it felt like inside his protective shell and the price he paid for protection, in the following passage:

Jeremy Pauling saw life in a series of flashes, startling moments so brief that they could arrest motion in mid-air. Like photographs, they were handed to him at unexpected times, introduced by a neutral voice: here is where you are now. Take a look. Between flashes, he sank into darkness. He drifted into a daze, studying what he had seen. Wondering if he HAD seen it. Forgetting finally, what it was that he was wondering about, and floating off into numbness again.

(p. 37)

Like Jeremy Pauling, the patients I have discussed in this chapter frequently experienced and often attempted to describe the numbness resulting from the use of autistic protections. There was always a certain quality of poignancy conveyed as they complained of isolation from their own internal experiences and objects, as well as from the potential healing effects of their contact with me. I believe this experience must be distinguished from the triumphant pleasure of manic flight that we often observe in these very same patients who, while operating on other levels, evade and avoid feelings of shame, guilt, or persecution.

Like Jeremy Pauling, Hendrick often experienced his life in flashes; Carla called this "checking out" on herself; Hope referred to these states as "losing" herself; Robert described this as "falling through windows"; while Vickie complained of feeling "disembodied" and "gone." When we listen carefully to our patients, I believe we can detect their desperate appeals for our help in finding a way out of the autistic tomb and the numbness that incarcerates them.

Just as the analyst must discriminate between unintegration and disintegration; between paranoid-schizoid and depressive anxieties; between internal and external realities; between "attacks on linking" and links which have yet to be formed or which are at best tenuous in nature; between active and passive; between words as communication and words used defensively as action; between the varying dimensions and geoanatomical locations of mental experience, we need to be able to make the fine discriminations between these various primitive states of mind in order to be maximally responsive to our patients in the thera-peutic relationship. In the following chapter I will highlight such discriminations, which I believe contributed to Hendrick's experience of what Bion (1962a) termed the containing object.

4

The "flying Dutchman" and the search for a containing object[7]

The moving finger writes and having writ moves on; nor all thy piety and wit can lure it back to cancel half a line; nor all thy tears wash out a word of it.

Omar Khayyám, *The Rubáiyát*

In the seventeenth-century legend of "The Flying Dutchman," a sea captain returns home from a long voyage to his new bride. Mistaking her kindness to others as a sign of her infidelity, he is taken over by envy and delusional jealousy, and murders her in her bed. The Dutchman is unrepentant before the court as he proclaims his belief that man could sail to the edges of the earth 'til doomsday and never find one faithful woman. He is subsequently condemned to death, returns to his cell to await execution, and falls asleep in his berth.

Suddenly he awakens from a deep slumber in the dead of night to find the door of his cell open and the guards sleeping as though drugged. Fleeing the morning sun that will bring his certain execution, he finds his ship ready to sail in the bay. His loyal crew receives him and they are carried off by a light wind to the safety of the open sea. Secure at last, the Dutchman falls asleep once again in his cabin. He has a dream in which a voice speaks to him. All at once he knows the awful truth: his wife has been chaste, *he has killed sweet innocence*. He wants to die, indeed he tries to kill himself. However, a power greater than his own will thwarts his act of suicide. The Dutchman soon realizes that, in his madness in the courtroom, he has pronounced his own fate: he will wander over all the generations and all the seas looking for a woman who might be willing to die, so that he might know the meaning of love. But was it *just a dream?*

In Albert Lewin's 1951 film classic, *Pandora and the Flying Dutchman*, the Dutchman finds himself centuries later and nearly without hope of ever finding his salvation when he meets the actress, Pandora. As he finds their connection deepening, he attempts to sail away in order to spare this woman who loves him and whom he loves. However Pandora is not deterred. Once a woman without heart, she is transformed by her relationship with the Dutchman, and is willing to join him in his pursuit of peace, uncertain of the fate that awaits them.

Intrigued by this legend (and later the film) when first introduced to it as a youngster, I was reminded of it early on in the treatment of Hendrick, the patient I have already referred to briefly in Chapter 3. Hendrick put me in mind of Lewin's character, Hendrick Van der Zee, portrayed by the actor James Mason in the film. I thought of this middle-aged man as a sort of flying Dutchman, since he too seemed to have been searching for an eternity for one who, *metaphorically speaking*, could and would be willing to die for him.

By this I mean to say that, by the time Hendrick was referred for analysis, he had been in and out of numerous therapies for nearly three decades and had yet to find someone who would "take a transference": someone who might be willing to accept those painful and deadly aspects of his infantile experience and beyond, which fueled the hyperbolic projections that he meted out from the first hours of the treatment. Unable to find such a person, Hendrick seemed condemned to a living death, an omnipotent immortality of aloneness originally taken up in the name of survival.

Perhaps one might consider the case of Hendrick – not unlike the legendary tale of the flying Dutchman – as emblematic of a situation observed with many patients who, while in infancy, *failed to find an object who might survive their projections* and who therefore spend their lives alone if "immortal," always seeking one who might be able to sustain and transform their experiences.

Notwithstanding the classical oedipal implications of the "Dutchman" allegory, I wish to focus this chapter mainly on those aspects of the analysis of Hendrick in which oedipal elements were either altogether absent or, when present, appeared to function as decoys for the earliest infantile transference lying barely concealed beneath the surface. It goes without saying that, at other moments in the treatment, late oedipal (Freud) as well as early oedipal (Klein) triadic issues were present and attended to when these were perceived to be of immediate urgency in the transference as well as in the patient's daily life, and when these were not primarily defensively motivated.

Throughout this chapter, I reference certain theoretical/technical considerations that may have informed my work, such as Bion's (1962a, b) model of the "container-contained"[8] and his model of "projective identification as a form of primitive communication" between mother and infant (Bion 1959; 1967a) as it applies to the analytic relationship and the infant's (and later the analysand's) search for coherence.

Additionally I will underscore the analytic function of "taking the transference," which may be understood as referring not merely to a cognitive understanding of or an empathic attunement with what the patient is feeling and experiencing in any given moment, but as *an unconscious introjection of certain aspects of the patient's inner world, and a resonance with those elements of the analyst's inner world, such that the analyst is able to feel herself to be that unwanted part of the patient's self or that unbearable object that had formerly been introjectively identified with by the patient.*

I believe that this function requires that the analyst develop her capacity to allow for a tentative blurring of boundaries between herself and her analysand as well as an ability to maintain some degree of observing ego necessary to her interpretive functioning. However, I am convinced that any conscious attempt at "role playing" or going-along with the analysand by the analyst is bound to be experienced by the analysand as "unreal" and only serves to increase persecutory feelings and the defenses against these, and/or fosters an "as-if-ness" in the analysand. It has been my experience that, by being "real" with the patient, the analyst risks exposing herself to an awareness of her own infantile vulnerabilities and the dangers inherent in such awareness.

The above-mentioned concepts, meaningful to me in Hendrick's case, may indeed be apposite in the work with other patients who require that we do more than just comprehend their dilemma. It is essential that the analyst be willing to first experience and take up a given role in the transitional space (Winnicott 1951) of the transference/countertransference, and subsequently that she be able to articulate how she is being experienced, so that a membrane between inside and outside, between phantasy and reality, and between self and other may gradually evolve in the mind of the analysand.

Beginning

By the time Hendrick came to me, in his late forties, he had been engaged in one form of psychotherapy or another since late adolescence. A markedly depressed and angry man, I found him standing in my waiting room, a physically imposing raw-boned 6 foot 6 inches. He lumbered into my office with an air of menace and sat, stoop-shouldered and sullen, inspecting the premises with suspicion. His face bore the scars of a hellish case of adolescent acne which – in concert with his unusually huge feet and hands – gave him an awesomely scary appearance. His expression was brooding and, although his posture was slumped, he appeared ready for combat, fists clenched and eyes scanning for opponents.

At that time, Hendrick, who held an advanced degree, was on the verge of being dismissed from his position in a medically related field due to his belligerent behavior especially toward female co-workers, many of whom he had reduced to tears on more than one occasion. Hearing this I felt forewarned of what was in store for me if I agreed to work with this man.

In part, Hendrick was seeking help because he was apprehensive about his professional future, fearing that he might be labeled "unemployable" if he could not learn to control his interactions with fellow workers, which he characterized as "bullying and intimidating." He was also concerned about the poverty of his personal life, having recently returned from a holiday trip in the country, saddened that he had no one to share nature's beauty with either during or afterward.

However, even more relevant,[9] Hendrick seemed to be expressing the extreme nature of the vulnerabilities that lay hidden beneath his tough facade when he told me that he had "a hole in his head and a hole in his body." He felt that he was "just too much for anyone." It was soon to become clear that these declarations constituted the major threads woven throughout the fabric of his sense of self.

It seemed, at least in our initial interview and for some time onward, that Hendrick's human contacts outside those at work were limited to his mother, his sister and brother-in-law, and their children. He briefly referred to his mother as "a zero" and said little about the remainder of his family. His father had died of cancer when the patient was 15, yet he claimed that he did not remember anything about him.

Hendrick also confided that he had never been able to consummate a sexual relationship with either a woman or a man. He had lived with one woman, together with her young son, for a brief period of time some twenty years prior to the analysis. Although they had slept together in the same bed, "there was no intercourse." In spite of this, Hendrick had been quite content to be "the man of the house" by providing this woman and her adolescent son with some of the comforts she could not otherwise afford. It seemed that they had enjoyed each other's companionship and affection. However, she had broken off their relationship quite suddenly after an incident in which Hendrick had become uncontrollably enraged at the boy for "drinking up all the milk in the refrigerator."

Here I felt I was being privileged early on to a glimpse of a very-little-Hendrick who had failed to connect in a deep emotional way with his parents, and who subsequently consoled himself with the benefits of a pre-maturity that functioned to cover over his infantile despair, disappointment, and wrath. I also took note of the possibility that, if I were to collude with Hendrick's empty shell of genitality, I might run the risk of simply reinforcing his defensive organization.

Prior to and for some years after the above relationship ended, Hendrick spent nearly all his weekends engaged in a myriad of public bathroom escapades in which he would participate in anonymous sex-play with "parts of people" through what he called "glory holes," or he would lurk on the periphery of school playgrounds with fantasies of dominating young boys. Although he never acted-out these fantasies, Hendrick damned himself as a pedophile. I took this reported behavior as an expression of his attempts to distance himself from the pain of real relationships and to gain dominance, in phantasy, over those vulnerable aspects of his self.

Hendrick told me that he "had always felt repulsed by the thought of a woman's physique, especially her breasts and vagina." He assumed that he was "hopelessly homo." He hated this sense of himself, since he equated homo-sexuality with being a "fucked-up-little-kid." He admitted having no friendships to speak of and, although he visited his family weekly, he said that he felt "estranged and misfit."[10]

Apparently, Hendrick had learned of analysis in his college days, only later on observing a colleague benefiting greatly from such a treatment. Perhaps not surprisingly, Hendrick was rejected by several analysts before finding his way to me. Nevertheless, his determination to have an analysis was very moving for me and, from that first meeting onward, I perceived in him a certain *unconscious cooperativeness*: a genuine desire and an ability to communicate in a primitive way that helped me to connect with an inchoate aspect of his personality and its as-yet-undigested experience.

Certainly Hendrick's conscious cooperation was expressed in his devoted attendance in his analytic hours, as he was rarely late (even though he had to drive for well over an hour each way to get to my office) and missed sessions only infrequently when required to attend meetings after work. Of course, it was of some concern that he denied having dreams or phantasies about anything, and could only describe his sensations in idiosyncratic terms. For example, tears were referred to as "moisture," sexual excitation as "twitching," and a picture formed in my mind of an infant whose mother was unbearably humiliated and embarrassed to the point of shame at the sight of her baby's body and its functions, inventing some clandestine way of attending to him and of communicating with him about his physique. Emotions were something else altogether. These seemed so overwhelming as to be absolutely unspeakable.[11]

Hendrick had little verbal memory of his childhood experiences. Consequently, from our first meeting forward, he consistently and violently projected powerful experiences into me, unable to find other means of commu-nication. For quite some time whenever I attempted to respond to him he would retreat into sleep, as if he expected me to push his "too much" experiences back defensively. Thus, I came to think of him as the flying Dutchman, when it seemed he had been doomed to solitude, emerging periodically to find someone who could "love him enough to die for him," then disappearing for fear that someone might. I also felt strongly that there was a lonely and precarious innocent protected inside this often-monstrous and menacing fortress. To illustrate this, I will present some material from our first hours of contact.

First contact

At the end of the initial interview, Hendrick stood over the chair in which I sat, extending his hand, at the same time challenging me to shake it and daring me not to. I sensed that either way I would be faulted and condemned to death. While taking his hand, I felt terribly small, frightened, helpless, vulnerable and, yes, bullied and intimidated. Subsequent hours were no less disturbing as Hendrick repeatedly cursed at me, in his booming baritone voice, about everything from my physical appearance to the layout of my room, my reserve, and of course the fee he was paying me (even though he knew that this was considerably reduced).

When I could recover my wits long enough to actually think about these early experiences with Hendrick, I grew more and more convinced that he was attempting to get across to me some sense of what it was like to be a very-little-he, constantly under threat from someone upon whom he depended for his very survival. As I managed to convey this to him in some detail, as it seemed timely in those first few hours of the analysis, this line of interpretation seemed to usher in, bit by bit, Hendrick's earliest memories of his mother.

In the interest of clarity, before going on to convey a sense of Hendrick's experience of his mother, I wish to add that my earliest interpretations were based largely upon intuition, rooted in emotional experience, induced by the patient's style of presentation and fortified by my convictions regarding *the communicative function of projective identification* (Bion 1959; 1967). The patient's responses to such interpretations served either to verify or to annul them. However, I feel strongly that the accuracy of any intervention is only of value so long as it results in movement and increasing openness in the session and in subsequent sessions, as well as an expansion of the patient's inner world and his functioning outside the analysis over time.

Mother

By all accounts, Mother was prim, proper, and reserved, a spinster of 30 years, when her family finally arranged a marriage with "a nice Jewish boy." She gave birth to Hendrick, her first child, when she was 35.

In one Monday hour, just after the patient's birthday, he told me that his mother had visited his apartment for the first time. After she had gone, Hendrick found a package containing a blender, left unceremoniously on his kitchen counter. He knew that Mother must have left it there for him – a birthday gift, one she had known he needed – but he was struck by the sense that she had left it there without so much as a word, as if anonymously. "She's afraid to touch me! There's never any direct contact between us. She won't even let me kiss her!"

Recalling the previous week's work, in which some important links had been made between past and present situations and his experiences of me around the anniversary of his birth, it seemed that Hendrick was now giving me a sense of the mother he had known as a child, as well as a sense of the mother-me he now experienced in the transference. I said that I thought it had felt to him that I had given him a much-needed tool for bringing together and understanding his experiences in the last week, a kind of birthday present. However, he had not discovered this until I was gone, and so my leaving him for the weekend had seemed an evasive act on my part, as if I did not want any part of him or his affectionate gratitude. Hendrick replied that he thought I had to take some time away from him or I'd "get sick."

The patient recollected that, from the time he was 2 or 3 years old, his mother had been "sick" and both his father and uncle "had considered confining her to a sanitarium, something that was unheard of in those times, especially in working-class families" residing in that conservative part of the country. It appeared that Mother's "sickness" was characterized by frequent and violent fits of ire, which began with verbal assaults aimed at a little Hendrick and culminated in bouts of vomiting. On these occasions, when Mother began to erupt, Hendrick would run and hide from her, but would soon return to her side when she became physically ill. As he watched helplessly while she "spilled her guts into the toilet" Hendrick was afraid that she might die.

His associations coalesced into a profile of a mother filled with uncontained and unbearable grief and rage, overflowing at times onto her young child. I could imagine that his flight in terror of what he could neither comprehend nor tolerate left Mother with no other solution. It appeared that her affective eruptions were transformed into their somatic counterpart, finding receptivity only in an inanimate object (the toilet). Her ensuing depression, sensitively perceived by her son, put Mother at risk for suicide and Hendrick returned to her side to give comfort, fearing for her life. He told me that on such occasions he would say, "I'm sorry Mommy." Tragically, her only reply would be, "There's no such thing as sorry!" I wondered for nearly two years what might have filled this mother with such irresolvable despair.

Waiting

One week, in the beginning of the third year of the analysis, an intermittent electrical short occurred in the device provided for patients to announce their presence in my waiting room. This device consisted of a button that, when pressed, would light up in both waiting room and consulting room. The short developed ten days before a holiday break. However, since my consulting room is situated such that I can usually hear the door to the waiting room open and shut, and since Hendrick would customarily arrive just before his hour, I was prompt as always, coming to get him from the waiting room without delay.

Nevertheless, it was curious that this patient had not called my attention to the inoperative call light, since he had always seemed exquisitely sensitive to even the slightest change in the setting (for example, the appearance of a new leaf on a plant, a thirty-second delay in my arrival, or a barely crooked picture on the wall would send him into a state of tantrum).

62

On my first day back from the break, Hendrick arrived quite early and I failed to hear him come into the waiting room. Thus, he was left waiting some minutes beyond the time for the commencement of his session. Finally, a frustrated Hendrick knocked loudly on the waiting-room door. When I went to get him, he stormed in, furious with me for leaving him out. As it was Hendrick's first day back, I took this up as an expression of his anger with me for "leaving him out" for so long over the break. "Bull shit!" he shouted, "You're just trying to avoid the obvious. *It's broken*. Why the hell don't you fix it? Of course, you're a woman, you can't fix it! You're a zero, just like Mother." He went on to accuse me of attempting to avoid criticism and said that he thought I was surprised that he would even mention it.

I confirmed that it was surprising that he had not referred to it before. Hendrick seemed puzzled and I clarified that the problem had existed for some ten days prior to the break. I added that it seemed to me that he had been quite lenient with me, not making any fuss until today. Upon hearing my response to his outburst, Hendrick allowed full expression to his fury, perhaps sensing that I did not experience his fussiness as "too much" to bear. "You're lying to me. It wasn't broken before. You're trying to drive me crazy!"

Hendrick continued to batter me with accusations and insults, in total disbelief that he had failed to notice that the light was out. He said that he *always, always* watched the light like a hawk, first to make certain that it went on so that he would know that I knew he had arrived; then watching for it to go off so that he would know when I was coming to fetch him. "I always watch for the light," he yelled at the top of his lungs as he sat up on the couch, his eyes bulging red with rage and hurt. "You can't tell me I don't, that I didn't notice it wasn't lit. That's just not right!"

It seemed to me that, in part, Hendrick was communicating his wish to remain unaware of some new development that had occurred before the holiday, some development that had been reversed as a consequence of the long break in our contact. As Hendrick continued to rail against me for some minutes, I felt helpless to interpret the meaning of his outburst, sensing that I would not be able to reach him through such an impenetrable barrier of paranoia and misunderstanding.

Suddenly he slipped into his shoes, stood up, stated that he couldn't stay any longer and marched off toward the door. There he hesitated for a few moments such that I felt a window open up in his barricade, just wide enough for me to say, calmly but firmly, that I felt *we both* needed to understand more about the source of his anguish: that we were not finished talking. I wondered aloud if he thought he could stay, although this felt dangerous to him. Hearing this, he returned to the couch, at first sitting up. As we spoke he became calmer and eventually lay down once again.

I conveyed to Hendrick my sense of a little-he who felt terribly betrayed by me right in that moment as well as over the long break in our contact; that he felt that I had then and was now deceiving him about who I was; that he had just

63

experienced a breakdown that he feared I could not bear to acknowledge and therefore could not put right; and that he was feeling confused and lost and needed me to light his way back at that moment.

In response to this avenue of interpretation, Hendrick plaintively replied, "It's broken!" I said that I thought he was letting me know that he also felt that somehow *I was broken*; that he worried that it might have been he who had damaged me beyond repair, and thus I could no longer help him. His apparent interest in what I was now saying encouraged me to add that he was furious with me for letting him down so painfully and perhaps feared that his anger might have made me dangerous and crazy. Perhaps this made him feel that he must get away from me right away.

Now thoughtful, Hendrick wondered if he hadn't noticed the broken light before the break because he just hadn't been looking for it. I found his insight stunning and concurred with him, reiterating that he had been vigilant in the past, watching to make sure that I noticed him and also to make certain that I would not harm or startle him with my presence, but that it seemed he was now considering that something *had* changed before the break and that he *had* been able to relax his vigilance.

Hendrick suggested that he "might have been more trusting lately." Maybe he "hadn't been looking for the light for some time." I said that it might have been that the long break in our contact had rendered me once again untrustworthy and that with my trustworthiness in doubt he had needed to get confirmation, especially on this day, that I was still there for him: evidence that I would not hurt or frighten him. Responding in a boyish tone, grinning from ear to ear, Hendrick ended the hour saying that he "liked that story," "but . . . " he added, "maybe something in me *doesn't* like the idea that I *can* trust you."

Here we capture, in full view, Hendrick's terror of change, even a change for the better. Could he dare to experience me as benign? And even if he did, could he tolerate the feeling of losing such a benign object? Or must he deny his experience, killing me off along with a trusting part of himself in the process. Could I contain his rage at my absence and imperfection, or would I condemn him to eternal aloneness through some horrendous act of retribution?

It seemed, in the end, that Hendrick did feel that both his anger and disappointment were received and sufficiently transformed. I had not been destroyed, neither had I condemned him. Such experiences of a containing object may have created a space in which Hendrick could consider an aspect of himself that was asserting itself *against* our connection, trying to break us up by provoking a sense of mistrust in him, not as a response to my failures and lapses, but rather emanating from a place within. The experience of being contained also appeared to facilitate the development of an internal dream-space within which Hendrick could now better accommodate his experiences.

First dreams

Indeed, in the following hour, Hendrick brought two dreams, the first of the analysis. While one was offered right from the start of the session, the second seemed to be presented in response to my interpretation of the first. In the inaugural dream:

> *Hendrick was watching as another man was snuggling up very close to a woman. He felt jealous of the couple and envious that this other man could have such a relationship with the woman. He was also in awe of the man both because he was touching and was being touched by this woman. Hendrick felt left out, hurt and angry.*

Although Hendrick offered no associations to this dream, I deemed it appropriate to speak to him about how the "he who felt left out" in the dream might represent not only "a he who felt terribly hurt and enraged about being left out of our close connection over the break," but also "a he who was watching over us as we came close to one another in the previous hour": a he who was at this very moment watching over us, and who was trying to let me know about some very painful feelings he was having.

Some may wonder why my interpretation of this first dream did not address the patient's phantasies and feelings regarding my husband, with whom I share the office suite. However, although I was cognizant of this factor and its potential effects, at the same time I was convinced by the way in which this dream was presented – especially with the absence of associations – that at this point in the treatment Hendrick was just beginning to develop some mental space for otherness. It seemed to me that the internal representation of the "third" as an aspect of the patient signaled Hendrick's inability to bear the presence of another lying outside of his omnipotent control. Therefore, I feared that I might be pushing him ahead precipitously by introducing "the father" at this point, rather than allowing him to develop further at his own pace.

Hendrick's response to this interpretation – of the earliest oedipal (triadic) situation and its internal representation – was embedded in the telling of the second dream. In that dream:

> *Hendrick looked on as a child was being torn apart by two women who were fighting over him. He said that it made him think of Solomon's judgment in the Bible.*

In brief association, Hendrick added that the child in the dream was a little boy who reminded him of photos he had seen of himself when he was very young. The women looked like Mother and perhaps one of his maternal aunts.

I said that I thought that he was letting me know that a very little-he was feeling torn between two experiences of me: of the mother-me who could be touched, who could touch him, and who could be trusted in this moment; and of another me who had driven him crazy with neglect. This led to further exploration that brought more definition to Hendrick's experience: the "short" had signaled the presence of the mommy-me who was incapable of making a connection with him and perhaps the absence of the daddy-me who would be able to repair our connection.

Here, in analyzing the second dream, I thought it more timely to begin to introduce the presence of the "father" in the transference. Indeed the way in which I chose to address both dreams recognized the active process of splitting employed by the patient in order to contend with these complex experiences: splitting of the self in the first dream and splitting of the analyst in the second dream. However, as I attempted to integrate Hendrick's view of himself and myself, one can observe how he resorted to a denial of our separateness in order to form, in a manner of speaking, a more "perfect union" in which he saw us as two helpless babies, together and undifferentiated. This I believe gives credence to my original sense of this patient as being in a state of mind which could not yet allow for two-ness, let alone the presence of a "third."

It also seemed to me that Hendrick had taken my failure to repair the "connection" prior to his return from the break as proof that, although *I could be confident of his love, he lacked the signal that might have given him confidence in mine.* He was convinced that I did not care about his pain; that I was no "mommy," but really only a baby who, like himself, could not make connections and could not fix things or put them right ("There is no sorry!"). In addition to this formulation, I said that it seemed that waiting for me to fix a broken-hearted little-he was nearly intolerable, and added that it appeared that he had quickly lost faith in me and in the analysis.

The reader may notice that, at this point in my interpretation, the emphasis was not on Hendrick's attack upon me and our connection, but on *the unbearability of the feelings that my perceived failures evoked in him.* I believe that this line of interpretation encouraged the patient to more fully express his feelings – rather than to act them out – with less fear of separateness and persecution. This forward movement may be seen in the material that I will report from the following hour. However, before continuing with that hour, I would like to make one additional technical point.

Frequently I refer to the patient in my interpretations as a "little-he" or myself as a "mommy- or daddy-analyst" and the like. I have found that this language is most helpful in addressing certain aspects of the patient and his experiences when these are communicated both verbally and non-verbally by him and intuited by the analyst. In my view, the way in which the analyst intuitively perceives of a given patient at a certain moment in time is the product of the patient's attempts to communicate his inner states and the coalescence of such communications into a portrait taking shape on the canvas of the analyst's imagination. Perhaps the more primitive the mode of expression, and the more limited the verbal articulation of the patient, the greater the need for the analyst to continuously and silently monitor his or her inner responses while in the presence of the patient in order to apprehend the *process* as well as the *content* of any given analytic moment.

Here I am also suggesting that another analyst with a quite divergent life experience might view this same patient in a very different way. Such is the individual nature of each analytic couple. Perhaps the value of each permutation of analyst and analysand, like the value of each interpretation, can only be assessed in retrospect and in light of both the patient's experience (as this is expressed in the minutes and hours to follow) and his ability to function in post-analytic years.

Murder

On the very next day, the handyman finally came to repair the signal light. However, by the time of his hour, Hendrick found it once again "out of order." In spite of the fact that I was able to collect him from the waiting room on time for his hour, Hendrick was openly furious with me. Now a new element appeared in his tirade: to all of his earlier complaints, he added yet another about the child patient who had been waiting with him in the room. He had felt that, unlike that "darling little child" who was taken from the waiting room for his session by my husband a few minutes earlier,[12] an unwanted he "with a hole in his head and a hole in his body" was left out, once more waiting.

Hendrick's ranting conveyed a sense that he was being made to feel less favored: deformed, cast off, and forgotten. He was outraged that I had ignored him yet again, while this "little shit" got all the attention, as if I favored the "little one" and had myself (equated with my husband)[13] responded to that "other child," while leaving him to wait, in a sort of purgatory, for all eternity. Hendrick was further disturbed by the feelings this event brought up in him. He resented this other child, younger and more desirable than himself. He said, "How could you leave me out there with that kid? I might have done *something terrible*. If you don't care about me, *at least you could have a thought for that kid*. Don't you know? *I'm dangerous!*"

I felt near the end of my rope, so unreasonably and irrationally ashamed and guilt-ridden that I could scarcely collect my thoughts. At last, I wondered if perhaps my experience at that point was, in part, an approximation of Hendrick's own unbearable state of persecution, which he now felt I was capable of bearing for him. All at once I was reminded of his sister Jeanette, six years his junior. I could imagine that Hendrick might have re-experienced, in that moment with my husband's little patient, some painful sibling rivalry. Perhaps he had been frightened by some violent feelings and fantasies stirred up in him by this experience in the waiting room. Murder came to mind!

I said that I thought he might be attempting to tell me about a little-he who was terrified of murderous feelings felt toward that baby-sister and how angry he was with a mother-me for putting him in such a position where he might harm this baby: one in which he had to contend with unbearable feelings of guilt and shame. Much to my bewilderment, Hendrick calmly inquired, "You mean Annette?"

I asked myself, who *is Annette?* I was certain that Hendrick's sister was named *Jeanette*. Confused, my mind raced through the cast of characters in his life. Sure that there was no Annette among them, I finally said that I thought perhaps he was introducing me to a new figure toward whom he had felt such things. Much to my surprise, Hendrick exclaimed, "Annette *was* my sister: the *one that died!* Didn't I tell you about her?"

I caught my breath while Hendrick continued to inform me about another baby-sister, one who had been born when he was not quite a year old. Annette had been a Down's syndrome baby, severely afflicted both mentally and physically. She had been so compromised that Hendrick's parents could barely cope with the chronic respiratory ailments that plagued her throughout her first year. Consequently, following the family physician's recommendations, they had committed the baby-Annette to a state institution and subsequently moved to another city in the same state. Mother's depression, now compounded with grief and guilt, had reached a crescendo when the family received word, one year later, that Annette had died of pneumonia.

It was soon to become clear to us that Hendrick had been severely neglected when still a baby, as nearly all of the family's emotional and physical resources had been drained away by the needs of the new baby-Annette. He had been so jealous of all the attention that his sister necessarily received from his parents that he had grown to hate her with a vengeance, and thus had blamed himself when she suddenly vanished and subsequently died. Later on in the treatment, we were to come upon other aspects of the disappearance and death of Annette that had a lasting impact on Hendrick, as exemplified in the following material taken from sessions in the fifth year of his analysis.

Dying

After the long Summer holiday break during the fifth year of the analysis, Hendrick returned in a terrible state. Session after session, he would come in and lie on the couch, his hands folded across his chest as if he were dead, not uttering a sound for long stretches of time. Occasionally he would emerge from this deadened state to roar obscenities at me, only to sink once again into some unreachable place. In moments of calm, the only comprehensible narrative to emerge concerned some seemingly innocuous memories about his Aunt Helen – Mother's younger sister – and the family's move to the West coast when the patient was around 6 years of age.

Hendrick reported that, during the break, he had spent much of his free time with Aunt Helen, since his mother and sister had also been away. This situation reminded him of the summer of his seventh year, when he, the then-baby-Jeanette, and Mother had stayed with this aunt in California while Mother searched for a new home for the family to live in. He could recall beginning school that year and nothing more.

I had an uneasy sense that there was much more, but could not articulate what I felt. However, whatever it was did seem to be somehow connected to and provoked by the break. Gradually some inconsistencies began to emerge regarding the family's move to California. Hendrick was absolutely certain that he had entered first grade in California in the Fall, yet was equally certain that the family had not moved to California until after Christmas that year. We wondered together how that could be.

The mystery lingered, as did the dead and deadening silences punctuated by Hendrick's sudden rages – mostly just before and after weekends – up until the Christmas holiday break. The week before this break, Hendrick asked, for the first time, if I would be leaving someone on call during my absence. He was worried that his fits of rage had been too much for me and seemed obsessed with the fantasy that I no longer wished to see him and would leave him permanently to whoever was on call for me.

Hendrick also complained of fears that he would die during my absence and he awoke nightly, falling out of bed, gasping for air. He often thought, in those days when he was "choked awake," that he might be suffering from some undiagnosed pulmonary failure or that he was having a heart attack. I was reminded that his sister Annette had suffered from chronic pneumonia, the cause of her early death.

"Bitch, bitch!" he cried out one day. "How can you do this. You're late! Why don't you get with it. Why don't you just check the atomic clock in Denver and fix yours, would you? Of course you won't, why should you? I'll never be able to count on you. You just don't care. You hate me. I'm just too much. Now you're dumping me so you can finally be rid of me. Why don't you admit it, I'm repulsive to you! You're gonna dump me on some other bitch who doesn't care. I'll just die."

A deluge of maledictions was followed by abysmal mutism, during which I felt very badly about myself. In spite of the fact that I knew I had received Hendrick on time, I felt so wrong, so out of sync with his needs, and so criminally negligent that I could hardly bear being with him. Each day that followed, I dreaded his coming and our hours together, and felt all the more guilty for my apprehension of him. I came to understand that Hendrick was communicating his own unbearable sense of being abandoned because he was a "bad baby."

One day I caught myself daydreaming in the session about a place I had once lived, very much "out in the country," although close enough to town that people often drove there to "drop off" their unwanted animals. At first I chastised myself for not being able to bear staying with Hendrick's material. At last I gradually began to make meaning out of my own chaos, created in the wake of my counter-identification with the abandoning-object being forcefully projected into me.

I was finally prompted to tell Hendrick that I thought he was letting me know how it felt that I was leaving an absolutely unwanted and broken little-him to die alone in a strange, deserted place with someone who would merely preside over his death. I added that I thought that it seemed that I was going away, never to return, happy to be rid of him. Or perhaps that he was left feeling that he was such a big baby that he had damaged me and I no longer could bear him.

Hearing this, Hendrick concurred, although still quite terrified, "Yes, like Aunt Helen. I'm dead if you leave me with that woman." I said that I thought he was trying to communicate some crucial bit of his experience, perhaps of a little-he who could just be left aside and forgotten, a little-one who had died long ago, unable to bear the terror and rage over being abandoned. Perhaps his silences were now an attempt to kill off not only these unbearable feelings but that part of his mind that could experience these feelings and fears.

After some minutes, during which I felt totally and hopelessly lost in uncertainty, Hendrick seemed to come back to life on the couch. When he spoke it was in a half-connected manner. He said, "Maybe I could take some time while you're gone to talk to Aunt Helen about our move to LA. No one ever talks about things in my family." Now tearful, he added, "No one ever talks about Annette. They just left her with Aunt Helen. *She* took her to the Institution, not my mother. Then we left town and never saw her again. She just died."

I felt chilled as Hendrick spoke. At once it occurred to me to say, "I wonder if perhaps *you* were also left with Aunt Helen?" As if a jolt of electricity had gone through him, Hendrick jumped up and replied, "That's it! *I know* what happened when we moved to LA! Mother left me with Aunt Helen! She took Jeanette and went back home without me, went back to my father to sell the house, *but she left me here* with Aunt Helen." Now crying, he added poignantly, "I know that must have been it, because I would have had to start school. But I think I thought then that she was leaving me to die, just like she'd left Annette."

It seemed possible that Hendrick — defensively identified with the baby-sister who had not survived his jealous attacks, the little-one with the mental and physical defects (the hole in the head and the hole in the body) — had been convinced that *he too* was being left to die in the care of his Aunt Helen. This belief was somehow extended to his current fantasy that I would leave him for dead with another "aunt," my substitute, over the holiday break.

This motif of holes — holes in his head and holes in his body — was recurrent in this analysis for many years. In Chapter 3, I have attempted to convey the flavor of the work in progress in the analysis toward developing a container for Hendrick's most elemental *bodily terrors*. Although the bulk of that work consisted of interpreting the patient's experience of me in the transference, I also addressed Hendrick's contribution to the perpetuation of his feeling of emptiness. However, there were other aspects and forerunners of this emptiness that he would one day introduce me to, as one might glean from the following material at a later point in the analysis.

Breasts

From about the fourth year of the analysis onward, Hendrick's material increasingly spoke to some intensely positive experiences both of himself and of me. He was becoming less fearful of men, developed caring friendships with women, felt physically attracted to them, began to date, and had genuinely warm and appreciative feelings toward members of his family, including Mother. Along with these changes in his behavior toward and experience of others and of himself, his appearance, too, had altered dramatically. He now appeared almost dapper, walking with a kind of masculine grace, and he had developed a warm and engaging smile, which he displayed with regularity. Additionally, a terrific sense of humor about himself and me seemed to evolve. *Hendrick had begun to play!*

However, at times, especially around the breaks, Hendrick would still cut-off all contact with me. I did consider the possibility that he was denying and obliterating our connection, as well as anything generative in himself, as a retaliative strike against me when I was felt to abandon him for another during the breaks. I also wondered if the internal saboteur we had encountered early on in the treatment was now rearing its ugly head once again.

At these times, the patient would talk about how he had enjoyed viewing male pornographic videos, especially those depicting young boys in various masturbatory acts, and the return of the impulse to visit the "glory holes" at the University. This would nearly always get a rise out of me. However, oddly enough, I felt hard-pressed to think of these reports as a denigration of things female, or as an envious assault on the good breast or a retaliative strike against the bad one. Yet, in ruling out these theoretical models, I really was left at a loss to know how to conceptualize his behaviors. Consequently, I confined myself and my interpretive activities to the description of these attacks, suspending judgment about or hypothesis as to their origins for a very long time.

Finally, on one silent occasion when I was calling Hendrick's attention to what had been his feelings of connection to the good-mother-me which had – as he had indicated – "filled him up" before the weekend and which he seemed somehow to be cut-off from or emptied of by the time of our Monday hour, the patient responded by asking me if he had ever told me about *his mastectomy*. Hearing this, I wondered for a moment if I had triggered some psychotic delusion in my patient with my observations, or perhaps I had mis-heard him.

Fortunately, I did not have long to wait to gain some clarity about this, as he began to tell me a most remarkable bit of his history, one that I could never have anticipated in my wildest dreams. He prefaced this by saying that, as I was speaking, he had recalled that at the age of 15, shortly after his father's death, he had been given Stylbesterol by a dermatologist in an attempt to clear up his acne. Tragically, the drug had triggered a grotesque development, one even more debilitating to an adolescent boy than a run-away case of acne: he began to grow breasts. This turn of events was especially disastrous for him, since he had once been labeled a "sissy" by his father when, as a very little boy, he "couldn't learn how to throw a ball."

His father, deflated in his expectations for his son, had literally thrown up his hands and walked away from him in frustration. Hendrick recalled feeling that his father had lost patience with him, yelling thoughtlessly, "You throw the ball like a girl, you little sissy!" With the growth of his breasts it had seemed to Hendrick that his father had been right: he was a girl.

To make matters worse, the doctors in charge of his case had paraded young Hendrick through countless rounds of consultations and hospital colloquia, since his was such "an unusual case." Finally, it was determined that bi-lateral mastectomy was called for. Indeed he was to be painfully and shamefully "cut off" from his newly-acquired breasts. It occurred to me that the growth of his breasts, and the subsequent surgery to reduce them, had made him feel like a freak. These new "holes in his body" seemed to tap right into the wounds he had endured both as a baby, when he had lost the breast-mother to his younger sibling, and also, when as a little boy he had experienced the loss of his father's love and esteem as a cruel castration.

Furthermore, Father, who died of metastatic bladder cancer when the patient was 15, had been absent from the home, confined to hospitals and convalescent facilities for some time prior to his death. At this crucial point in his development, Hendrick felt unable to be a man just when the reality of his father's absence and death seemed to demand that he take his place as "the man in the family." Later, at the age of 32, coinciding with Jeanette's marriage, my patient fought his own battle with bladder cancer from which he recovered completely, although he was left with the feeling that Mother now preferred his brother-in-law since she looked to him, rather than to Hendrick, to handle her affairs.

Hendrick's identifications seemed to have been with the depressed, dangerous, rageful, crazy, screaming mother who was felt as asexual, cold, prim and proper; with his dead baby-sister with the hole in the head and the hole in the body; and with the disillusioned, dying and later dead father. Although ideally he was also the good son and "father" who had never left Mother, and the big brother who was devoted to his little sister Jeanette, this ideal self existed in a state of conflict with that "big" brother-he who had hated his little sister Annette and who had wished or even willed her gone and dead, and the "dirty" son who was a danger to all women, especially his mother: the son who was "too much to handle."

Hendrick, thrust into the role of the "man in the family" after his father's death, unconsciously had taken the Stylbesterol incident not only as validation of Father's proclamation of his deficient manhood, but it also came to represent Father's revenge upon him for having taken his place close to the mother. It occurred to me that, paradoxically, this phantasy had enabled Hendrick to bring his father back to life in his mind. Thus he could put off, indefinitely, his grief over the finality of death and the unthinkable experience of the end of all possibilities for reconciliation with that beloved parent. I now understood that my patient's provocative behavior might have been intended to "get a rise out of me" as a way of resurrecting his dead father in the transference. This new way of thinking about Hendrick seemed to go a long way toward helping him gain access to his much-delayed process of mourning, as illustrated in the following material from the seventh year of the analysis.

Compensation and compromise

During the seventh year of his analysis, it was necessary to suspend Hendrick's third session of the week for a period of three months in order to accommodate my teaching obligations at the Institute. In the last session of the next to last week of this interrupted schedule, he came into the room in a sullen mood. He lay down on the couch, silent for some minutes, ran his hands over his face and through his hair and, in dismay, simply said, "Not good. Pretty bad."

After a brief pause, Hendrick smiled for a moment. Then, in a bitter tone, he said, "My raise came through yesterday, *our* raise, I suppose!" I clarified, "Perhaps you are letting me know that it's just no good when we're apart. When I'm not here for you, perhaps you feel there's no one to be happy for you and with you in your success. It seems I take away some of your good feelings – the raise – which you cannot sustain by yourself throughout the break in our contact." Hendrick agreed, saying that he thought it was a sad state of affairs if he couldn't miss an hour without feeling it so much. "How will I ever be able to end this analysis? How will I ever be able to give you up?"

I said that it felt impossible for him to leave me when his hope that he could reach a point where the leaving wouldn't hurt so much had dissolved in the pain of the break. Hendrick said that he'd never thought of it that way before, but supposed that he would miss me no matter how ready he was to leave. He said that it was especially hard when he has no one to take my place. Then he began to tell me about a good workout he'd had at the gym, although he modified this, adding that he had spent too much time on the tread-mill. His left foot, which he'd previously traumatized, was hurting him once again.

I told Hendrick that it seemed that there was a vulnerable little-he that felt hurt when left to tread onward, all by himself. He smiled and went on to say that when his roommate, Matilda, went out on the previous night she looked very pretty. She'd been more friendly lately, too. She looked beautiful in the dress she was wearing, coming down the staircase on her way out to dinner with friends. He thought she was being provocative. "I guess that really means I can be provoked," he said. "But it's OK, these days. I take it better than I used to.

I sorta like it, in fact. Too bad she'll be leaving soon. I think we could have gotten it on together. It's hard to believe that I could love a woman. Me! You know, I feel like maybe I could have a real relationship with a woman now. I think I've grown some in these past twenty-five years and things might be different today than they were then."

I said that a "pretty-me" was felt to provoke him, as I left him for my weekend out with others. Perhaps he felt more able to tolerate his feelings of jealousy, excitement, and rage. Hendrick nodded, "Yeah, even my embarrassment. Like at work today, I was talking with Heather – you know, that pretty woman in the resource center? She was telling me about a client who's a transvestite. It was OK when we talked seriously about the case, but then I became embarrassed and uncomfortable when she was guffawing at him, this man in a dress. I just had to change the subject. I couldn't stand it! I told her that I really liked the story that her husband had written about this line backer on the [football team]. I really changed the subject, didn't I? Just couldn't take it."

I considered that Hendrick might be expressing the embarrassment he experienced in that moment when I acknowledged his feelings of attraction toward me. Thus I decided not to push the issue for the time being. Instead, I said, "It seems that you could hardly bear the ambiguity. It must have touched you in a sensitive place, one you could hardly tolerate. The idea of this man in a dress – not really a man, but not a woman either – parading around with people guffawing at him." Hendrick agreed, "I just can't stand that. It brings up too many feelings. All those doubts I have about my own identity. I guess it's an old wound."

I said, "Perhaps these feelings resonate with that early experience of being paraded around in front of people, people you felt were guffawing at you: some half-man/boy–half-woman." Hendrick exclaimed, "Yeah. It really felt like they were pointing a finger at me, calling me a sissy, just like my father. I felt really scared. After all, he abandoned me. Not really. But, you know, he did give up on teaching me to throw the ball. He really wasn't there anymore, I mean after he died." Tearfully, Hendrick went on to say, "I guess he finally did abandon me, in a way, when he died."

Now more pensive then angry, Hendrick asked, "What did I get out of it anyway, except the plastic surgery. Huh! I haven't thought about that for a long time, what it felt like, my mother parading me around in front of all those doctors – all those Daddies – like I was some freak. What did I get out of it? And, on top of already feeling like I was a failure as a man . . . a sissy." As he spoke, I thought about another word that sounded like sissy: sister. I wondered if it could be that what he'd gotten out of being a "sissy" was the reassurance that his dead baby-sister was still alive in that sissy-he. I'd considered this possibility on many other occasions, when it seemed that the sense that he had "a hole in his body and a hole in his head" was sustained by a process of identification with the baby-sister who was born both physically and mentally deficient. This identification might have functioned to restore the baby-sister he feared he'd killed: to return her to the mother maddened with grief, to deny the phantasied effects of his murderous aggression, to sacrifice himself in her stead. And what greater sacrifice than his masculinity?

But what of the phantasy of keeping his father alive by sacrificing himself to the humiliating presence of the daddy? I thought the latter more immediate and chose to address that first, to see where he might take it. I said that perhaps he was letting me know something of what he may have gotten out of it. Perhaps a feeling of that daddy coming alive again in all those daddy-doctors, pointing their fingers, humiliating him, calling him a sissy – a feeling that Father was still alive and, in a way, still somehow interested in him; still calling him a sissy, but not giving up on him, not abandoning him, instead helping to restore his manhood.

Touched by this, Hendrick said tearfully, "Too bad he didn't stick around. Too bad he gave up. When I think about that word, sissy – *SSSSis-sy* – it reminds me of the sound of a woman peeing." Hearing this, I recalled that Hendrick used to complain incessantly, in the first years of the treatment, about his inability to urinate in the presence of other men. This had always signified for him that he could "never be a man among men." I had since wondered what had transpired with this paralyzing symptom, which he had not mentioned for so very long.

I finally suggested, "It seems there is a connection between this feeling of being a sissy and the problem of peeing like a man among men." Hendrick replied, "That's one of the real tangible gains I've seen here. I'm not 100 percent yet, but at least 90 percent better. That's *really* important." I said that I wondered if he was letting me know about how he felt now – not quite 100 percent a man, but at least 90 percent – and how real that feels, how important that is, how it gives him some hope about being able to have a new connection with a woman.

After a pause Hendrick said, "Men are funny about peeing, you know. In the gym, after sports, and even now when I go to work-out, some of the younger guys wear their underwear into the shower. Some even go home to shower. I used to think they were worried about showing – well – *you know*. I never had *that* inhibition." Here it seemed that a split-off and denied inhibition was making itself known in the moment, when he could not utter the word "erection" but instead said "you know." He went on to say, "I was always confident about my lower body. I've really worked on that. Although I never felt I could quite keep up in my upper body, but my lower body felt right, strong."

As Hendrick spoke and gestured toward his upper and lower body, I had the thought that there was a little-he who transfers a bit of his "OK lower body" to his "not-OK upper body" in phantasy. In other words, his excitement was felt, not in the engorgement of his penis, but in the reddening of his nose, in the blushing he had frequently complained of, and the flaring of his nostrils, which he often associated with embarrassment rather than excitement.

Hendrick continued, "But there's something else about peeing. Guys always think that they should have a real strong stream. All at once, you know? And you're not supposed to dribble. I'm so much better at that now." In response, I told Hendrick that as he spoke I was reminded of how, when he was a boy, he had difficulty playing basketball: he was tall and did everything well, except that he could *never dribble*. "Perhaps you are letting me know something about how fearful you are that you might have an erection while dreaming, or a spontaneous emission, and about how that is prohibited in your mind." He replied that he recalled being punished when he "came in the night" and was accused of "wetting his bed." I said that he felt he had to be a straight shooter, had always missed the basket, and had felt like a failure.

On hearing myself, I became aware of the double meaning conveyed unwittingly in the words I had used. Hendrick *was* a straight shooter – a good "mamma's-boy" – and this caused him to miss out on connecting with the "basket" as with women, disabling him in his attempts to have intercourse. Hendrick made his own connections: "Hah! That's right! I couldn't even pee with another man watching, because I might dribble. It's weird but it feels right. It's funny what I make of things. Dale [a previous therapist] used to say that it's the difference between *what is* and *what appears to be*. You know how I always make something out of the way people sit, how they move their legs in response to mine? Like Heather. She sits with her legs open, not crossed like most women. Men would never cross them, they go like this or like that," he said, as he demonstrated various positions. "But Heather is an aerobics instructor, so she's different, and that's good. It's kind of neat that I can talk to her like I do, that she likes me and we get along. I used to be intimidated by women like her. Especially since I read so much into how they sit and move their legs or don't. Dale didn't agree with my interpretations, he didn't understand. That's all I had to go on. All I *have* to go on, when everyone keeps their distance."

As Hendrick cried audibly, I was moved to say that I thought that perhaps he was telling me about that sensitive little-he who felt kept at a distance by me when I failed to pursue his reference to his attraction to me. Perhaps he felt that I was embarrassed by his erection – his directness – and that he had to hide it from the mother-me; could it be that he was letting me know how it feels when I deny him access to my body, when I limit our contact to words alone: he watches, sniffs, and listens for my presence, possibly to ascertain my stance: if I am open to him. Perhaps his eyes, nose, and ears are even more acutely tuned in than those of others who can get physically close to me. For him every movement sends a message, every sound conveys an attitude.

When Hendrick responded, saying, "Maybe that's why I go crazy over loud music. Too much said, too threatening," I thought he might be telling me something about how he is being over-stimulated by my voice, my words, and my now-open attitude, and I waited quietly for him to say more. Then he suggested, "I think I need to be touched so I can relax. It's easier to get feedback from people if you're touching. You can feel things you can't know from a distance. I bought some single tickets to the Dodgers (a baseball team in Los Angeles). It'll be good to go. I know I won't feel so alone anymore. Now I can strike up a conversation with people, drink a beer, eat a hot dog, listen to Vin Scully. But I'd really like to snuggle up with someone, a woman. Can't imagine how I could've settled in the past for just pushing on the back of the seat in front of me, getting off on that. Pitiful!"

This exchange marked a turning point in Hendrick's analysis, as he seemed now to be quite in touch with (instead of "dodging") his longings for direct contact not just with my mind but with my physical presence as well: the touch of another, especially a woman. It seemed that by calling a spade a spade – talking to him about his longing to be in touch with me – Hendrick felt his desires had been liberated, and his intimate contacts with women were henceforth pursued with greater vigor.

Ending

Midway in the ninth year of the analysis, Hendrick's dreams, his associations, and some emerging plans for future changes in both his professional and personal situations, which would necessitate his moving out of state, led us to set a date for termination. The last several months of the analysis were highlighted by some deeply moving sessions which were as satisfying to both patient and analyst as a good feed can be to mother and infant alike. Hendrick and I seemed at last to have found that "rhythm of safety" (Tustin 1986b: p. 268) wherein mouth and breast, after painstaking trial and error over time, finally achieve a peaceful and harmonious cooperative space in which it feels safe just to be. I believe this "rhythm" to be an essential precursor to a satisfying genital sexual relationship (Gooch 1991).

As fate would have it, in the next to last week of the analysis, I needed to cancel the third hour of the week due to illness, and I telephoned Hendrick at work in the early afternoon to tell him that I could not meet with him that day. I added that, if he did not hear otherwise from me, we would meet the following day as usual.

At three o'clock the next day, Hendrick called my office, leaving a message to say that, since he had not heard from me, he assumed we would *not* be meeting. However, if this was an incorrect assumption I could leave a message for him *if I needed him*, as he would be out in the field but would check in before the time he would ordinarily be leaving to come for his session. He added that he hoped I was feeling better.

I left Hendrick a message that *we would be meeting* at the regular time and he arrived promptly for his hour. He began by thanking me for the call-back and commented on the fog that was already rolling in from the sea. I said that I thought that perhaps he was letting me know that I had not made myself clear in my communication to him on the previous day, to which he replied that he thought it was he who had not been clear. He added that he wondered if we might extend his termination date by one session, to make up for the lost hour. When I said that I thought he was telling me about the difficulty he experiences in ending our contact and the conviction that we need every one of his last hours to deal with this difficulty, he said that he doubted he would ever really feel ready to end. He admitted that he was inclined to put off the inevitable feelings about the cessation of our connection as long as possible.

Hendrick went on to say that he'd thought it strange that I canceled the hour, since he could not recall my having missed a session in many years. In fact he could only recall one time during the entire analysis. This was an accurate recollection. Hendrick added that it had occurred to him that he'd been trying to comfort me when he said that he hoped I would feel better soon, and added that he thought that maybe he was so caught off-guard by this unusual reaction to disappointment, that he had not paid attention to what I had said about the Thursday hour. I said that it seemed to me that he might be suggesting that the reversal in his feelings and behavior with respect to me was somehow linked to his reversing my communication, so that he ended up thinking that *I would call him* if we were going to meet, that is, if *I needed him*. He smiled and I added that I thought perhaps his request for an extension of our date for termination somehow figured in here as well.

Hendrick paused for a brief moment, then said that he was thinking that I might have already scheduled a new patient in his hours, and that I resented his asking for an extension. I responded, telling him that I thought that he was trying to communicate something of his worry that when we ended I would not be willing or able to make room for him to return if he should need to, that my cancellation had prematurely pushed this feeling of being on his own, a feeling he was not quite prepared for and which he had to send back to me for further consideration. Here I was calling attention to Hendrick's use of projective identification, provoked by his sense that I was pushing him away prematurely.

Thoughtfully, Hendrick replied that he'd had lunch with Katrina, a colleague. They'd spoken about a client who had vowed to do something and had mustered the resolve to carry it through in spite of his doubts, to try to make a go of it. Hendrick said that he liked this client and had respect for him all the more because of this. After a moment, he said that he was now aware of other things that had disturbed him about my cancellation. He'd been awakened by a barking dog the night before. The dog's owners had not returned home that day and had left their dog out until the wee hours, howling. He also was bothered by excited teenagers gathered out on the street on that hot summer night and needed to talk with me about this.

Hendrick suddenly felt the front of his trousers. He said that he'd needed to urinate when he arrived and had gone to the restroom before coming in. He was now wondering if he'd gotten "something" on his slacks. He seemed to link this with feelings of embarrassment, experienced during a meeting with his supervisor who had made a fuss over him, acknowledging him for his expertise in a certain area of his work. He was afraid that he wouldn't be able to sustain the good feelings of accomplishment and pride he'd felt in that meeting with her once he left her office.

I suggested that Hendrick might also be expressing his fear not only that he would not be able to handle the hurt and resentment of being left out howling and the pain of missing me at the end of the analysis, but also that he was not certain that he could hold onto the feelings of excitement about and pride in his accomplishments and the feeling of self-respect he had gained by going through with the analysis. I added that I thought his being able to go through with the termination as well, in spite of his doubts, had made him feel so full of himself, and at the same time so pissed-off with me, that he was afraid of bursting open and spilling out, perhaps making a mess of himself and "going mad" again.

Hendrick concurred that he was indeed afraid he'd go crazy at work without my help, or that he'd fall back on his old "bathroom habits," or lose his newfound attraction for women. Then, after a pause, he talked about a meeting he felt he'd handled poorly that day. The meeting had something to do with suicide intervention. He said that he couldn't deal with the fact that he was bound by ethics and professional standards to rescue people from suicide. He thought that "if someone wanted to die, their wish should be given respect."

Recalling the patient's own latent suicidal tendencies, which had surfaced from time to time over the years, I said that it seemed that he was reminding me that I too was bound by professional and ethical considerations to save him from that part of himself that wished to die when left all alone, that I was professionally and ethically bound to rescue him from death by extending the analysis.

However, there was also a he who wished me to respect his judgment and to let him go. I also said that it seemed, on another level, that he was calling my attention to a he who regarded his leaving analysis as something of an act of suicide. Hendrick confided that he had felt his need for constant contact with me all these years, and that he was afraid that – when he could no longer rely upon me, when he could no longer come and talk to me about his dreams – he'd die of loneliness. When he remembered all the times, all the dreams, and how I had almost always been there for him, he felt grateful. However, at the same time he was pissed-off that it only made him want more, especially the kind of more I would never give him. He wished he could keep his hours, still pursue dating and some kind of social life, and be with his family as well.

Concluding notes

Hendrick was able, at last, to follow through with the termination of his analysis. Like the Dutchman, his once interminable search for a containing object had come to an end. It truly seemed that he had, at long last, found someone who would accept and could survive and help him to transform his jealous rages, his terror of spilling out, his disillusionment and his profound experiences of loss, as well as his states of healthy excitement. *Having found this in the analyst, he could at last – through a process of introjective identification – experience this capacity in himself.*

Bion (1959; 1962a, b; 1967b) wrote about the consequences of the mother's inability to provide an adequate container for her baby's fears of impending doom related to its early experiences of loss. This capacity of the mother – *to receive the baby's anxiety, unwanted parts of the self, sense, and even those aspects of his mental apparatus that pose a threat to his existence; the ability to transform this raw sensory data into the stuff of which dreams, thoughts, and memories are made; and the knack for returning them to the baby (sufficiently detoxified for his under-developed system to be able to tolerate) in an un-imposing manner* – serves to make up a good-enough "container," operating in a state of "reverie" or unsaturated attentiveness that is *adequate relative to the constitution of the individual infant.*

Although one might wonder if Hendrick had indeed been cursed with some constitutional affective and/or cognitive deficiencies, it appears that these innate handicaps might have been at least partially mitigated by good-enough mothering. The maternal function, which Bion referred to as "alpha," acts as a semi-permeable membrane, processing the infant's sense experiences, detoxifying them and returning to him the purified and digestible "alpha elements" that, when introjected, go to make up an "alpha membrane" (Meltzer 1978, p. 79) or "psychic skin" (Bick 1968) essential to the development of a mind for thinking thoughts with the capacity to separate conscious from unconscious, internal world from external world, phantasy from reality, wakefulness from sleep and dreams, with fluid communication between these dualities of mind/body.

In her depressed, disturbed, and preoccupied state, Hendrick's own mother was perhaps unable to adequately function as a container for her infant's early experiences. Thus, he became cynical early on, "killing sweet innocence" when disillusioned by the absence of this much-needed object. Such patients often vow to go it alone, perhaps missing out on the benefits that might be derived from affectionate attachments later on in life. Their hardened, impermeable cynicism – which has functioned as a survival mechanism (Symington 1985; Mitrani 1992, 1996) to protect them against further experiences of psychic pain that they simply were unequipped to endure – constitutes a challenge that the analyst must take up if the patient is to be "rescued" from his endless voyage on the stormy sea of aloneness. Perhaps, if the analyst is to meet this challenge, (s)he must be *willing and able to be transfigured by the patient*, taking the transference as it comes; *to suffer for the patient* – that is, to be mortal for him – and *to sufficiently transform his experiences* such that he may eventually feel confident enough to suspend the constraints of omnipotence that bind him together so that he can relinquish his immortality and regain his humanity among and with other ordinary human beings.

5

Chloe: from pre-conception to after birth[14]

> I wish either my father or my mother, or indeed both, as they were in duty equally bound to it, had in mind what they were about when they begot me.
>
> Laurence Sterne, *Tristram Shandy*

Since Freud (1940), there has been much written on the topic of pregnancy and motherhood, considering the baby as compensation for the lacking penis; as reparation to and identification with the mother; as a bio-psychological expression of femininity; and as a crisis/phase in female development involving endocrine and general somatic as well as psychological alterations that revive certain psychic traumas and conflicts from infancy, childhood, and puberty (e.g. Benedek 1952 and 1959; Bibring 1961; Blum 1981; Chodorow 1978; Deutsch 1944; Erickson 1965; Leifer 1977; Pines 1972 and 1982; Stoller 1976). Both the pathogenic and normal developmental aspects of pregnancy have been explored and their impact on the early development of the mother–infant relationship considered, along with the significance of the relationship between the sexual couple and between the mother-to-be and her own mother.

More recently, Raphael-Leff (1991; 1993) made substantial contributions to our understanding of both the intrapsychic and interpersonal elements of the female reproductive experience. Her work with women in groups, as well as in individual psychoanalytic therapy, has provided a clinical laboratory for examining the fantasies (both conscious and unconscious) that are common in women prior to conception, during technologically assisted procedures, throughout gestation, and even beyond the birth of the baby. She has been able to develop a thoughtful set of guidelines for evaluating the need for psychotherapeutic intervention in cases of either normal or complicated pregnancies.

However, to my limited knowledge, few if any authors have focused – *in*

82

verbatim detail – upon the long-term analytic process with women in this phase of feminine development. As one can appreciate in the case of Hendrick presented in the previous chapter, the emotional state of the mother during the pre-, peri-, and post-natal periods of the infant's development has a profound impact on the baby's and later the adult's capacity for love and work, regardless of its own constitutional limitations. If we did not believe this to be true, there would be little point in attempting to mitigate these inborn features through the process of psychoanalysis.

In this chapter, I hope to extend our comprehension of maternal development through a detailed exploration of various aspects of the analysis of one young woman, whom I call Chloe, as she struggles to learn what she is about, before, during, and after becoming a mother. As such, the material that I present encompasses that period during which this analysand and her husband were attempting to conceive a child, continuing throughout pregnancy, and into the weeks immediately after the birth of their baby.

In a personal communication, Dr. Trilby Coolidge (1999) suggested that my choice of pseudonym for this analysand – the Greek for verdancy – reflects "the flourishing greening of growth" of this period of the analysis, from pre-conception, through and immediately after birth. I believe that one may consider this interval not only as a fertile window of opportunity for growth in the analysis of ordinary women, but also as an extra-ordinary opportunity for growth in the analyst as well.

Thus, following the presentation of some relevant background material, I will be focusing on Chloe's maternal evolution and on my own evolution as an analyst as well. Along these lines I will briefly underscore some of what I observed and learned from this particular patient about myself, alongside the importance of Chloe's psychological gestation and birth to the actual enterprise of parenting, thus stimulating further thinking about some of the challenges encountered in the analytic treatment of prospective mothers.

Relevant history of the case

Chloe was referred to me just before her thirty-first birthday after a string of four prematurely interrupted therapies, all initiated by her therapists. Consequently, she came to me quite despondent and with a ready-made and highly-charged negative transference. For example, at the time of our first consultation, Chloe was engaged to a somewhat older and quite schizoid man, Peter, with whom she was in love, and he with her. The material around this time spoke to their difficulties with sexual intercourse. According to the patient, their love-making was contrived and lacked spontaneity. Chloe felt that it was "not about her," that she could not arouse Peter, and when he would infrequently make love to her it was unsatisfying and all too brief.

While fully acknowledging the pain of this situation and its significance in Chloe's relationship with Peter, I also took this up as an expression of her experience of our connection. I told her that I believed she was also letting me know that she felt she could not excite and enliven me to connect with her in a meaningful way, and when I did it was "not about her." That is to say that it was flat, by the book, time-limited and squeezed into a schedule not made with her needs in mind. I was most surely a mother-analyst who had received her only out of a sense of duty, while she was an undesirable baby, not enough, not right, and always under threat of being cut-off and deserted.

Indeed when such abandonment anxieties would threaten to overwhelm her nearly to the point of decompensation, Chloe would defend herself mainly through splitting and projective identification, often filling me with feelings of being under constant threat of being left. On these occasions, I was all wrong for her while she was often angry and depressed, silent, thoroughly disappointed and let down. However, it seemed at the time that my willingness to absorb some of my patient's complaints in this way helped in the gradual development of her trust in me as someone who might be willing to stand by her, for better or for worse.

Thus, within a few weeks' time, and in spite of our overtly dis-comforting connection, Chloe's material began to speak to her desire and need for additional hours and we agreed to meet on a four-times-per-week basis for a relatively low fee, which was all she could afford while she and her partner were starting up a new consulting business. It may be relevant to mention, as the reader will see, that Chloe had inquired about and thus was aware of my usual fee and took the initiative to say that she would raise her fee at such times as she felt able to do so.

Relevant historical context

As I learned more about Chloe's beginnings, I came to conceive of her initial transference constellation as a version of her experience of being born to parents whose first child, a son, was destined to die from the start. That baby-boy had hung on for nearly two years before succumbing to the effects of a serious congenital defect, several years prior to my patient's conception. In a way, Chloe also felt doomed from birth: she was a girl and therefore "never enough" to replace her brother. I could imagine that a bright child, such as Chloe must have been, might become convinced that such a "replacement child" was needed by her parents in order to assuage their guilt over having produced a defective baby-boy, and to modify their grief over having been helpless to save him. I even went so far as to silently conjecture that Chloe may have (in a manner of speaking) "inherited" both her parents" guilt and their grief, as she seemed always to have felt herself to be defective as well as helpless to relieve the parents of their despair.

Although at first I considered that this dynamic might stem from some narcissistic aspect of the patient's mentality, I also contemplated what Klein (1952a) implied when she stated that:

We have grounds to assume, from early days onwards, the mother's unconscious attitude strongly affects the infant's unconscious processes.

(p. 116)

Klein even went so far as to suggest that "It is an open question whether or not the mother's mental and physical state influences the foetus as regards . . . constitutional factors" (1952a, p. 116f) involved in the development of the rudimentary ego and pre– as well as post-natal modes of object-relating and behavior.

My assessment of the situation was further complicated as I learned of the existence of another brother. This brother was a "difficult baby," four years Chloe's junior. By all accounts, he was a great disappointment to the parents. Perhaps, when it seemed to my patient that this sibling could not secure their love either, Chloe took it upon herself to become her baby-brother's father-protector and loving, self-sacrificing mother-substitute.

Taking into account Chloe's inclination to self-sacrifice and other-protectiveness, it seemed possible that she had been a major contributor to her own experience of the analysis as "not about her." However, I also kept in mind Chloe's description of her father as a "diagnosed manic depressive – erratic, seductive, manipulative, and crazy" – and her characterization of Mother as a "depressed and passive woman" who, in the patient's experience, had left her children "wildly unprotected" from Father's excessive demands and his outbursts of violent behavior.

One year into our work, Chloe's fiancé began his own analysis. The couple were married the following year and, shortly thereafter, Chloe ceased to complain of those earlier difficulties with him. Additionally, both Chloe and Peter grew steadily more and more successful in their respective professions. Accordingly, Chloe raised her fee by increments as her finances consistently improved. However, these raises usually coincided with the resolution of what she called "bad patches" in which she complained of feeling hopeless about the analysis, her ability to do "this kind of work," my competence, and/or my commitment to her. Not surprisingly, these bad patches nearly always preceded or followed weekend and holiday breaks.

Pre-conception

Concurrent with the sessions I will report, Chloe and Peter were immersed in the process of *in vitro* fertilization after many months of attempting to conceive by "natural" means. Obstacles to conception existed on both sides of the couple,

85

as Chloe had lost a fallopian tube due to an ectopic pregnancy years earlier and had significant scarring on the remaining tube, while Peter's sperm lacked both quantity and motility. During this particularly difficult time in her life, while being pumped full with all kinds of hormones, Chloe suddenly reported that she was beginning to feel better a week or so before the Fall holiday break.

Chloe then went on to briefly mention a call from her father, how she had felt manipulated by him, and how "crazy" and incoherent he had seemed to her. This material felt evanescent and seemed to go nowhere, or so I thought at the time. Then, much to my surprise, she announced that she had begun to see an acupuncturist, a nutritionist, and a masseur, and had decided to take up meditation as well. She claimed that these activities helped her to feel better.

While listening, I began to suspect that all of this was a bit manic, especially since Chloe had made a fleeting reference to something she was "not looking forward to occurring on the upcoming weekend." Although the patient had quite a history of being forsaken – both in childhood and in her several therapies – and her response to weekend and holiday breaks had generally been quite pronounced, this time it appeared that by-and-large everything was just rosy. I, on the other hand, was feeling uncomfortably left out.

Considering the possibility that Chloe might be handing-over to me her own unbearable feelings of being abandoned over the weekend, I interpreted her need to hold at bay some uncomfortable feelings. I supposed that she might be afraid that, should she become aware of these feelings, she might be overwhelmed by them in my absence during the weekend and, perhaps even more so, in anticipation of the longer holiday break ahead.

Although Chloe did not appear to be the least affected by my interpretation at the time, when she returned on Monday she reported being quite angry with me over the weekend. Clearly still furious with me, she complained that I had been a "provocateur and a predator" in the Thursday hour. I had refused to acknowledge any progress made by her. Furthermore, I had been "prodding and poking" her into feeling "stuck and bad," just when she has begun to feel better about herself and more hopeful about the positive impact of her analysis.

The way in which Chloe presented her perceptions of the preceding Thursday hour made it quite clear that she had experienced me as a sort of "crazy father" who preys on her good spirits, turning on her and destroying any positive sense she might have had of herself. Although she denied feeling that *I* was crazy, she seemed gradually to relax with me toward the end of the hour after hearing this interpretation, and the following new material began to emerge.

Chloe reported at length an incident that had given rise to a suspicion that her housekeeper had been stealing "painkillers" from her medicine cabinet. As she spoke, I considered the possibility that, in part under the influence of her own unwanted feelings of being abandoned for the weekend and perhaps her unbearable experience of a "crazy father," I had in some way been attempting to cause her pain. Evaluating this and other possibilities – including the likely prospect that Chloe had actually received some unacknowledged benefit from our work together – I felt worse and worse about myself, so much so that by the end of the hour I was resigned to the probability that Chloe might interrupt the analysis. I was even able to feel for the moment that she might be justified in doing so.

Of course, it was not that I was so surprised that the patient had not welcomed my attempts to penetrate her manic defenses (if indeed these were present), nor was I taken aback by her rage that I had done so. Instead I was moved to reconsider the motivations for my interpretations and was therefore feeling remorse in the face of the possibility that, while attempting to avoid contact with my own infantile sufferings and the resultant insecurities these engendered in me, I may well have been poking and prodding Chloe into feeling these for me. Perhaps one might conjecture that this was an enactment of her connection with Father that day on the telephone.

Coinciding with my restored ability to attain some clarity of mind in the Tuesday hour, the patient could now be observed to be splitting herself in two. By this I mean to say that, while bestowing upon Peter the role of the angry, hurt, and betrayed party who wanted to dismiss the housekeeper for her act of thievery, she on the other hand appeared unbothered by the theft, claiming that she had given up using painkillers while in the process of attempting to conceive.

Although (and perhaps because) I found this communication personally relieving on some level, I considered that Chloe might unwittingly be responding to some sense that I had reached the limits of my tolerance for persecution in the Monday hour, and thus was now attempting to relieve me. Henceforth, I had a thought that I – not unlike this maid who steals her means of coping with pain – had been experienced by my patient as a thief: rudely and illicitly depriving her of her way of defending herself in my absence.

It then occurred to me that Chloe might have needed to know that I had not consumed her means of protecting herself: that her painkiller-defenses would be there should she need them. I also considered the possibility that her "feeling good about herself" on Thursday had not been merely a defense, but a genuine feeling just beginning to grow in her: some expression of her faith in what we had been doing, as well as a sense that she could take care of herself in my absence.

Just before the hour ended, I managed to say that I thought it must be very painful and difficult for her to bear feeling so betrayed by me, when it had seemed to her that I was attempting to erode her self-confidence and her growing sense of hopefulness and security. On Wednesday Chloe let me know just how she had taken my interpretation on the previous day. She began the hour by informing me that she had "managed to calm Peter down." She had "obtained a confession from the housekeeper, who promised never to take anything again without first asking for permission." However, she knew that "their trust in this housekeeper had been seriously damaged" and that they would "eventually have to ask her to leave."

I said that perhaps she felt she could not trust such a woman, especially with a baby. She agreed and said that she thought it "too bad, as [this housekeeper] had been so good to her in the past and if [she] were to give birth, [she] would need her more than ever." She then added that she felt badly about the prospect of dismissing the housekeeper, as she sensed that this woman "felt really unlovable at the core" and regretted that she might be adding to such feelings by firing the housekeeper, thus making her feel even worse about herself.

In what Chloe said, I recognized my own tendency toward feelings of being bad and even unlovable, and acknowledged to myself that I might have given in to the temptation to undermine my patient's good feelings about herself when these threatened inevitably to leave an unlovable-me in danger of abandonment. I also recalled that Chloe had seemed quite wary of me when she arrived to the session that day, even though she seemed to have put aside her more overtly angry feelings – about that me who was experienced as preying on her nascent good spirits – by turning my interpretation into a "confession."

With this in mind, I told Chloe that, although there was a she who – perhaps for my benefit – had put aside her anger with me and who no longer appeared to mind that she'd been robbed, she seemed to be letting me know that there was also an unbearably enraged-she who felt irreparably betrayed, was furious with me for depriving her of her means of dealing with acute and overwhelming pain, and who silently demanded my resignation.

As Chloe was nodding in agreement, I added: "It also seems that you might be attempting to quell your inclination to dismiss me since you may feel gratitude toward me, may still feel you need me, and perhaps – although I can't be sure of this – you may perceive me, like your housekeeper, to have some deep-seated sense that I am unlovable and are right now trying to protect me from what you fear to be my inevitable collapse." As Chloe was silent for the remainder of the hour, I was not certain if or how she had received what I said.

The next day I opened the door to the waiting room with much trepidation. However, I grew hopeful when Chloe greeted me with a genuinely warm smile and handed me her check. I noticed that she had opened up the check, which had been folded in two as usual, before giving it to me and, although I did not look at the check just then, I noted to myself that Chloe might have intended that I do so.

As she lay on the couch, Chloe said that she felt much better. She had talked to her father about some incident in which "he acted especially paranoid." She wondered at length why no one could help him, mentioning her "angry younger brother" who could not be helped either, regretting that neither of them believed in analysis. She said, "I just know someone could help them, but I guess they have to be willing to change."

While she spoke I had the growing impression that, unlike her usual reaction of despair and hopelessness to such experiences with Father and Brother, this time she sounded hopeful. Something in her tone – in contrast to the content of her communication – expressed a feeling that there was indeed help to be had, that people could change if only they could be reached. However, I said nothing here since I could not be certain at this time that I was not just imposing my own hopefulness upon her.

As she went on about her brother's resistance to therapy, I wondered to myself if this was Chloe's way of letting me know something about an isolated part of her that couldn't trust me, didn't believe I could help her, and thus resisted my interventions. However, I also considered – once again because of something in her tone of voice and gesture, conveyed from the moment she had arrived that day, something I couldn't quite put my finger on – that she had once more begun to feel good, in part because she experienced herself as finally being able to get through to me.

Before I could speak my mind, Chloe said, "I've been thinking about 'Great Stuff' [the name of the project she was then working on]. Feeling better about that too. Oh, I know I *was* going to back away, just let [my partner] go on without me. I had decided that I didn't want any part of it, even if [our client] did renew the contract. I *was* just going to divorce myself from it and let [my partner] go it alone. But I've had second thoughts, some new ideas when I left here last night about what I might be able to do to improve the project, and I think I've decided to stay on after all."

Once again, Chloe seemed hopeful. Finally, she exuberantly blurted out, "Oh, by the way, did you notice? I raised you!" Then, as if she was aware of the peculiar way this had been phrased, she giggled and said, "That came out funny! I really meant to say, I gave you a raise!" At this point I looked at the check, which I had placed face down on the table next to my chair. I saw that the patient had indeed raised my fee by $15 per session. At this point I felt I had enough information to be able to address her material.

First, I thanked Chloe for the raise, extending my appreciation and acknowledging that she must truly be feeling better and more secure with regard to her resources. Then I added that I was wondering if perhaps there might be some significance in the way that her announcement of "the raise" had first been expressed.

Turning her head toward me, craning her neck as if interested to hear what I thought about it, Chloe asked directly, "What do you mean?" to which I replied, "Perhaps you are letting me know that you're feeling pleased – perhaps even satisfied and also grateful – when you can experience yourself as having raised me well this week." As she giggled with delight at this notion of mine, I was encouraged to add, "It seems you might be feeling that you've finally gotten through to me, that I've been helped by you to be a better analyst, that you've finally been able to help me to understand something essential to your experience."

Chloe nodded and seemed very moved as she reached behind her head for a tissue, dabbing at her eyes for several moments. After a long while I said, "I believe that this sense of being able to 'raise' me is quite important to you, since you have so often been made to feel like a failure in your attempts to help your loved ones. I wonder if your feeling moved right now is connected to a sense of having been acknowledged by me: feeling thanked as well as thankful." Then, in a very direct way that was unusual for her, Chloe said, "Yes! I believe that's true." She paused for a few moments and finally laughed, adding, "It's funny. What you said – about my 'raising' you – reminds me of how, when my brother was a little kid, he used to tell me that I hadn't done a very good job of raising our parents, otherwise they would have been different by the time he was born."

What appeared to be Chloe's confirmatory associations to my interpretations seemed to be overtly filled with hopefulness, and I was moved to say, "Perhaps you are also letting me know how hopeful you can be when it seems that I can change and how, in turn, you can be more optimistic about your own future development."

Discussion

One can follow, in the above detailed material, the process whereby this patient tenaciously persisted in her endeavor to help me to better understand her, in spite of certain obstacles emanating from my own personal dynamics as well as her defensive system. I will here attempt to elaborate my thoughts about that material.

In the Thursday hour, prior to the last week before the up-coming Fall break, Chloe reported a typical encounter with Father. When she seemed oddly untouched by this and went on to talk about various activities that made her feel good – while I felt myself growing increasingly uncomfortable – my initial hypothesis was that she had managed to avoid feeling demoralized by her father by passing on to me – via the mechanism of projective identification – those feelings of helplessness and inadequacy that might otherwise have diminished her sense of well-being.

I assumed that the realization of Chloe's phantasy of ridding herself of these feelings had been facilitated, in part, by her report of those activities (that is, massage, acupuncture, meditation, and diet) contributing to her "feeling better." Since the analysis was not mentioned in this list of helping activities, I concluded that I was being made to feel helpless and inadequate, or even useless to my patient.

Only later on could I appreciate how, while feeling insecure and puny, I had defensively grasped for my theory – of separation anxiety and the defenses against it – to protect myself from such disagreeable feelings, and in doing so may have pushed back, too soon, Chloe's experience of inadequacy with respect to a father who seemed hopeless, adding to this my own sense of inadequacy. In doing so, I believe that I had unwittingly identified with that father who – perhaps demoralized and driven crazy with guilt over the defective first baby that he had produced, and was subsequently unable to help to survive – had created in Chloe the feeling of not being enough, not being right, and always under the threat of being cut-off (that is, dying).

Additionally, on quite another level, I think I had failed to consider the possibility that Chloe's "feeling good" might have been due, in part, to a growing sense of her ability to help herself in my absence. It has crossed my mind that often in our attempt to establish an object that is capable of tolerating helplessness and dependency long enough to be able to experience and to think about it we may overlook the importance of cultivating the patient's ability to transform thought into appropriate and creative action. Along these lines, I believe that, by attributing Chloe's extra-analytic therapeutic activities exclusively to a system of manic defenses, I had overlooked the realistic consideration that, while undergoing fertility treatment, obstetric patients are often encouraged and even advised to engage in such activities as Chloe described.

Fortunately, when Chloe returned on Monday, she was determined to have me contain these feelings of inadequacy. Such feelings must have resonated with my own deepest sense of being unworthy and unlovable, and therefore at risk of being rejected. The patient's choice of the word "predator" may indeed have linked up with my own childhood experience of a predator-mother. Consequently, I felt terrible as I recognized that my interpretation, however plausible, may have emanated from a complementary identification (Racker 1953) between an aspect of my own internal world and Chloe's.

Subsequently, in that hour, I was able to hear the story of the thieving house-keeper as a clear communication of Chloe's experience of me in the previous hour and her present-if-unconscious intent to dismiss me. Now owning my internal predatory object, I felt that perhaps my patient was justified in defending herself against me. Looking back, I believe that, at this point, I was just barely able to contain both my own "bad" internal objects as well as those of my patient.

In the next hour I became convinced that Chloe was unconsciously aware of the strain under which I was operating. It seemed clear to me that her act of splitting-off and projecting into her husband her own injured and angry retaliative-self was, at least in part, initiated on my behalf and perhaps motivated by her desire to relieve me of the sense of persecution that I was scarcely able to contend with. Indeed her defensive action served to allow me some mental space for thinking about her experience of me, and I was subsequently able to address her sense of betrayal and disappointment.[15]

It then became apparent, in the Tuesday hour, that this interpretation was experienced by Chloe as a "confession" of my guilt and implied a "promise" to curtail such behaviors in the future. This "confession" and "promise" apparently had mollified her rage at me and, as a consequence, she was able to tell me – via the material about the housekeeper – more about her feelings of need for and gratitude toward me as well as about her perception of me as "feeling unlovable at the core."

While I was inwardly able to acknowledge her perception as accurate, I refrained from a confession or self-disclosure, instead acknowledging the significance of her communication interpretively. I was then left to bear "not knowing" what effect if any I had on her, which may have replicated her own often-felt experience of being left "wildly unprotected" by her mother.

Much to my surprise, the Thursday hour seemed to speak to Chloe's experience of the analysis as "Great Stuff." Although she had felt near to giving up on me and the analytic process, she was now perhaps more hopeful as she was able to feel her own sense of agency with regard to making our "project" work. At last she could experience her own contribution toward moving the analytic process along. She had "ideas" and clearly felt that, unlike the parents of the past, she could persevere to do a good job of "raising" me in order that I might become a better analyst to that continuously emerging and growing baby-part of herself.

I firmly believe that, through our analytic work, Chloe was able to gain a much-needed experience of her own capacity to be a parent – her capacity to conceive a child and to help it to grow – at a crucial time in her life that constituted the overarching context of the analytic work during this period in the analysis. Perhaps feeling "richer" for the experience of the previous analytic week, Chloe concluded that she could afford to pay a higher fee.

A note on being "raised" by the patient

Most significantly, this experience with Chloe impressed me with the importance of both recognizing and interpretively acknowledging our patients' own sense that they may possess the ability to tune into us; that they may have accurate perceptions of us apart from those distorted by the transference; and that they may also have a quality of insight as valuable as our own, combined with a healthy desire to help us as well as to obtain help from us. Bion once (1975b) suggested that we know little about raising children.

> However experienced we are we still know very little indeed about how to bring up children, of whatever age. However, we are beginning to know that we do not know. That is something.
>
> (1975b, p. 147)

The literature in psychoanalysis, beginning with Freud, and most notably in the body of work by Melanie Klein and her followers, is filled with allusions to and theoretical models based upon the premise that the relationship between analyst and analysand bears some likeness, at least in the transference–countertransference dimension, to that which exists between mother and infant, between parent and child.

In many other analytic orientations, with few exceptions (e.g. Casement 1985a; Jacobs 1991; Searles 1975; and Winnicott 1948), the analyst is equated with the parent, while the analysand is assigned the role of the child or infant. Casement (1985a) even goes so far as to suggest that, over time, we may even experience the realization of the potential of psychoanalysis "for enabling a rebirth of the individual personality" (p. 27).

It may be clear to many that such a "rebirth" need not be limited to the personality of the analysand alone. Perhaps we are beginning to know that we know little about "raising" patients and perhaps even less about their ability to "raise" us. That is something!

Conception

Indeed, Chloe and Peter's inability to conceive a child seemed to parallel the impasse experienced by the analytic couple, as well as the less than fruitful connection between Chloe and her mother as a nursing couple: one in which the scars of Mother's loss may have obscured her mental conception of a baby-Chloe, impeding her emotional development. It might also be of interest to note that immediately following this period in Chloe's analysis – during which I re-examined my work and was able to conceive of my patient in a new way – my relationship with her took a marked turn for the better. By "better" I mean to say that a "rhythm of safety" (Tustin 1986b, p. 268) – a phrase that denotes the satisfying working relationship that develops between the mother's nipple and the baby's mouth, when the sensations of "hard" and "soft" as well as other opposing experiences begin to come together in a creative way – seemed to have finally been established between us.

Perhaps not so coincidentally, shortly afterward Chloe and Peter were able to conceive a child by frozen embryo transfer. Curiously, just as a more fruitful union seemed to have been established between Chloe and myself only after my "errors" had been identified and rectified, Chloe's successful conception of her baby took place in the second of two attempts. The first – occurring prior to the material reported above – was botched by the physician who, having neglected to perform a "mock transfer," failed to account for Chloe's individual anatomical configuration.

By her physician's own admission, his way of proceeding with the first embryo transfer had set up such an irritation and subsequent uterine contractions that the initial batch of embryos had – in his own words – "never had a chance to latch on." However, after discovering and correcting for his error, he performed the second transfer with more care, and the subsequent implantation was successful.

It may be important to clarify that, although on the one hand I do feel that I had indeed erred with Chloe, I also would agree with Winnicott's (1963) paradoxical notion that, if the analysis goes well and the transference is allowed to deepen, the patient will get us to "fail" in the ways that (s)he needs us to, that is in the area of his/her omnipotence.[16] Quite independently, Tustin (1987) also insisted that our errors are the "growing points," as indeed mine were for Chloe and no less for myself. Ample evidence of Chloe's continued growth may be seen in the following sessions, which took place during the sixteenth week of Chloe's pregnancy, just prior to the date set for her amniocentesis and ultrasound examination.

Words and other pictures

Chloe began the Thursday hour, the last of the week, by telling me of yet another telephone conversation with Father. It appeared that, although there had been a painful disagreement between them some days beforehand, Father now behaved "as if nothing had happened." Chloe then went on to speak about the group of pregnant mothers she had met with that day and her discovery that all of these women were already dreaming of their babies.

While listening to my patient, I was reminded of how unusually silent Chloe had been in the Wednesday hour. In that session I had attempted to reach her without much success. I had addressed the possibility that, although there was a vocal-she who was looking forward to the amniocentesis on Friday, there might also be a silent-she who was at the same time dreading being poked and prodded by yet another painful needle: an experience she had often had of me, and perhaps was protecting herself from at that very moment. I also said that I wondered if she might be fearful that I would extract some painful feelings and certain fears that were deeply embedded within her silence, and how this could upset her equilibrium.

With these recollections of the previous hour and the current material in mind, I now told Chloe that I thought she was somehow presently communicating her concern and dismay that, unlike other mothers-to-be, she did not yet feel firmly in contact with her own baby, even in her dreams. In response to my speculation, Chloe admitted that she had been extremely troubled when she realized that she could not dream about her baby. The patient then added, "I did have a dream last night, but I'm afraid it was not about the baby."

> In the dream, Chloe was trying to get her mother's attention, but Mother was very depressed. Then Chloe was looking all over for this boy or man. She thought she saw him and followed him everywhere, trying to catch up. But while trying to find him, she missed her bus.

Chloe offered that she did not know the man in the dream, he didn't look familiar. She made reference to her mother's recent return to the East coast after a short visit, which in turn reminded me of something she had told me in the Tuesday hour: that her younger brother had not come by for dinner the night before Mother left town and how Mother had been upset and disappointed by his absence.

In that moment, an image was thrown up in my mind of a baby duckling swimming in a pond, while a mother hen longingly looked out from her place on the shore. This image was one related to something my own mother had once told me in an attempt to describe her sense of estrangement from me when I was a small child. I had not thought of this in a very long while and wondered in silence how this association of mine might be connected with what Chloe was now telling me.

I was soon able to offer my tentative thoughts: that this dream was very much about her baby, about how much concern the patient had for her mother, and how this concern was currently playing a big part in Chloe's experience of her own pregnancy. I went on to hypothesize that, in the dream, she seemed to be telling us that while searching to connect with her deceased elder brother – in the hope of restoring him to life and reuniting him with her mother who had been so despondent over his death – perhaps she sensed she was missing an opportunity (missing the bus) to connect with her own baby. I added that it appeared to me that she was profoundly affected by the ghost of this dead brother, presently obtruding itself between herself and her baby, just as this ghost had seemed to impose itself upon her relationship with her parents. Perhaps this ghost had been obstructing our connection as well.

Chloe's response seemed to be one of curiosity and interest, such that I was encouraged to wonder aloud if she might be looking forward to Friday when the amniocentesis and the sonogram might help to bring her into closer contact with her own baby. Chloe replied that she had been looking forward to the pictures and video that were to be taken during the sonogram: *moving images* that might enable her to connect with and to find out more about who this baby was, especially the sex of the baby. "Maybe it will be a boy."

After a period of silence – during which I grew concerned that I might be losing her again – I recalled how Chloe had openly expressed, in the Tuesday hour, very many questions regarding how we might carry on the analysis just before and immediately after the birth of her baby. This association of mine prompted me to further interpret the dream from yet another vertex, one that might bring us into closer contact.

I now proffered that Chloe might also be communicating – through the dream, as well as in her silence – something of her worry that, while paying so much attention to the baby gestating in her body, I might be missing that baby-her who is very much alive in her mind and who needs a mother-me to "see" her, to bring her out, and to support and hold her together, especially when we are so uncertain about what will happen to us and the analysis, how we might manage to sustain our connection after the birth of the baby in her tummy.

95

Chloe's response took the form of an awe-filled silence, punctuated by an inarticulate and almost dreamy murmur of appreciation uttered at the end of the hour. It seemed that we had both been extremely moved by the poignant significance of her material, as well as by the quality of our contact that day. Indeed Chloe seemed more and more to have in mind what she was about.

On Friday I received a message from Chloe on my answering machine. She seemed unabashedly joyful as she reported that the amniocentesis had gone well. They didn't know the sex of the baby yet, but she wanted to leave me a message to tell me a dream she'd had on Thursday night so that she would not forget it by Monday. She added that she had trouble sleeping that night as she had been so worried about the procedure.

In the dream Chloe had come in for her session and we were sitting face to face. She said, "I don't think I want to do this anymore. I'd rather read a book." And I responded, "OK, I'll just sit here with you and read a book, too." However, as she began to read, she noticed that some of the pictures were missing. She looked up at me, at which point I asked, "Are you ready to start?" To which she replied, "Yes." Then I took out an egg timer, turning it over to begin at the beginning of the hour.

I considered this message remarkable in many ways. First, it was unusual for Chloe to call me between sessions, since she had rarely dared to overtly exhibit an awareness of missing me or needing me to be in her life in any way during the breaks. Second, she had often resisted reporting her dreams, this because she treasured them so, thought about them with care, and often anticipated – especially in the first three years of the analysis – that I might misinterpret them. It also seemed that, if I had a view of her dreams that ran counter to her own, I was felt to undermine any understanding she had of these precious productions. Thus, certain valued and tender aspects of Chloe's inner experience were frequently shielded from possible insult.

In contrast, this time Chloe eagerly shared not only her experience of the amniocentesis, but also an important dream that afforded us a window onto her current experience of the analysis in many of its positive and negative aspects. Furthermore, it might be said that Chloe's dream seemed to be functioning as a container (Bion 1962a) for all of these aspects of her experience, rather than as an enclave in which she might keep them in protective isolation.

Finally, Chloe seemed to be determined not to allow any interference between us and our process of communication (for example, the "face-to-face" position of the two of us in the dream, which omitted the couch that she had so often felt as interfering with my "seeing her" and her "seeing me," and that may have represented some obstructive and obscuring object).

I believe that, in this dream, Chloe expressed something of her appreciation of and need for the word-pictures I draw for her, which seem to be of interest to and may be understood and appreciated by many aspects of her personality.

In the following material from the Monday hour, my initial impressions were confirmed and further expanded upon by the analysand.

Chloe came in and lay on the couch, reiterating that the "amnio" had gone well. However she could not understand how people could say that it doesn't hurt. "Of course it hurts! It's a needle penetrating your skin. But it was wonderful to be able to see my baby's brain and its spine. Everything's developing well. Being frozen doesn't seem to have stopped my baby's development from progressing normally. During the procedure [the baby] faced the probe and held up one tiny finger. Not quite a 'high-five,' but it made me very happy!"

Chloe then went on to tell me that she had also met with her accountant and found that her business had broken-even for the first time. No great profits, but they weren't in the hole either. She also reported on various business meetings that had gone well: "No 'big deals,' but things are progressing slowly and surely." Chloe seemed satisfied. She'd been asked to write an article on pregnancy for a magazine: specifically about her concern that something in her past may have had an adverse impact on her fertility. She was eager to write about her experiences.

Additionally, the patient spoke of a Sikh guru with whom she exercised yoga. She expressed her disagreement with this guru, whose opinion it was that soap operas and *People Magazine* were "bad." Chloe felt certain that there were "Worse things than living inside another person's life. It's much better than crack cocaine or heroin." She also took umbrage at some advice that the guru had given a friend who had been unable to conceive. "[The guru] said 'you just have to surrender!' But I don't think that's true, that all you have to do is give up and the baby will come. If she could [surrender], she would. It's just not that simple."

Lastly, Chloe recounted her efforts to purchase a membership at a gymnasium for Peter: a surprise for his birthday. She explained that some establishments seemed sneaky, trying to get her to commit to a three-year programme, charging a penalty for a "lesser commitment." Only one had said, when she told them that she didn't think she could commit to a long-term contract for Peter, that "they would be there when and if she was ready, and there would be no penalty."

Now returning to the dream, Chloe added that she thought it was a good dream, "contained in time and space, and not all over the place," and consequently she happily found that she could "remember and understand some of it." At this point, the links between and therefore what I felt to be the essence of her communications suddenly gelled in my mind. I said that she seemed to be letting me know that she had come to feel that numbing herself was less healthy for the baby-her than being "gestated" in my mind, perhaps even depending upon me to think about her; that she had felt moved by the "pictures" I drew for her with my interpretations; that she was now able to feel content with and to appreciate the progress she was making, slowly but surely, and all the little things: the little-Chloe she could not yet fully comprehend, as well as her own baby who, falling short of making a "high five," could only hold up one little finger.

While Chloe listened with interest, I added that she might also be letting me know of her need for me to appreciate that our probing- and even sometimes needling-analysis hurts when it penetrates her protective shielding, even though the pictures of the baby-her, glimpsed through the analytic process, are felt to be well worth the pain.

It seemed Chloe was feeling that something good had come of our discomfort. She seemed to be making her way out of that hole of despair that had, in the past, gobbled up her sense of security. Indeed, although on the one hand there was a Chloe who balked at the experience of analysis and would often behave as if she preferred to engage in a cognitive-intellectual exercise, on the other hand there was a she who needed and sought out the "pictures" I drew for her with my words, as well as the structure of our analytic relationship – confined in time and space – within which she seemed able to observe her own mental structure maturing, slowly but surely.

Chloe also appeared relieved to "see" that, even though she had been emotionally frozen early-on, she could now develop normally. Additionally, she seemed to appreciate that even if some part of her was unsure at times – could not commit herself to the analysis, and subsequently retreated from the emotional turbulence created in the wake of our connection – I would not "penalize" her for protecting herself; that I would not retaliate, but would instead be ready and willing to begin at the beginning, whenever she felt able.

The absent and present father

The material I wish to describe next had as its context an event in my life about which Chloe happened to have some knowledge, and which truly had an effect on her life in an unusual way. Midway through Chloe's second trimester of pregnancy, my husband – with whom I share an office suite –was called away for a period of time due to a family emergency and Chloe had learned of this situation from a friend. As fate would have it (and just to complicate matters) my husband's absence coincided with the vacation of Peter's analyst.

The week after my husband's departure Chloe's material began to speak, either directly or indirectly, to both the real and imagined consequences of these absences. In this hour, which took place during the twenty-second week of her pregnancy with her now-known-to-be baby-girl, the "absence of the father" became central to Chloe's sense of self and her relationship to her fetus, as well as our connection in the infantile transference.

In this session, the first of the week, Chloe began by telling me that she had been feeling "as big as a house" over the weekend. This feeling had been precipitated by a visit to her obstetrician on the previous Friday, during which he had scolded her for "gaining too much weight." Chloe was mortified by this event, since she had been careful about issues of nutrition even before conception, and ate only when hungry and quite healthfully at that. Up until this meeting with her physician, she had not felt herself to be "too big." In fact she was not in the least unduly preoccupied with her pregnant shape, and was even looking forward to "showing" her pregnancy, which it seemed was related to being able to "see" her baby.

Whereas Chloe had always been extremely petite and knew rationally that she may have even been a bit underweight before becoming pregnant, she now felt terrible about herself and quite anxious, although about what specifically she knew not. She had never experienced herself as "one of those women" who were "overly concerned about their appearance, always on a diet" or whose self-esteem relied heavily upon their good-looks. This variety of self-consciousness was new for Chloe and she was indeed feeling very low.

While I began to consider some super-ego entanglement, Chloe went on to say that she was looking at photos from her brother's wedding. "I didn't 'show' then and I looked really cute: just like a little girl." When I said that it seemed she might be having some difficulty thinking of herself as a "big" grown-up woman – a mommy – Chloe introduced a dream she remembered from over the weekend.

She was taking pictures with a Polaroid, but something was wrong with the camera. The film was somehow liquefying and leaking out all over, gumming up the camera. Consequently, no pictures came out. She was horrified and couldn't think what to do about it, and she woke up in an anxious state.

By way of association, Chloe said that she and Peter had recently purchased a Polaroid camera to take pictures of her as she "grows." She added that she had been a "print model" when she was a little girl. She also told me that, on Friday, she had taken photos with the Polaroid of each of the children in the mentor programme in which she volunteered. She'd written the name of each child on the back of the photo so that it might be easier for her to remember who each of them was.

As Chloe went on, I was reminded of a leaky-bathtub dream she had brought the week before. In that dream she said that:

She was taking a warm bath when she suddenly noticed that there was a leak in the tub. The waters were draining away and she woke up frightened that she would be sucked down into the hole.

After a brief pause, Chloe turned on the couch and pointed to the wall opposite: the one between my husband's office and my own. She said, "I wish I could ask you how you're doing with Dr. M away. It's strange knowing that there's no one there, that we're here all alone."

Chloe then continued to tell me about feelings of frustration related to the new computer she and Peter had just purchased. In spite of the fact that she was an expert with such things, she was having great difficulty getting this new equipment set up and running properly. She'd failed in her inaugural attempt to "integrate the new software with the new hardware" they had purchased. What had made matters worse was Peter's impatience with and anxiety over her initial failures.

Chloe added that she might have been alright had it not been for Peter's frustration heaped upon her own. "He lost patience with the time it was taking me to work out this integration in the beginning, and when he gets anxious I just can't think. Peter's solution is to throw it all away and start over again. He wants to get rid of it, take it back, get another. He scares me when he's like that. He just collapses. I know it's hard for Peter with his analyst away, but it scares me for many reasons, especially when I'm feeling bad about my weight." Then, after a pause, Chloe commented that it seemed that I was being inordinately quiet.

Over time, I wondered aloud if perhaps Chloe was worried about a leaky-me with my husband gone, the empty room next door. Perhaps she wondered if I too – like Peter – had collapsed without what she imagined to be my central means of support. And if I had collapsed, how would I be able to help her to integrate her experience of herself as a "cute little girl" with her growing experience of motherhood? How would she be able to adjust to her baby if Peter became frustrated and anxious? And how could I keep the baby-her in my mind while I lacked the support of my husband?

Seemingly relieved, Chloe replied: "Yes, I think it must be hard for you, not being able to talk to anyone – except patients – all day long." I said that it seemed, at least in part, that she was fearful that the vulnerable mommy-me was leaking out and could not be found in our session when there was no sturdy-daddy next door. How could I stay solid without the daddy to hold me together. Perhaps a liquefied and leaky-me was felt to be gumming up the works of the analysis and would no longer be capable of producing the "word-pictures" she needed to be able to capture her experiences; to identify, to hold and fit them together throughout this time in which she was struggling to adapt to and integrate all the changes occurring in her body as well as in her perception of her self, no longer just a cute little girl, but also a mommy growing a baby inside.

Some thoughtful moments passed by before Chloe began to voice her concerns that Peter might be feeling jealous of her connection with their baby. "She's kicking now. We felt a foot last night. He has to put his hands on my belly in order to feel it. He's always afraid he might miss it. I think he's frustrated that he can't do other things while he waits for the baby to move. I can read a newspaper or watch TV knowing that I won't miss the baby moving and kicking, but he can't do both at the same time. I wonder if Peter gets frustrated that he might be left out. It must be very hard on him."

As Chloe now seemed to be in contact with a "baby" who is left out, I said that I wondered if the concern she was voicing about her weight was also her way of communicating her experience of the "wait" over the weekend, when there is a baby-she unable to be "felt" by a daddy-me who is off doing other things, not feeling her movement. On the other hand, perhaps she is also considering that I might have felt left-out over the break in our contact, not being able to "touch" that baby-she who she imagines is all I have while my husband is away.

Somewhat dispirited, Chloe admitted that she had sorely missed my support when feeling so criticized by her obstetrician on Friday, and could have used some help with all the negative feelings about herself that this incident stirred up. She added with some hesitancy that she had also wondered, on occasion, if I might envy her pregnancy, and wondered if I had children of my own. "Maybe you would like to feel the baby, but you can't do that and be my analyst at the same time."

Then Chloe grew silent, appearing worried about something more. After a few moments she said, "I don't think that Peter is upset that I've gotten too big. He says he likes the way I look." A prolonged silence followed during which I found myself fidgeting with my clothing. Then, Chloe once again made mention of my husband's absence, wondering how I felt while waiting for him to return. The thought occurred to me that she might also be making reference to my "weight" and the connection this may have with my husband's departure and my "wait" for his return.

Quite tentatively I said, "I wonder if you have some concern that if you were to really grow as 'big as a house' – perhaps like me [I am somewhat *saftig*] – that your husband might leave you, just as you can imagine that mine has?" Chloe gave a big sigh of relief and said, "It's irrational, since I know that Dr. M will be back, but I had entertained the thought, just for a moment, that you had broken up." She added that she'd been embarrassed by this thought, which had occurred to her on and off for the past several days, and had been afraid to voice it in the last week. However, she now realized that this idea had fed her fear that the change in her "cute little body" might affect her connection with Peter.

After a brief pause, Chloe told me with some uneasiness that she had felt sleepy that afternoon and, although she was glad right now that she had come to talk with me about her worries and was feeling relieved, in part she had wished, at the time, that she could just stay at home and take a nap. What followed this admission could be described as an uncomfortable silence, during which I felt somewhat pressured to "give" my patient something.

Following a period of sorting-out this pressured feeling I was having, I wondered aloud if Chloe had earlier felt under some pressure to come to see me this day, perhaps in part due to a certain sense of duty toward me: an obligation to fill-up that empty "room" in my life, created in Dr. M's absence. Chloe said that she thought this was true. She had not wanted to hurt my feelings by canceling her hour. However, she said that she had also wondered if her problems might be felt as a burden on me at a time when I might have my own worries to contend with.

The role of the father

Regarding the role of the father, Tustin (1992a) wrote:

> In my experience, the father in the family has an important part to play in supporting the mother and infant through the pains and tribulations aroused by the lack of perfect fit with each other and the realizations that they cannot absolutely control each other. Children in such families [where the father is absent] have never learned to put up with the world as it is, and to adjust to it. It is only by such adjustment that psychological changes can take place, which enable them to become agents of change in the outside world.
>
> (pp. 119–20)

On yet another level, she suggests that the father serves the function of a bounding presence, intervening between mother and infant to prevent the prolonged perpetuation of and dependence upon an undue sensuous closeness that might otherwise interfere with the normal development of a sense of two-ness.

Certainly, both these essential functions of the father are crucial to normal development of the nursing couple and the internal structure of the mind of the child. However, it is important to recognize that there is a fine line between the experience of the paternal provision of support and boundary and an experience of an intrusive or a predatory third party at a time when two-ness is just coming into being in the mind of the infant.

Tustin suggested that the deficiencies in the mother's capacity to contain emotional experience – both her own as well as her infant's – and the gap in her self-confidence may be compensated for by the presence of the father or exacerbated in his absence. She posited that the absence of the father – either physical or emotional, whether during pregnancy or immediately after parturition – may result in the mother's use of the fetus or baby as an object to plug up the gap in her sense of self in order to assuage the elemental terrors emanating from her own birth and early infantile experience as these are activated through her maternal identificatory preoccupation with her baby. McDougall (1980) beautifully illustrated this situation in the case of her patient Isaac, whom she refers to as "the cork child with the abysmal mother."

Experience with patients like Chloe has made clear the importance of the father's role – and not just that of the mother – in the development of an internal psychic container for life's events, and has brought to light some of the fatherly dynamics that are especially influential in the integration of hard and soft sensations in primitive proto-mental life, a subject briefly touched upon in Chapter 2 and which I will here elaborate upon in greater detail.

Proto-mental integrations

In 1981, Tustin discussed the importance of integrating the various sensation-dominated happenings encountered in the infant's experience of the environment, both before and after birth. She called our attention to a primary sensorial component inherent in the task of early integration. Thus, while Klein (1957) highlighted the integration of the experience of the good and bad breast (objects) and those corresponding aspects of the self taking place in the depressive position, Tustin (1981) stressed the primary integration of the sensations of hard and soft occurring even before the onset of the paranoid-schizoid position.

Such sensations as Tustin referred to − either physical or psychological – are perceptible by the infant and the fetus even before birth and are perhaps the precursors of what Klein conceptualized as the part objects – breast/nipple and mouth/tongue – in relationship with one another in phantasy. Thus the sensations of hard and soft may be thought of as existing in opposition to one another at such a time when the fetus or the infant cannot be said to be entirely distinct from the mother (Winnicott 1960) – at least from the vertex of the baby – and when phantasy is as yet in a predominantly proto-mental state (Bion 1977b). Here I use the qualifiers "not entirely" and "predominantly" in order to emphasize a "neither-here-nor-there" situation akin to what Tustin (1992a) called "flickering states" of awareness of separateness.

In other words, such sensations may be said to be registered before psychic or somatic birth has been negotiated in phantasy proper. In this regard, Tustin clarified that:

> In the sense-dominated state of early infancy the infant's primary distinctions are between "comfort" and "discomfort," "pleasure" and "unpleasure." "Soft" sensations are pleasurable and comfortable. "Hard" sensations are unpleasurable and uncomfortable.
>
> (1981, p. 185)

She continued to suggest that:

> When on the basis of a cooperative suckling experience, "hard" entering nipple and tongue are experienced as working together with "soft" receptive mouth and breast, there is a "marriage" between "male" and "female" elements that takes place. Out of this union of hard and soft sensations a new way of functioning is born.
>
> (1981, p. 186)

Tustin described the product that emerges from the infant's integration of hard and soft and she submitted that this integration prefigures all those which follow, ushering in the important mental functions of projection and introjection:

> Gradually, "soft" sensations become associated with "taking-in," with receptivity. "Hard" sensations become associated with "entering" and "thrusting."
>
> (1992a, pp. 100–1)

She went on to suggest that later on these form the basis for the infant's bisexuality in the following manner:

> Hard thrusting becomes "male," and "soft" receptivity becomes "female." When on the basis of a cooperative suckling experience, the "hard" entering nipple and tongue are experienced as working together with the soft receptive mouth and breast, then a "marriage" between "male" and "female" elements takes place. Out of this union of "hard" and "soft" sensations, a new way of functioning is born, that of firm, adaptable resilience and toughness. This means that reality can begin to be processed, and [the necessity for] sensation-dominated delusions will wither away. The world will begin to "make-sense." And in this "making sense" of the outside world, the parents play a very important part.
>
> (1992a, p. 101)

Tustin also implied that these psycho-biological integrations run parallel to certain neuro-physiological integrations taking place within the brain. Additionally, she proposed the inception of projective mechanisms wherein – after Freud's (1920) model – the soft-pleasurable sensations become associated with "me-ness," while hard-unpleasurable experiences become associated with "otherness," in much the same way that psychotic children will eat only soft foods, while rejecting and spitting out the hard lumps.

However, Tustin (1992a) underlined the critical nature of this early phase of the awareness of two-ness in which the soft-me is extremely vulnerable. She concluded that, "If the maternal sheltering is disturbed at this time, the infant feels exposed to 'nameless dreads' (to use a telling phrase of Dr. Bion's)" (p. 102).

Discussion

One can see in the beginning of the hour presented that the awareness of the absence of my husband, like the sense of a lack of certain qualities in her husband (the lack of patience and frustration tolerance), was associated with the inability to think about "the baby" both in herself and myself. It was feared that we would fall apart, that our maternal capacities would leak out through the gap created in the absence of the "father." There was even an indication, in the material about "taking it [the computer] back and starting all over again," of the patient's fear that her baby would be "rejected" by the father if she did not readily settle in with the two of them and their style of living.

As in the dream of the film that "liquefies and leaks out all over and gums up the camera," certain fears were expressed regarding a dysfunctional relationship between hard and soft: the lack of integration resulting in a "no pictures" situation, which was connected with the analyst's silence. My "quiet" was thus experienced as a disquieting event brought about by my husband's absence.

Here we can see the development of the awareness that, without the presence of the father, the mother cannot think, just as Chloe felt that I could not interpret her experience – that I could not produce the necessary "word-pictures" that serve both to confirm her growth and my capacity to understand her – when my husband was felt to have collapsed out from underneath me, leaving me (and subsequently the baby-her) unsupported. Chloe's worries over her weight were associated with my "over-weight" and the phantasy that I had been abandoned by my husband, leading to the fear that she too would be abandoned or would leak out of the hole created by the father's absence.

Fearing that I had been abandoned, she felt obliged to compensate for my husband's absence. Here the negative aspect of what might be considered an "oedipal triumph" can be seen. Chloe felt it was her duty to plug up the gap in my life by inserting herself into it out of a sense of duty. She then abandons her own sense of need in favor of what she perceives to be my own. Once this situation is addressed, the patient is able to turn her attention back once more to her own needs as well as a concern that these may impose a burden upon the analyst.

Interwoven into the material presented, one can detect the threads of the various themes related to the role of the father: his function in the integration of hard and soft sensations (Tustin 1981); as a support system for the maternal environment; as an auxiliary container for the baby's anxieties; as a jealous rival or an excluded third; and as a protective boundary between mother and child. This material helped me to further appreciate the role of the father in sheltering the mother and consequently the infant or even the fetus during the various critical junctures of development and the integration of various aspects of self-experience, both before and after birth.

It seemed that Chloe's preoccupation with the absence of the father and/or with his inability to tolerate chaos in the nursing couple on their way toward achieving a "rhythm of safety" may have resonated with Chloe's early experience as a fetus or infant whose mother was unable to think about her baby, perhaps in part due to her own preoccupation with the event of the loss of her first child, and compounded (or at least left unmitigated) in the absence of sufficient paternal support.

Arguably, one might even infer that Chloe's fears about her own baby – as well as the baby-Chloe, experienced in the transference – may have been inextricably linked to her own early unmentalized experience (Mitrani 1995b) of liquefying and leaking out through the gap created by trauma to her father's as well as her mother's whole-some-ness of mind. The process of teasing out each of these fears in the analysis could be said to supply an "object lesson" (as Tustin once referred to it) or a mental structure in which the patient could begin to sort out her own emotional experiences. By helping her to do so, perhaps the analysis provided her with a sense of a firm and resilient bounding paternal-object as well as a sense of a comforting and receptive maternal-object, working together to hold and contain the baby-Chloe securely in mind.

Premature labor

As the weeks passed, Chloe was increasingly able to hold her own baby in mind and she began to gain confidence in her ability to be a mother. As many of her more-than-expectable fears regarding "all that could go wrong" both with the baby and the birthing process were articulated and linked up with her early experiences and phantasies, a deep appreciation of "this thing that is so important, so big . . . this thing that some people take so lightly . . . so for granted" but that "everybody does" grew in Chloe, as did the baby she had named "Colleen."

In the final weeks of the pregnancy, Chloe's physical discomfort waxed as her interest in the world outside waned. Occasionally, she longed to be able to wear her old clothes again, to retrieve her own interests, especially in her work. Her life and thoughts, as well as her body, were taken up with Colleen. Decisions about whether or not to collect cord-blood; whether to have a "dulah" present at the delivery or not; whether she would have anesthetic or would just tough it out; whether to have help after the birth or to try to go it alone were made in each hour as we sifted-out and addressed the transference significance clouding over and/or accentuating these practical issues. All the while Chloe let me know how she missed having me and her analysis to herself: it had not been "just the two of us for too long."

Just as the patient was forced to exchange the comfort of the couch for the large double overstuffed chair that more readily accommodated "the two of them," the work increasingly consisted in our attending to both the baby-Chloe and the baby-Colleen. Our time was evenly divided between the analysis of Chloe's experiences and what she made of them, and progress reports consisting of measurements: Colleen was now approximately seven pounds and lay in the womb, head down, at zero-station, while Chloe was 90 percent effaced.

Eventually, Colleen seemed "to demand more than just equal time" and we found that we were often interrupted in our conversation by fetal kicks and pokes that made Chloe "sore" both physically and emotionally. Sometimes a part of Colleen – a foot or a hand – would wedge itself in an uncomfortable place beneath a rib, and Chloe would poke or tap back in self-defense with the hope that the baby would move aside. But Chloe's crowded womb – not unlike my crowded consulting room – was full to capacity, with little space to expand.

At other times, Chloe would tap on her tummy when she feared Colleen was lying too still, and this seemed to get things moving again. In turn, her behavior stimulated me to interpret her impatience and anxiety over not knowing what Colleen was up to "in there."

As her wait for the unknown became more and more unbearable, Chloe experienced a short period of false labor, which she misinterpreted as a premature labor. On one occasion she rushed to the hospital, but was soon sent home to wait again. Chloe longed to be done with her "confinement" and to "get on with the next development."

A birthday

Colleen also seemed to have similar aspirations to move ahead, and on a Sunday near the end of the thirty-ninth week of gestation I received a phone call from Chloe. She happily announced that Colleen had "drained the sea" and "decided to come onto dry land and breathe the air with her parents." Chloe would not be in for her Monday hour, but hoped to speak with me soon.

On Wednesday, Chloe called to let me know the details of the birth: in her struggle to emerge, Colleen had become hung-up on the pelvic arch and despite a long labor, a Caesarian section was performed. Everything Chloe had imagined would be easy, was hard; everything she had anticipated would be hard, was easy. The baby was beautiful and perfect, calm and alert, 7 pounds 2 ounces and 21 inches in length. They were nursing well just two hours after birth.

Chloe kept in contact with me by telephone during her hours – of course as the baby would allow ("Colleen doesn't like the telephone cord: it's not *her* cord. I guess I have to go now!") – while convalescing from her surgery at home. Chloe's mother, who had flown to LA immediately after the birth, was an enormous help to her. Mother slept in a little no-frills guest house without complaint, and she cooked and helped with the baby and the household chores, and Chloe felt that a wonderful bond had begun to form with her own mother as never before.

Post-partum observations

Chloe's first day back took place on a Thursday, eighteen days post-partum and exactly three weeks to the day since our last face-to-face session. Aided by Peter, carrying the Moses-basket and diaper bag, Chloe held a tiny but chubby Colleen in her arms. Settling into the chair, Chloe immediately opened her blouse to nurse, although Colleen had appeared content just to be held and Chloe's breasts seemed relaxed and not in the least engorged. Colleen took the nipple and sucked gratuitously, making little squeaks and grunts. Chloe held her with her head supported; however, the baby's feet were left dangling.

"Colleen hated the drive over, but we're finally here." Chloe looked quite well, with lipstick applied, hair arranged, and glasses on, as she reported that Colleen had her first visit to the pediatrician on Wednesday. Proudly she announced, "She's eight pounds four ounces – one pound two ounces more than she was at birth. The doctor says she's a very healthy baby and that we can begin introducing her to our world. He said, 'A healthy baby can be introduced to your world, while an unhealthy baby introduces you to hers.'"

Although it did not escape me that Chloe might be letting me know that she had felt that a part of her had been left dangling with the early birth of her baby, I chose only to acknowledge how proud she seemed to be able to tell me what a good mother she was. In response, Chloe beamed, adding that Colleen had also found her fingers for the first time on Wednesday, and how she felt this was better than a pacifier. "It seems to help her when I'm not right there." It was as if Chloe felt that I would allow her to invest in herself without always having to rely upon me to comfort her, just as she seemed able to allow some space for Colleen to do the same.

Then, with some discomfort, Chloe said, "She's frightened of every new thing. But she's comfortable here, she knows this place, your voice." Addressing Chloe's anxiety, I ventured to interpret, "Perhaps, alongside Colleen, there is also a very-little-you here today who felt left out of our close contact too abruptly and for too long. And in feeling insufficiently supported by me, that little-you is a bit fearful of this new and awesome world called 'motherhood,' where everything is a potential threat, that is until you find that you and Colleen can survive."

"It's true," she said tearfully, gathering up Colleen's tiny feet in her hands. "I really missed seeing you these weeks." Looking down at Colleen she admitted, "This is the hardest thing I've ever done. But other women do it all the time, so it must be do-able. It's so ordinary and yet so extra-ordinary. Colleen had her first bath yesterday, the umbilical cord dropped off. Peter didn't like that. He was surprised that he didn't really get to cut the cord, just cleaned it up a little. He didn't really separate me from Colleen. It's funny how I don't like it when others hold Colleen. I miss her."

I replied that it was soothing to Chloe to feel that Colleen was still a part of her, "not really fully separate and perhaps, on another level, that we still have this connection as well." At once I noticed that Chloe had begun tapping Colleen on the feet and body, jiggling her slightly as the infant grew quiet, rather than stroking or rocking her to sustain her slumber. This behavior seemed to get a response from Colleen, who squeaked and wiggled, kicking her feet and stretching her arms.

I wondered if Chloe was somehow communicating how she had experienced my interpretation, perhaps as a baby-she who isn't left for very long without stimulation. However, I also considered that this might be Chloe's way of confirming my interpretation, by demonstrating how she is still able to reinstate a (for her) comforting sense of at-one-ment with Colleen by tapping her feet and jiggling her body, just as she had once tapped her tummy and the fetus inside to get it to move out of an uncomfortable spot within, or simply to encourage her to show some signs of life.

During the hour, any squeak or murmur coming from Colleen when she was off the breast was met by a return to the breast. Chloe commented, "She can't be put down for long. I think she's afraid to sleep." When I wondered aloud if perhaps a baby-Chloe was worried and needed comforting when Colleen was too still or asleep for too long, the patient enthusiastically replied, "Yes! It was really hell the first night. I was never sure if Colleen was sleeping or if something was wrong with her. But when my mother came it was a real help. She was thoughtful and calm." I took this last comment not only as a sign that Chloe was beginning to form a positive identification with her mother, but also as a transference communication and an indication of her experience of my intervention.

Chloe arrived the following Monday with an entourage consisting of Peter, Colleen, and the nanny Sally, whom she had hired to help out, especially so that she might be able to regularly attend her analytic hours. She somewhat hesitantly left Sally with Colleen in the waiting room after asking, "Are you sure you'll be alright?"

Lying on the couch for the first time in months, Chloe told me how hard it was to get to my office. Peter had trouble strapping the car seat in, "He says he just can't handle these 'baby things' and he was upset that he would be late for his analysis. Colleen got upset too when the traffic stopped-up. There were so many trucks and buses that we couldn't even see your building. Peter got so mad, and then Colleen started to scream." It was clear from what Chloe was saying that someone had become agitated at the prospect of being late for the hour, stuck in traffic.

I was at once reminded of the time when Peter had wanted to get rid of their new computer, when the "integration of the hardware and the software" had not gone smoothly. I said that perhaps when Peter became angry and impatient she had felt as if he might abandon her and her baby at any moment. Perhaps in feeling unsupported herself she could no longer hold Colleen in her mind and her baby seemed to fall apart as well. Chloe agreed and with much clarity suggested that they were like "three babies, each in need" of their respective "mothers," with no mother in sight.

Quite happy to finally have me all to herself, Chloe said that she could only marvel at the way in which Sally could calm Colleen down, when neither she nor Peter was able to do so. "I think I sometimes make things worse for Colleen, as if my anxiety sometimes slops over onto her and she has to deal with my insecurity as well as her own. It's hard to admit that someone else can calm her when I can't, but it's also relieving to know that my baby must be just fine out there in the waiting room." She further explained that she had instructed Sally to switch on the call light if there was a problem she couldn't handle.

I wondered aloud if perhaps Chloe was letting me know how she felt torn between a resentment of me that might go hand-in-hand with the discomfort of her awareness that she needs me to absorb her overflowing anxiety so that Colleen might be relieved of that duty, and her gratitude toward me when she feels me to be available and able to do so. Nodding, Chloe added that it was good to be able to be alone with me and to finally feel free to say what she is thinking without worry about how it might affect Colleen. I thought, but did not say, that Chloe might be feeling relieved that I could both bear her resentment and accept her gratitude.

With restored good humor, Chloe then confessed, "I've been thinking of selling Colleen to the [*Islamic jihad*.] She's really a little terrorist. She's holding both me and Peter hostage. But when she gets better at articulating her list of demands, we can be freed." I had to laugh as I offered my thought that she might be expressing how uncertain she feels about her ability to understand her baby's needs, what terror this needy baby evokes in her, as well as a hopeful expectation that their communication will improve over time.

After a moment, Chloe said, "Poor little girl. Some things seem so scary for her, even her own bowel movements. It may sound funny, but I think she imagines that her intestines are going to come out and it won't ever stop." Here it seemed to me that Chloe was truly able to be in contact with and to tolerate and understand her baby's experience in a quite sophisticated way.

In the following hour, Chloe brought her baby in with her, explaining that Colleen hadn't yet had enough to eat. She nursed the infant until she appeared satiated, and stroked her gently until she slept. I noticed that the tapping and jiggling had ceased. Instead Chloe was able to place Colleen in her basket and to reclaim the couch and the analysis for herself.

By the date of the one-month anniversary of Colleen's birth, Chloe was able to attend a full week of analytic sessions while her baby remained with Peter or Sally in the waiting room without incident. However, in the Monday hour following this week, she brought a dream:

She had left Colleen in one of four elevators. She was frantic, trying to find her baby, but could not recall which one of the elevators she had placed her in.

Chloe recalled having felt guilty when she realized she had not thought of her baby for some minutes during the Thursday hour of the previous week. "It was so relieving to be able to talk to you," she said, "But I'm beginning to understand that what's good for me does not necessarily coincide with what's good for Colleen. We're two separate people now, although I know my state of mind affects her tremendously."

110

While keeping in mind one possible layer of meaning contained in the dream, I replied that it seemed that she might be attempting to help me to understand how she felt, as if she were abandoning her baby while enjoying our connection. "It's rare that I 'forget' about her. I'm almost always putting her first. I always try to park in the upper parking lot when I come here, even though it's not what I used to do. I don't think the fumes from the gasoline in the underground lot can be very good for the baby."

I said that it seemed she also needed me to understand something of the concerns she carried over the effects upon Colleen of the analysis that takes her deep below the surface of her experience. Although this may be felt as relieving for Chloe, she is worried that the analysis might be toxic to the baby Colleen. After a few moments, she said that there was another part of the dream she had forgotten until just then.

There were two women with her while she waited for her car in the underground parking garage. One woman was very impersonal toward her baby and they just chatted, while the other was trying to get Chloe to allow her to hold the baby. This woman, unlike the other, was very gushy, almost suffocating. At that point Chloe put Colleen in the elevator.

Hearing this addition to the dream, I recalled having leaned over to look at Colleen when Chloe rose to leave one day during the previous week. The patient had asked me if I wanted to hold her baby, to which I replied "perhaps another time." Meanwhile, Chloe went on to tell me other thoughts related to the dream: "The parking lot reminds me of last week, when Peter got into an argument with the parking attendant in the outdoor lot. He refused to give him the keys to our new car. Now I feel uncomfortable parking there since Peter was very angry and unreasonable with the guy."

Over time, we could begin to understand how Chloe needed me to bear with her while she struggled uncomfortably with feelings of competition with me as the woman in the dream who is trying to take away her baby, or perhaps as the parking attendant who wants the keys to the new car; how she perceived me to be both too far, like the cold and impersonal woman in the dream (when I declined her offer to let me hold Colleen), and too close, like the gushy woman who suffocates her with interest, or the toxic fumes in the underground garage (which may represent my unconscious desire to have physical contact with her or her baby, possibly perceived by Chloe as a contaminant to our analytic relationship). She may also be of two minds: struggling with conflicting desires, in part wanting me to be less "impersonal" and more involved with her and her baby, at other times feeling suffocated when I am felt to be on the verge of exceeding the bounds of the analytic relationship.

Certainly I considered the possibility that the latter might be the negative side-effect of her way of getting around the former. That is, had she felt me to be avoiding getting closer to her when I put off indefinitely any physical contact with the baby with whom she identifies, she may have sought an underground connection with me (one constructed in phantasy) that may have, in turn, stirred up certain persecutory phantasies, turning me into a toxic and suffocating stranger. Additionally, Chloe's anticipation – of a violent conflict between us as well as an irrational power struggle for control over who would hold the baby-her as well as the baby Colleen – may have provoked certain maneuvers aimed at hiding the baby from me during one of the preceding hours (one of four elevators).

Nevertheless, in spite of the turmoil or perhaps because of it, I felt certain that this young woman was well on her way to parceling out and comprehending both her own and her infant's fears, as well as the need for each of them to have a mother/analyst who could understand and bear with them in their ongoing individual and conjoint struggles to develop healthfully.

In the next chapter, I explore yet another aspect of the ordinary relationship between mother and infant: that of the aesthetic conflict. I will present vignettes from the treatment of a number of patients that may serve to accent the infant's need for a mother who can bear the ecstatic elements of the experience of at-one-ment, as well as the terrors inherent in the awareness of two-ness.

6

Unbearable ecstasy, reverence and awe, and the perpetuation of an "aesthetic conflict"[17]

"Beauty is truth, truth beauty" – that is all
Ye know on earth, and all ye need to know.
John Keats, "Ode on a Grecian Urn"

Although much has been written on Tustin's notion of the "tantrum of two-ness," far less attention has been paid to her concept of the "unbearable ecstasy of at-one-ment" and the importance of the containing function of the mother with regard to that elemental experience (Tustin 1972). As the title of this chapter reflects, along with a discussion of the experience of ecstasy, I will take up the central contribution of a little-known paper by Bion, in which he makes a unique distinction between what he called "reverence and awe" and the more commonly discussed Kleinian concept of *defensive idealization*, and I will also introduce into the mix Meltzer's notion of the "aesthetic conflict."

I hope to show that each of these *specific* themes – separately and in conjunction with one another – have some essential bearing upon the provocation or mitigation of envy, the process of introjection, the development of both healthy and pathological internal object relations, and the resultant nature of the super-ego and individual self-esteem. The clinical case material, presented both as background for and in illustration of the phenomena described, will lead up to certain conclusions which may have some bearing upon our attitude and technique in psychoanalysis.

Although I do acknowledge that many authors – perhaps most notably Kohut (1971; 1977) and before him Lacan (1949) – have made substantial contributions to our understanding of the idealizing transference, it would not be possible to provide an extended survey of the literature on this topic. Neither shall I attempt to develop a comprehensive exposition of the central issues in aesthetic

113

appreciation, which are beyond the scope and focus of this chapter. Instead, I hope to offer one view of how some selected concepts, put forth by Bion, Meltzer, and Tustin, overlap, intersect, and perhaps modify one another – which may reflect the personal and professional intersection between these three contemporaries who were rooted in the Kleinian tradition and working on the cutting-edge of object relations in London[18] – and how these have impacted one analyst's thinking in the consulting room.

To begin with, I would like to present a segment from the analysis of a patient whom I call Jessica, as an introduction to the theoretical discussion to follow.

Jessica

Over one weekend break in the sixth year of a five-times-per-week analysis, Jessica – a woman in her late thirties – attended a concert of classical music. Featured on the programme was a female violinist who was to play Jessica's favorite concerto.

Jessica adored music. She had herself been formally schooled in the violin since the age of 2. She had, in her youth, played with numerous amateur orchestras, and nearly all the members of her immediate family were musically inclined. This is by way of saying that, for Jessica, attending concerts was nearly always an intensely emotional experience.

On this particular occasion, Jessica sat quite close to the stage, directly in line with the spot where the soloist would be standing. After the overture, in anticipation of the concerto to come, Jessica found herself glancing about the audience, soon realizing that she was looking for me.

When the soloist walked on stage, Jessica was stunned. The woman who stood before her was incredibly beautiful, an ethereal vision of long black hair flowing over porcelain white shoulders left bare above a deep-blue strapless satin gown. As the violinist began to play, Jessica could not decide which was the more lovely: the sound of the music that flooded her ears, or the sight of this Rumanian gypsy dancing and swaying to that music, which bedazzled her eyes. Jessica was enraptured and ecstatic.

After the concert, as the sights and sounds of the evening lingered on in Jessica's mind, she thought once more about my perceived absence, and her ecstasy gradually degraded into a profound sadness. At that moment she was aware of a deep and almost unbearable feeling of regret over not having been able to share this experience of sensual wonder with me.

In the Monday hour in which these events and feelings were reported, Jessica talked about her mother, a beautiful woman of Rumanian descent. She said that her mother – who was nearly always depressed during the patient's childhood – had little sense that she (the mother) was either beautiful or desirable. The patient thought that this might be partly due to her father's openly-expressed intention to obtain a divorce from her mother even before Jessica's birth. I recalled that Jessica had earlier told me that her mother, who was the only child of a borderline psychotic woman, had been both physically and emotionally abused.

Jessica's violin lessons were initiated, encouraged, and supported by her mother, who also participated actively in her music studies by accompanying Jessica, when possible, at the piano. Mother also sang – at one time semi-professionally – but had always longed to play the violin, and was thrilled when her daughter seemed to demonstrate both an interest and talent in this direction.

Jessica said that she had felt good when she left the hour on Friday, and she now thought that this might be one reason why she had hoped to see me that evening at the concert. Since she could not find me, she concluded that I must not be there, and felt disappointed at not being able to share the beautiful concert experience with me. She now was aware that she wanted very much to convey this experience in the session, but she feared – much to her dismay – that I could never really have that experience, since I had not been there.

The patient also made reference, both direct and indirect, to my perceived physical beauty. As she did so she burst into tears, which seemed to pour out of her in an uncontrollable way, streaming down her cheeks, and soaking her hair and the collar of her dress. When she noticed this, Jessica expressed a concern that both her hair and dress had been ruined, and she reported a sense of dread that she would not be able to pull herself together when our time was up in order to face the day that lay ahead of her.

While Jessica spoke, I was reminded of a dream she had reported the week before about a teacher on whom she had had a crush in elementary school, a beautiful woman with prematurely graying hair. Additionally, I noted the fact that – like the violinist – I am of Rumanian heritage. While wondering *if* and *how* Jessica might sense this, I recalled the uncanny feeling in the Friday hour of the previous week, when it seemed that we were so closely attuned to one another that the sensation of our "touching" was unmistakably palpable.

I also recalled that this hour was one of those rare and memorable ones when our thoughts – her associations and my interpretations – seemed to be burgeoning, one from the other, in such a graceful and organic way that it had felt at the time like we were creating a modern ballet or a poem. Jessica's comments at the end of that hour had spoken to her experience of something "beautiful" about our contact as well.

With this in mind I said to Jessica that I thought that she was communicating something of the ecstasy she had experienced, not only at the concert but also in our Friday hour, when she had perhaps experienced herself, me, and our connection as a thing of beauty. Jessica nodded in agreement with this and added that she had felt foolish when she left at the end of the hour, thinking that, while she was sorry to end the analytic week, I probably felt tired, and would be looking forward to my weekend off.

115

To this I replied that it seemed that she had come away from the Friday hour with two contrasting experiences of me: one as a beautiful mother-analyst who loved and supported her, and the other as a tired, depressed, and unsupported mother-analyst who was relieved to be rid of her. Since she was not certain which experience was true, she had searched the concert crowd for my face, in hope of finding me there sharing in the beautiful experience of both herself and myself making lovely analytic music together, swaying in tune with one another, rocked safely in the rhythm of the melody of the Friday hour. I also said that perhaps she had taken my absence from the concert – like my absence during the weekend break in our contact – as a confirmation of my depression and fatigue.

Jessica responded to this saying that she had felt awfully overwhelmed after the concert but that she didn't know why. Hearing her, I recalled that our Friday hour had been so rich that I needed to make notes on it afterward, in part to preserve it, in part because this is one way in which I feel I can help myself to contain whatever leftover emotion might otherwise spill into subsequent hours with other patients. I was then moved to say that I thought Jessica might be telling me that she needed to see her feelings of admiration toward the beautiful mother-me reflected in my presence at the concert.

Perhaps Jessica needed to see that I could also feel myself to be beautiful, but, when she imagined me absent from the concert, her worst fears were realized. Perhaps her experience of the mother-me as tired, depressed, and relieved to be rid of her for the weekend had seemed painfully confirmed. In that moment, her feeling of ecstasy had dissolved, spilling over in an overwhelming encounter with disillusionment, perhaps leaving a very little baby-Jessica feeling incapable of the task of holding herself together over the long weekend.

One might say that "beauty" and its associated attributes – goodness, hope, and truth – are the cornerstones of mental health. However, the experience of the beautiful mother must first be had *with* that mother, not merely *of* her (Reid 1990). This notion is analogous to Winnicott's (1958) observation of the baby's need to first experience being alone in the presence of the object, in order that it might gradually develop the capacity to be alone, rather than being overcome with loneliness and despair. Winnicott also discusses the baby's need for a mirroring object, which I believe is closely related to the issues under examination in this chapter.

As the hour unfolded, it became clear that Jessica needed me to partake in the experience of myself as a beautiful mother-analyst, to catch the overflow of the ecstasy she felt in my presence in the Friday hour, and to confirm this experience when its reality was threatened by the pain of separation – by the presence of the absent object (O'Shaughnessy 1964).

The aesthetic conflict

I was put in mind of Jessica's experience while reading a paper by Meltzer (Meltzer and Williams 1988). In that paper, on what he called "the aesthetic conflict," he stated:

It has probably escaped no-one's attention that the percentage of beautiful mothers recorded in the course of psycho-analysis far exceeds the national average and that this appellation clearly refers back to childhood impressions often completely out of keeping with later more objective judgments by the patients of their middle-aged parent.

(pp. 8–9)

Here Meltzer prompted our consideration of the possibility that the view of the "beautiful mother," often presented by patients in analysis, harkens back to some early proto-aesthetic experience; one that is however not without conflict. He went on to say that the baby:

"Rocked in the cradle of the deep" of his mother's graceful walk; lulled by the music of her voice set against the syncopation of his own heart-beat and hers; [responds] in dance like a little seal, playful as a puppy. But moments of anxiety, short of fetal distress, may also transmit itself through heart-beat, rigidity, trembling, and jarring movements; perhaps a coital activity may be disturbing rather than enjoyable, perhaps again dependent on the quality of maternal emotion; maternal fatigue may transmit itself by loss of postural tone and graceless movement.

(p. 17)

In this passage Meltzer indicated that the baby knows its mother inside and out – as both the bad and the beautiful – and is impacted on a sensual level by each of her physical, mental, and emotional qualities even before its birth. This notion reverberates with findings from current fetal observation (Mancia 1981; Piontelli 1985; 1987; 1988; 1992a; 1992b), psychoanalytic/clinical inference (Bion 1976a; 1977a; Freud 1926; Hansen 1994; Maiello 1995; Mitrani 1996 and 1997c; Osterweil 1990; Paul 1981; 1989; 1990; Share 1994), and in an imaginative conjecture by Bion most notable in his *Memoir of the Future* (1979b).[19]

Indeed, Meltzer (1988) purported that "Every baby 'knows' from experience that his mother has an 'inside' world, a world where he has dwelled and from whence he has been expelled or escaped, depending on his point of view" (p. 21), and he went on to posit that, after birth:

The ordinary devoted mother presents to her ordinary beautiful baby a complex object of overwhelming interest, both sensual and infra-sensual.

> Her outward beauty . . . bombards him with an emotional experience of a passionate quality, the result of his being able to see [her] as "beautiful." But the meaning of his mother's behavior, of the appearance and disappearance of the breast and of the light in her eyes, of a face over which emotions pass like the shadows of clouds over the landscape, are unknown to him.
>
> (p. 22)

Meltzer seemed to suggest here that the mother is an enigma to her baby. The baby *may* have known her, and yet – perhaps shaken by "the impressive caesura of the act of birth" (Freud 1926) – he has suddenly become uncertain of what he knows. Is she a beauty or the beast?

When Meltzer proposed that:

> This is the aesthetic conflict, which can be most precisely stated in terms of the aesthetic impact of the outside of the "beautiful" mother available to the senses, and the enigmatic inside which must be construed by *creative imagination*.
>
> (p. 22, italics mine)

it seems that he was implying that the baby's sensory experience of the beautiful or good mother must be confirmed by what he finds inside the mother, and that his experience of his mother's inner world – her mood, her emotional and mental life, her attitudes about herself and him – is colored by *creative imagination*, that is, by his own unconscious phantasies via the process of projective identification.

However, further along, Meltzer appeared to append the above conclusion, submitting that the baby must wait – like Kafka's "K" – "for decisions from the castle of his mother's inner world" (p. 22). With this addition, it would seem Meltzer was suggesting – and, I believe, is correct in doing so – that *it is not just the baby's "creative imagination" that imbues the inside of the mother and the baby's pre- and post-natal experience of her with meaning* since, as he so astutely observed, the baby must derive his cues from the mother's conscious and unconscious communications; that is, the baby must wait for his mother to confirm his greatest hopes or his gravest fears.

To put it another way, the baby asks, "how does Mother view or experience herself?" and must anxiously await the answer *from his mother*. I believe that the baby's "question" and the mother's "answer," in conjunction with one another, constitute one aspect of the type of reality testing that Melanie Klein (1963) referred to as *the means by which the baby finds validation for the enduring existence of the "good breast"*: the good internal object, and the good experience that the breast represents.

An example of this type of reality testing, and the consequences of a distorted message being received from the "castle of the mother's inner world," may be seen in the following material from the analysis of Carla, a patient whom I have already introduced in Chapter 3.

118

Carla

I would like here to demonstrate how Carla and I came close to understanding one aspect of the most primitive origin of her fear of being spilled and gone, as well as the template for the development of her leathery protection against the threat of such dissipation. Both this anxiety and the defenses against it appeared to be connected to a primary experience of the mother as it became enacted in the transference relationship, which I will now attempt to describe.

In the third year of her analysis I noticed that, almost invariably, when Carla returned from the weekend breaks, she would greet my arrival at the waiting-room door with a warm and enthusiastic smile. Then, she would scan my face quite intensely, passing through the doorway on the way to my consulting room. The intensity of Carla's scrutinizing gaze often left me feeling unusually self-conscious. Carla was very beautiful and always perfectly made-up when she came for her sessions, and I frequently was given over to wondering if my lipstick was on crooked, if I had forgotten to powder my nose, or if perhaps I had applied mascara to just one eye and not the other.

These banal ruminations were discomforting and intractable, and I found myself tempted to dismiss them as irrelevant. However, as these were uncommon if not altogether absent preoccupations with others of my patients, I opted to allow them to brew a bit to see what percolated out of them. This led to the emergence of some fleeting thoughts: might I be envious of this young and beautiful girl? Might Carla be looking for something in my face that might reflect her own? Was I felt to be failing her in some way that was both disconcerting and implacable?

No matter how many times this sequence would occur, by the time my patient had settled on the couch, I noticed that her enthusiasm for me and her analysis would suddenly be transformed into a tough, leathery air of indifference and disgust, as if she resented having to submit to *my* "rigid requirement for yet another hour and another week."

One day I had the opportunity to turn our attention to this shift in her attitude toward me. I said that I wondered if the change might somehow be connected to feelings and thoughts provoked in her by what she seemed to see in my face when I came to the door. She replied with despair, "It could be, but I can't think how. After all, *you always look the same.*"

Carla then went on – as if changing the subject – to tell me that she had been happy that she had managed to arrive in plenty of time to get to the restroom before her session. However, when she found that "it was all locked up," she was left feeling as if she might burst open.[20] Then, by way of denying the urgency of her need and the significance of her disappointment, she added resolutely that it was "*really* OK."

At that moment, it seemed to me that the story of the locked restroom contained clues to the meaning of her radical transition from joy in the waiting room to disdain on the couch. I now considered that Carla had been filled to bursting with positive feelings about our connection, which she could barely hold inside when she arrived. However, she had soon been disappointed when she felt me to be emotionally shutting her out – just as she had felt shut out of the restroom – as she searched my face for signs of *my own joy* as evidence that I might have been open to the overflow of her excitement, that I might therefore be able to provide her with some relief from these as well as other (perhaps less positive) overwhelming feelings. Instead, she seemed to find me "always . . . the same" or locked-up.

I told Carla that it seemed to me that she had been hoping that my face would reflect the enthusiasm with which she had come to see me that day – especially when she felt that it was not too late for her to get some relief – but that her hopes had somehow rapidly turned to disillusionment. She nodded in agreement, so I continued, telling her that I thought that she might be bringing to our attention a very little-she, unable to bear that feeling of disillusionment, a thin-skinned little-one who had consequently resolved to toughen up for fear of bursting open.

Carla responded by saying quite poignantly that she had only hoped that I would be as happy to see her as she was to see me. I acknowledged her hope and added that she also seemed to need to feel that a flowing-over and joyous baby-she could be seen and held in my facial expression, so that she would not spill away and be lost again. I soon added that I thought that this need to be held together was so intense and urgent that – when it seemed to her that I *could not* reflect and reciprocate her joyous feeling for me – she had transformed herself to match what must have felt to her to be a locked-up, leathery-tough, mommy-analyst. I felt that perhaps this transformation was intended to enable her to create a sense that she could catch and hold herself by bringing us closer together with no gap in between.

Carla wept softly and finally told me that, as I was speaking, she had flashed back upon the image of her mother's face looking just as it had when, as a very little girl, she would watch her with loving admiration as she sat before the mirror on her dressing table. After a long pause Carla then told me – for the first time – that when her mother was a child she had been disfigured in a terrible automobile accident and, as a result, her face had always looked strange, disgusted, and remote, with a leathery skin full of scar tissue resulting in a frozen, unchanging expression of disdain. Carla then tearfully expressed the painful realization that she could never tell if her mother really loved her.

It seemed to me that – in some dimension of her experience – the baby-Carla may never have felt lovable or held lovingly, safely, and responsively in her mother's gaze, as Mother's unalterable expression might have hindered her ability to reflect her daughter's joyous states of ecstasy, admiration, and love for her.

Unfortunately for Carla, the ecstasy of one-ness with the mother (Tustin 1992a) may well have been left uncontained, rebounding off the expressionless surface of her mother's face, an ecstasy apparently unreflected in the mother's experience of herself. I am reminded here of a passage by Winnicott (1967), who was admittedly influenced by the work of Lacan (1949) on ego development when he wrote:

> What the baby sees [when he looks at the mother's face] is himself or herself. In other words the mother is looking at the baby and *what she looks like is related* [in the baby's phantasy] *to what she sees there.* Many babies . . . have a long experience of not getting back what they are giving. They look and they do not see themselves. There are consequences. First, their own creative capacity begins to atrophy . . . most mothers can respond when the baby is in trouble or is aggressive, and especially when the baby is ill. Second, . . . perception takes the place of apperception . . . [it] takes the place of that which might have been the beginning of a significant exchange with the world, a two-way process in which self-enrichment alternates with the discovery of meaning in the world of seen things.
>
> (pp. 112–13)[21]

I could also imagine that Carla's mother – grief-stricken, abandoned, and betrayed, with little in the way of self-esteem and self-love to reflect back to her daughter – may have failed to confirm the little girl's *experience of her mother's inner goodness.* Thus, Carla's faith in and appreciation of *her own* inner goodness and beauty – lacking resonance with a sense of a good internal object – may have dissipated and faded away over time.

Carla's perception that I "always look[ed] the same" seemed to evoke, in the transference, these very early painful feelings of being unlovable. At the same time, I became the receptacle for that maternal object with the frozen, disfigured face that manifested itself in the countertransference as extreme self-consciousness and obsessive doubts about my make-up being lop-sided or missing, and indeed may well have affected my facial expression, contributing to a vicious cycle. As our understanding of Carla's experience deepened over time, the way in which we saw each other and ourselves shifted. She began to feel better about herself and our connection, and we could begin to touch upon some of the omnipotent phantasies that contributed to the untoward sense of guilt and shame against which she so mightily defended herself.

Fuller (1980) reminded us that the negative of the *aesthetic* is the *anesthetic*, and he suggested that aesthetic emotion is connected to primal experiences of the self submerged in its environment, with the subsequent gradual differentiation of the self out from it. I believe that a premature or abrupt loss of that early fleeting experience of "at-one-ment with the beauty of the world" often leads to states of anesthesia where little can get in or out.

The most extreme consequences of such disruptions might be seen in those cases of infantile autism described by Tustin (1992a), where the natural processes of projective and introjective identification have been massively truncated. Indeed it seemed that, at best, all that my patient Carla could gain for herself, in adhesive identification (Bick 1968 and 1986; Meltzer 1975; Meltzer *et al.* 1975; Tustin 1981, 1986a, and 1990; Mitrani 1994a and 1995a) with her mother, was a tough, leathery protection against that penetrating disillusionment that threatened to puncture and deflate her own beautiful baby-buoyancy.

Chloe

Here I will briefly present some additional material from the analysis of the patient "Chloe," whom I have already introduced in Chapter 5. This snippet of her analysis is taken from the first year. As the reader has perhaps already gathered, this young woman was an exceptionally lively, passionate, and creative person. In one Thursday hour, the last of the week, Chloe was understandably frustrated with the limitations imposed on us and our communication by the weekend break and by the use of the analytic couch and verbal language, which did not begin to allow a place for all she was and all she had to give. Nor did it leave room to scratch the surface of the sensual, emotional, and mental needs of the baby-Chloe, as these were felt toward a mother-me in the transference.

At this early stage of the analysis, Chloe feared that she would give up, which she had let me know referred to her sense that she might anesthetize herself, cut-off or freeze in silence all curiosity as well as all desire for real contact. She was afraid of those times when she "stayed in her head," anticipating that I would fail to give meaning to her dreams and associations, which would leave her "feeling stupid."

My interpretations near the end of the hour addressed that wondrous and wondering she, so full of feelings, thoughts, and questions that she sensed had no place and would receive no response except in her own imagination, and the utter despair and helplessness she felt in the face of this experience, which was almost too much for her to bear. In the beginning of the following Monday hour, Chloe presented me with the lyrics to a song by Elvis Costello (1996). She thought, and I agreed, that Costello's lyrics spoke to her experience in nearly every relationship, including ours. I will quote here only the last verse and chorus of what I took to be her poetic confirmation of my interpretation, which ended in a poignant question:

Nonsense prevails, modesty fails, grace and virtue turn into stupidity.
While the calendar fades almost all barricades to a pale compromise.
If something you missed didn't even exist
It was just an ideal, is that such a surprise?
What shall we do? What shall we do with all this useless beauty? All this useless beauty.

It seemed to me that Chloe may have been re-experiencing that "something she missed, which didn't exist" and the shocking awareness that it was "just an ideal." But is it *just* an ideal? Or is it perhaps something else?

Reverence and awe

In a paper read at a joint scientific meeting of the Los Angeles and Southern California psychoanalytic societies in 1967, which was posthumously published only in 1992 as a chapter in the book *Cogitations*, Bion described an encounter with one patient who came to him after a previous analysis from which he had benefited, but with which he was nonetheless dissatisfied. At first Bion expected to find greed at the bottom of this patient's distress, but it soon became clear to him that there was something else going on.

Bion described his patient's outpourings, which were so fragmented "that they would have required an omniscient analyst to sort out and make sense of." Bion's interpretations were either labeled by the patient as "brilliant" or they were met with extreme disappointment and hostility to the point of depression. Bion finally concluded that:

> There is a great difference between idealization of a parent because the child is in despair, and idealization because the child is in search of an outlet for feelings of reverence and awe. In the latter instance the problem centers on frustration and the inability to tolerate frustration of a fundamental part of a particular patient's make-up. This is likely to happen if the patient is capable of love and admiration to an outstanding degree; in the former instance the patient may have no particular capacity for affection but a great greed to be its recipient. The answer to the question – which is it? – will not be found in any textbook but only in the process of psycho-analysis itself.
>
> (1992, p. 292)

In his customary style, Bion avoided saturating his concepts, leaving them somewhat ambiguous, and thus allowing us the freedom to use our own capacity for "imaginative conjecture" to fill in the blanks, so to speak. I will yield to the temptation to do so with the understanding that the reader may draw his or her own conclusions, which may very well differ from my own.

Bion seems to be saying that, in this instance, *he had met with a patient for whom Klein's theory of envy did not apply*. Indeed he made it clear that he did not see his patient's disappointment and hostility as constituting an attack on the good breast or the analyst's good interpretations. Neither did he seem to see the patient's fragmented presentation as the result of an envious attack on thinking or on the links that might have rendered his communications meaningful and relevant

(Bion 1959). Instead, Bion concluded that his patient was attempting to have an experience of an object who might be able to understand and transform the inchoate experiences of the as-yet-unintegrated-baby-he and was therefore seeking *the realization of his preconception* of an object who could contain these experiences as well as his innate capacity for love, reverence, and awe.

I would suggest that the containing capacity, initially found and felt to be located in this type of *external* object – when introjected – leads to the development of an *internal* object capable of sustaining and bearing feelings of ecstasy and love; an object that might form the basis of the patient's own self-esteem. This aim certainly calls for an analyst who *truly* thinks well enough of himself and his own goodness that he is not dependent upon the goodness and cooperativeness of the patient in order for such a positive self-perception to be confirmed, and in order for him to continue to function analytically.[22]

Discussion with Frances Tustin

At this point, the reader may be wondering where Tustin's ideas on the "unbearable ecstasy of at-one-ment" enter into all of this. During one of my final conversations with her, we had the opportunity to discuss this distinction that Bion makes between the manic defense of idealization and the healthy striving to be in contact with an object deserving of reverence and awe. Prior to this time, Tustin had not been aware of the existence of this paper of Bion's, which I chanced to bring to her attention as follows.

When we were together in England in October of 1994, just one month before her death, I knew that Tustin had little time to live and I wanted to express to her – one last time and in most explicit terms – how much her work had meant to me. I wished to do this partly out of my own need to show my gratitude toward her this one last time. However, I also felt the need to reassure her, since she seemed to be openly plagued by a fear that she had not given enough, and that what she had contributed would soon be lost or forgotten, or that it would have no effect on anyone after her death.

When I told Tustin how profoundly she had helped and inspired me in my thinking and practice as an analyst, she demurred, as if she felt I was in danger of idealizing her. She said that I gave her "much too much credit for [my] good work and hard-won success," and she heaped upon me many other compliments that, although sincere, left me feeling somewhat rejected.

Suddenly I felt a headache coming on, and my good spirits faded. When Tustin noticed that my mood had changed, she asked what the trouble was. Of course, since we were good friends, I was quite candid with her about what I had felt and about what had followed, and perhaps even scolded her a bit when I told her that I hoped she would be more mindful of the way she handled people's gratitude for and admiration of her.

124

After recounting my experience and those of the patients discussed in this chapter, we talked over how it was she who had, long ago and ever since, stressed the idea that the overflow of the "ecstasy of at-one-ment" (Tustin 1992a) could only be borne if it were adequately contained by the mother herself. Tustin had written that, in the most primitive states of mind, "beauty is associated with moments of bodily completeness in which there is an experience of ecstatic fusion with the earth-mother" (Tustin 1992a, p. 224). She warned that, if left uncontained, "for a variety of reasons, which may be part of a temporary passing phase, the mother's capacity to bear such extreme states is muted, then the infant is left to bear such states alone" (p. 106). At these moments such ecstasy might be experienced as a dangerous overflow of bodily excitement, equated with "a devastating sense of two-ness" (p. 106), too much to be borne in the nascent mind, perhaps disintegrating into a painful, if not unbearable, somatic agony.

In her work with children, Tustin noticed that when the beautiful experience of at-one-ment is unable to be kept in mind, not only does it leak out and dissolve into its antithesis – the ugly tantrum of two-ness – but the baby is now doomed to an eternal despairing search for that "ever-present auto-sensual bit" needed to "flesh out" its experience of being.

Tustin and I conversed at length about the relationship of the experience of "ecstasy" to that of the beautiful mother referred to both by Meltzer (1988) and by Winnicott (1945), as well as about Bion's ideas regarding "reverence and awe." In spite of her own considerable struggles with the fact of her own inevitable demise, she was ever mindful of the difficulty I was experiencing while facing the impending loss of her friendship and support and was concerned that I might be unraveling at the prospect of her death. It seemed to both of us – in that moment – that I needed to secure – in our last contact – her help in containing all of my love and gratitude for her.

Some conclusions

As a result of that last conversation with Tustin, I arrived at the tentative determination that the resolution of what Meltzer called the "*aesthetic conflict*" might be predicated, at least in part, upon the capacity of the mother to contain the baby's reverence and awe of her, along with her own capacity for tolerating her baby's hatred, envy, and the terror of loss. This may prove clinically crucial when we consider the process of internalization or introjection by the patient of the analyst and his or her functioning, which we hypothesize is essential to insuring a successful and lasting outcome of psychoanalytic treatment.

Of course, the mother's capacity to tolerate these feelings may vary relative to the needs of the individual infant, which in turn may vary according to the intensity of the infant's feelings and any innate capacity on his part to keep these in mind.

It might further be concluded that our ability to apprehend beauty (Meltzer 1988) is linked to the existence – at the core of the inner sphere of the personality – of a "container," not just for our painful experiences, but for those joyful ones as well; a containing object with the capacity to endure not just our feelings of hatred toward the object (and toward the self), but one that is enduring of and resonating with those loving feelings felt toward the perceived external object, one in which the capacity for realistic self-love and -esteem is rooted.

Kahlil Gibran wisely wrote in *The Prophet*:

And a poet said, Speak to us of Beauty.
And he answered:
Where shall you seek beauty,
and how shall you find her
unless she herself be your way and your guide?
And how shall you speak of her
except she be the weaver of your speech?
(1923, p. 74)

It must not escape our awareness that our capacity to love – and therefore to forgive ourselves – depends largely upon the way in which our loving feelings have been dealt with, accepted, and validated by an other. It seems, when all is said and done, that we are limited, in part, in our capacity for self-esteem by the limitations of our parents' capacity – and later our analyst's capacity – to contain and therefore to confirm our feelings of reverence and awe. I believe that herein lie several technical implications of enormous import.

For example, we must consider that if we interpret the patient's genuine reverence and awe of us – when we are felt as truly "good objects" – as a defensive idealization – as if we were instead being experienced as bad objects – this perhaps out of some *rigidly inappropriate adherence to theory*, we will fail in our function as a container (Bion 1977b) for experiences of true goodness, and consequently this essential internal function – the capacity to experience goodness – will fail to develop in the patient. Instead, what Bion calls the "'Super' ego" (Bion 1962a, p. 97)[23] will be augmented, and its devastating effects intensified, where forgiveness and the striving for life might otherwise healthfully prevail. Additionally, the development of an enduring faith in the existence of goodness and beauty, with increasing hope for their apprehension, will be stultified. When hopefulness perishes, nagging doubts about the goodness of the object – and therefore about the worthiness of the self – perpetuate in spite of repeated proofs of such goodness and worthiness. Moreover, increased envy and defensive idealization will proliferate hyperbolically (Mitrani 1993a).

Klein (1957) herself had suggested that, like envy, gratitude originates at birth and is its counterpart. Klein also points out that *envy diminishes gratitude toward the object*. However, it has been my experience that this avenue of thought is a two-way rather than a one-way street. In other words, we might also consider that *gratitude can serve to diminish envy*! If this is so, how – technically speaking – do we, through our contribution in the analytic setting, throw the balance one way or the other?

Along these lines, Spillius (1993) examined a few of the factors that may contribute to or actively provoke envy in our patients, and those which modify or mitigate their envy, as well as those elements in what she calls the perceived "giver/receiver relationship" which make envy more or less bearable. Her complex model highlights many of the feelings, perceptions, and mis-perceptions (both conscious and unconscious) that may persist in both "giver" and "receiver" and which contribute to the overall experience of envy and its interpretive handling in the analytic process.

The giver–receiver relationship

On the positive end of Spillius's bi-polar model, the "giver" derives gratification from giving and is aware that the "receiver" may resent being on the receiving end of the relationship. The "receiver" accurately perceives the "giver" as sensitive to and understanding of these resentful feelings and, in this way, is also able to acknowledge his envy, which he may then be free to balance out with his positive feelings. The "giver," acknowledging the coexistence of such positive feelings, willingly becomes the "receiver."

Thus, a benign process of giving and receiving is put in play in the analysis, as the "receiver" introjectively identifies with an object who gives and receives with pleasure. As I have stated elsewhere (Mitrani 1993a), Spillius seemed to imply that, in this benign cycle, both analyst and analysand partake in and are enriched by this process of *positive introjective identification*, as each in turn has the opportunity to take up the role of the "receiver" as well as that of the "giver."

In contrast to this, the negative end of Spillius's model proposed that the "giver" may experience little pleasure in giving. Instead he may feel imposed upon and drained by the demands of the "receiver," and as such may be motivated to give primarily by his need to feel superior; a need derived from, and perhaps covering over, a fear that what he has to give is bad. Should this attitude on the part of the "giver" be accurately perceived by the "receiver," "envy" will be exacerbated, resentment will be increased, and gratitude will be diminished. The "giver," now further deprived of gratitude, may give less or more aggressively, and the deprivation–envy cycle will continue with both "giver" and "receiver" taking in and identifying with a joyless object in an endless battle for superiority and omnipotent power as compensation for a pervasive sense of discontent.

Perhaps one can see here the importance of the establishment of an internal container for goodness, joy, and fulfillment – and even for beauty – in the mind of analyst and patient alike, in order for the positive pole of the "giver–receiver" relationship in analysis to be reached. Without this capacity to experience goodness, analyst and patient together spiral down toward the negative pole and may be stuck in a vicious cycle where envious experiences are endlessly exacerbated.

Finally, I think that as analysts we need to realize that *the degree of our awareness* of both our strengths and limitations, and *the extent of our willingness and ability* to consider, to accurately evaluate, and to acknowledge to ourselves the impact of the messages we send to the baby-in-the-analysand from the "castle of our inner world," are all crucial factors in providing an emotional experience for the patient that serves to mend old wounds and facilitate new growth.

In Chapter 7, I further demonstrate the impact of the analyst and of the analytic setting on the outcome of treatment. However, unlike those other cases I have thus far presented, I will report on the premature interruption of the analysis of a patient whom I call Joel. I also focus upon another form of extra-ordinary protection: one that has been at the core of Kleinian clinical research and theoretical developments concerning "negative therapeutic reactions" since Riviere's (1936) paper on the subject led the way down a path toward various formulations regarding what have been alternately termed narcissistic, pathological, or defensive organizations.

7

Never before and never again[24]

> To dare to be aware of the facts of the universe in which we are
> existing calls for courage.
>
> W.R. Bion

Wilfred Bion (1979a) once wrote:

> When two personalities meet, an emotional storm is created. If they make
> sufficient contact to be aware of each other, or even sufficient to be unaware
> of each other, an emotional state is produced by the conjunction of these two
> individuals, and the resulting disturbance is hardly likely to be regarded as
> necessarily an improvement on the state of affairs had they never met at all.
> But since they have met, and since this emotional storm has occurred, the
> two parties to this storm may decide to "make the best of a bad job."
>
> (p. 247)

In this chapter, I attempt to convey to the reader something of the experience
of the emotional storm produced by the conjunction between myself and one
analysand and our respective efforts to "make the best of a bad job," albeit in
deeply divergent ways. As I will be reporting extensively from an analysis that
was prematurely interrupted in spite of those efforts, one might say that this
chapter is *itself* an effort to "make the best of a bad job" by transmitting something
of what I believe I was able to learn from my experience about certain phenomena. These are: the compulsion to repeat past trauma within the area of
personal omnipotence (Winnicott 1974) provided in the transference; the fear
of breakdown (Winnicott 1974) that may arise in the course of an analysis; and
a corollary defensive organization that patients may fall back on at such times in
the interest of survival.

Toward this aim, I present material illustrating the development of and some
connections between these three phenomena as they became manifest in the

129

course of one analysis. Additionally, I highlight some of the factors that may have contributed to the emergence of the fear of breakdown in this analysis: those inherent in the analytic setting, those connected to the analyst's failures, and those related to the history and character of the patient. I begin with some background material from the early childhood and clinical history, followed by material from the early phase of the analysis of the patient whom I call Joel.

Joel presented himself in mid-life – after four previous (some quite lengthy) periods of analysis – as "still lacking certain authoritative information," which he thought I might be able to give him. Much to his surprise, and to mine as well, rather than an intellectual information-gathering exercise, he instead found himself "rapidly overtaken" by emotional experience. It is a sense of what Joel was "overtaken" by that I will here begin to convey to the reader.

Relevant childhood and clinical history

At the time that our analytic process "overtook" him, unhinging his life from one session to the next, Joel could only look back with longing over "a good thirty-year period of total uneventfulness." It seemed that he would never have expected that anything of importance could ever overtake him again, other than death someday, and that was perfectly alright with him since he was not fond of "events," and hated outright and quickly fled from those that rattled his psychic equilibrium and made a muddle of the internal arrangements of his life.

In spite of Joel's previous analytic encounters, the majority of such events seemed to lie relatively unearthed and far back in the dim, remote years of his childhood, which he surprisingly had little conscious desire whatever to recall, and when he did so unconsciously, then only with great aversion.

Many of Joel's recollections came as associations to various transference interpretations made regarding what I felt to be his communications about his experience of me (and also based upon my countertransference response to him). At times I appeared as a collapsed, depressed mother in need of fortification, moral support, and general enlivening in order that he might be able to keep her in contact with him; at other times as a narcissistic father requiring adulation, flattery, and demonstrations of reverence to forestall his turning his attention elsewhere.

Additionally, vivid experiences of being locked away all alone in a closet as a very little infant in order to muffle his cries (this apparently done by Mother in compliance with Father's demands for peace and quiet as well as for her undivided attention) came to the foreground around weekend breaks and holidays some months into the treatment. Alongside such transferential expressions of early traumatic situations (subsequently confirmed) of isolation and the consequent development of an anxious preoccupation with his objects, Joel's narrative revealed to me the following bits and pieces of his history.

130

One summer's day midway in his third year, little Joel woke up in his bed with a sore throat. Before he knew it he was being whisked off to the hospital where a tonsillectomy was performed. Tragically he never recovered from that event, which might be said to have been a prelude to an even longer hospitalization, only a few weeks later, in an isolation ward filled with iron tombs in which children like himself – their pale faces framed with halos of baby-fine hair poking out from one end – were encased. The rhythmic droning and whooshing sound of machinery blended with the footfalls and whispers of masked men and women, hopelessly in attendance, keeping busy wiping brows and putting glass straws to parched lips, waiting for death to take its toll.

Even after he had emerged from the mechanical lung in which he was encased, Joel's isolation continued. He had no one human being to hold him. He had only a few soft, stuffed animals – those taken from his former habitat and placed in isolation with him – to hold on to. All other affectionate contact was denied him. He was still a danger to others and was treated as such, his mother and father remaining safe behind a wall of glass.

They said he would never walk again, but he was determined to walk: *to walk away from them all, just as he felt he had been walked away from.* And walk away he did, encasing himself in an iron tomb of his own making, one as strong as his will to survive. He would create *his own* wall of glass, behind which "they" would feel isolated, angry, and forgotten. Eventually he would grow up to rescue and hold the weak and the soft, the little "animals" of the world. As a physician, he would make it his "business" to help the helpless, but *he would never love them!* It was as if he had secretly vowed *never, never* to be vulnerable to anyone again. People were unreliable. Thus, emotionally meaningful contact with them was to be avoided with due diligence. It felt to me, on one level, that *Joel was determined never to allow himself to know that he could not live without other people.*

It seemed, from all his accounts, that Joel's previous analytic engagements had been conducive to and collusive with his own tendency to avoid emotional contact with others. I had reason to suspect that his first analysis – aimed exclusively at the oedipal level – missed the mark, passing over the primitive infantile transference altogether; the style of the second fed neatly into the patient's desire for "authoritative information"; the third was quite authoritarian and stirred up intractable resistances, eventually leading to impasse; and the fourth foundered when it appeared to the patient that he was being actively prohibited from bringing up certain material that, for him, was essential to the expression of his experiences.

Nevertheless, it should be noted that Joel was genuinely grateful to and acknowledging of each of his former analysts and their work with him, and truly suffered each awareness of failure on their part, awareness that usually came into play in relation to something he felt he was receiving in the current setting with me, some experience that he had not been afforded previously, especially those that allowed for contact with aspects of himself formerly untouched.

131

From the outset, our therapeutic encounter ran contrary to the emotional isolation to which Joel was accustomed, except that he would simply not show up for an hour from time to time, and of course there were the usual weekends and holiday breaks, which in the beginning he found more relieving than distressing. This may have been due to my technique of interpretation, wherein I usually limit myself rigorously, at least for quite some time, to addressing the immediacy of the infantile transference in the moment, as the process unfolds between myself and the patient.

As I have previously clarified for the reader, I prefer to take this avenue of interpretation, rather than the road outward toward the historical/genetic aspects of the case, or inward to the intrapsychic internal–object–dynamics level of the material, both of which I find can be emotionally distancing for some patients who take this as a sign of the analyst's need for emotional distance. Furthermore, especially in the beginning with patients like Joel, I have discovered that pointing out the relationship between various objects in the analysand's inner world may lead to a defensive kind of intellectualization, since these patients rarely have the mental space to contain and to take responsibility for such happenings, which is why they attempt to "play" them out in relation to the analyst in the first place.

I believe the early establishment of Joel's intense emotional connection with me was also, at least in part, due to his apparent ripeness for contact – on an unconscious level – perhaps spurred on by his advancing age and physical symptoms, his increased awareness of loneliness, and certain unavoidable and distressing professional/interpersonal difficulties.

Early clinical material

In his Monday hour, two weeks prior to our first long summer break, Joel mentioned that he had had a dream that morning. He then went off on several tangents that led him and me away from that dream. On both Tuesday and Wednesday of the same week he began by making mention of this dream, but still seemed reluctant to report its content. In the beginning of the fourth hour of the week, Joel complained of fatigue and sleepiness, of forgetting his keys and "going off on tangents." I listened attentively, even somewhat anxiously, but the dream was still nowhere within third-earshot. Finally Joel announced that he knew we were out of time, but that he would begin with the dream on Monday.

I felt suddenly cut-off, dropped, abandoned, chilled, and hungry for more, and left quite in the dark as to how the end of the hour had arrived so soon and without my awareness. I thought, "Oh no, it cannot end here!" I glanced at the clock. But only thirty minutes of the session had elapsed! When I called Joel's attention to the remaining fifteen minutes, he laughed nervously and launched into the dream, as if he were diving into a pool of ice. In the dream,

Joel was attending a conference held at some exotic resort on the Amazon River in a primeval rainforest. All participants were housed in one building. Members of an "elite" group, including someone resembling a former analyst, were upstairs in spacious individual rooms, while those in the "out-group" were crowded together below on the ground floor, vying for position in one of four smaller rooms. Three of these rooms filled up very quickly. One by one, doors were shut in his face as he tried to enter. There was no sense of privacy as Joel could be observed from all directions. There was no way for him to get off by himself and, worse yet, the floor of the large room in which he stood was slowly being pulled away, revealing a gaping black pit below it.

Joel was terribly frightened as it seemed that the fourth room, the only one left in which to take refuge, was off to one side, occupied by two people: lesser members of the in-group who seemed to be quite chummy as they huddled together, smoking marijuana and ignoring him. Finally, a man named Billy appeared. He whispered in Joel's ear that he was going off to another room, one that he had secretly secured for himself, and he invited Joel to join him. Joel knew that this was illicit, but he had to save himself. He had to get away. He had no other choice.

Joel's associations to the dream – his expectation that I was leaving to go off to some conference during the break, his desire to attend one particular professional event if only he had someone to go with, his sense of being left out, and thoughts of purchasing marijuana to help him through the loneliness of the weekend – all carried an air of poignancy. Joel identified the "Billy" in the dream as a "sneaky orderly" he had known in the hospital during his internship, "someone who sold dope on the side."

Meanwhile, I silently recalled that "Billy" had indeed appeared in other dreams as a sinister figure. In one dream, he had appeared as an actor who hid dog shit by sweeping it under the carpet, and in another, which took place in a Catholic church, Billy had "taken communion," but had left the church without actually swallowing the Eucharist: an act of desecration. Joel had been the only one in the congregation to notice this, and had stood up in his pew, crying out to the priest for help. Without my mentioning it to him, Joel also recalled this last dream and reminded me of it in detail, as if to call to my attention the link between the two Billys.

At this point an image was thrown up of a very-little-Joel who felt on the verge of being dropped and broken by my impending absence and by my inaccessibility during the break; of his profound feelings of being ordinary (part of the crowd), unwanted, shut-out, exposed and endangered in some primeval setting, the floor being pulled out from underneath him to reveal an awful abyss.

Together we reached an understanding about his reliance on a "Billy-part of his mind" with which he had developed a relationship while "in the hospital" (perhaps also representing a resourceful-if-outlaw part of his personality that he had come to rely upon as a child suffering from polio). In Joel's dream, his renewed dependence on Billy seemed to be provoked by an experience of the two of us as "chums" in a perceived collusion to remain oblivious to his vulnerability and endangerment (like the two conference attendees smoking dope). The latter seemed to have been central to his experience during the week and was now anticipated as the inevitable nature of our final session together before the weekend (the fourth room) and the final week before the break (the fall into the black pit).

The dream seemed also to disclose the manner in which Joel was being seduced away from me into a secret room (the last fifteen minutes of the session), which, although forbidden, might have offered some means of survival. "Billy" rescued Joel by "selling" him drugs (forgetfulness and numbness in the sessions and the "idea" of marijuana over the weekend) to ease his pain of aloneness and also to provide him with some privacy from the impingements of our close analytic contact and its inevitable disruptions.

Concurrently, Joel's dream also demonstrated some unconscious awareness on his part that this sneaky Billy-part of him was not merely a rescuing angel. It was clear that this Billy-part of the patient acts *as if* he is taking in my interpretations in our analytic "communion," but leaves the hour without swallowing a word, thus constituting a "desecration" of the analysis, one which Joel was – at that very moment – trying to inform me about, perhaps in order that I might prevent such desecration from occurring.

Our understanding of this dream, arrived at in this and the immediate hours that followed before the break, seemed to deepen our connection and, for some time, Joel continued to help me to locate – and even to touch in moments – that bit of him that disavows the effects of his past while vowing *never again* to be a helpless–little–one: alone, isolated, rejected, and shut-out, though paradoxically under coldly intrusive observation while in a primitive foreboding black pit of despair. And yet, the repetition of this precise situation was gradually being created in the transference.

The compulsion to repeat

How can we understand this repetition? Freud wrote, in his autobiographical study (1925):

> I have contemplated a new solution to the problem of the instincts. I have combined the instincts for self preservation and for the preservation of the species under the concept of *Eros* and have contrasted with it an *instinct of death* or *destruction* which works in silence. Instinct in general is regarded as a kind of elasticity of living things, an impulsion toward the restoration of a situation which once existed but was brought to an end by some external disturbance. This essentially conservative character of instincts is exemplified by the phenomena of the *compulsion to repeat*. The picture which life presents

to us is the result of the concurrent and mutually opposing action of Eros and the death instinct.

(p. 57)

Further on, in his paper on "Inhibitions, symptoms and anxiety" (1926), Freud linked the compulsion to repeat with repression, wherein "old situations of danger are preserved" (p. 154), only later emerging in the transference constellation. In "Beyond the pleasure principle" (1920) he explained that in analysis:

The patient cannot remember the whole of what is repressed in him and what he cannot remember may be precisely the essential part of it. Thus he acquires no sense of conviction of the correctness of the construction that has been communicated to him. He is obliged to *repeat* the repressed material as a contemporary experience instead of . . . *remembering* it as something belonging to the past.

(p. 18)

The ratio between what is remembered and what is reproduced varies from case to case. The physician cannot as a rule spare his patient this phase of the treatment. *He must get him to re-experience some portion of his forgotten life.*

(p. 19, my italics)

Freud (1920) also observed that resistance to remembering does not lie in the unconscious,[25] which is altogether cooperative and revealing of itself in the transference. Instead it "arises from the same higher strata and systems of the mind which originally carried out repression" (p. 19) which he referred to as the *coherent ego.*

I would like to propose that *this coherent ego may lie in the realm of the preconscious and that some of its functions bear a striking resemblance to what some later authors refer to as a defensive organization.* I will later say something more about this defensive organization and the ways in which it serves to protect the individual from emotional turbulence, which may come as a result of the exercise of curiosity in analysis, and which threatens to bring about madness and breakdown.

Curiosity and emotional turbulence

Bion, writing about the problem of emotional turbulence (1976a), pointed out that:

Human beings clamour for some kind of authoritative statement to take the place of both ignorance and the exercise of curiosity; they hope, in that way, to put a stop to disagreeable feelings of ignorance and the repetition of the questions. The repeated questions may even be what is known as the repetition compulsion. But *repetition compulsion may in fact be a spark of human curiosity* which has hitherto failed to be extinguished by any authoritative statements from whatever source.

(pp. 229–30, my italics)

On one hand, Bion seems to be suggesting here that there is one aspect of human nature that is actively involved in a quest for psychic truth. I would imagine that this is precisely the part of the patient with which the analyst may be said to form a working alliance. On the other hand, Bion warned us that there are disagreeable feelings – emotional turbulence – provoked by not knowing and by the "exercise of curiosity" motivated by the awareness of not knowing. Relative to this, there is another aspect of human nature which strives to restore a sense of comfort, cutting off further inquiry by offering authoritative statements. Certainly these formulations seem apposite in the case of my patient Joel.

Other contemporary workers focusing on the area of internal object relations also seem to agree that there is a part of the patient, largely unconscious, that bears this spark of curiosity, that needs to know and to be known, and that actively aids us in our quest to understand them, even while – at the same time – another part of the patient continues to work to kill off all curiosity, to conceal, and to avoid discovery.

For example, Rosenfeld (1971) appeared to be referring to this curious, truth-seeking part of the patient when he wrote about the *helpless, needy, dependent libidinal baby-self*. In contrast with this, he delineates an authoritative "system of mind," one that resists the disagreeable awareness of experience and the emotional turbulence that comes with it, when he describes *the defensive, narcissistic or patho-logical organization*. Perhaps this latter structure might be viewed as one version of Freud's *coherent ego*, as the source of the authoritative statements mentioned by Bion, and as analogous to Winnicott's (1949) *enemy mind-psyche*.

Winnicott (1949) posited that disruptions in the infant's continuity of being produce an "over activity of mental functioning" (p. 246) and the precocious development of omnipotent phantasies of a defensive nature, produced "to take over and organize the caring for the psyche-soma; whereas in health it is the function of the environment to do this" (p. 246). It is precisely *the organization* of these very early infantile, omnipotent, unconscious, defensive fantasies – as they are conceptualized, particularly by Kleinian and post-Kleinian analysts – that I refer to in this chapter as *the defensive organization*, a concept which I will now further clarify.

136

The nature of the defensive organization

As I have pointed out, defensive organizations have been widely investigated, theorized about, and clinically illustrated, especially in the Kleinian literature,[26] since Riviere's (1936) seminal paper on the negative therapeutic reaction. As I have indicated above, Rosenfeld (1964) described these as structured, organized patterns of manic defenses, relied upon to ward off anxieties of a paranoid-schizoid and depressive nature. He observed that defenses such as omnipotence, grandiosity, denial, splitting, and projective identification – when maintained throughout infancy and childhood without mitigation – may become a well-organized, rigid, and stable aspect of the personality. In the case of Joel, this organized aspect of the personality is clearly presented in dreams in the form of the character "Billy."

As one can see in Joel's dream, when faced with abandonment, the impressionable baby-self may come under the control of such a defensive organization, which employs either seduction, "terror, persecution and dread" (Meltzer 1968), or the threat of insanity (Money-Kyrle 1969) to play upon and perpetuate the patient's fear of once again becoming dependent upon – and having feelings of affection for or gratitude toward – a needed object outside their omnipotent control.

Betty Joseph (1975) referred to these patients as "difficult to reach" since we can rarely find them outside their protective shielding and, when we do, they are quite thin-skinned and are therefore easily injured by the slightest error in tact or timing. Furthermore, patients in the grip of such a powerful influence often experience episodes of negative therapeutic reaction, particularly at the very moment when the relationship with the analyst begins to deepen and productive work momentarily proceeds. During these episodes, we often hear our patients complaining that the analysis is worthless or, even worse, noxious.

Segal (1981) attributed these complaints to the work of unconscious envy in the patient. However, we must be cautious when interpreting such communications, for what may appear as an envy-driven attempt to denigrate the analyst's work and worth may well be intended as an act of appeasement or reassurance toward that inner protective force, which simply cannot bear the development of this fruitful alliance between analyst and analysand. Perhaps such a new alliance, by providing an alternate means of living and coping with and within relationships, threatens the old protective organization of objects with obsolescence.

O'Shaughnessy (1981), in her paper on defensive organizations, reported a lengthy case of one patient which underlines the necessity for prolonged analysis within such a defensive organization in the transference. She implies that this allows for an environment in which ego development may proceed while anxiety is "in recession": contained by the analyst and/or in the analytic relationship.

In a trio of papers on the subject, Steiner (1982; 1987; 1990) characterized the defensive organization as a buffer against or refuge from untenable anxieties; as a mental state lying midway between the paranoid–schizoid and depressive positions. He suggests that this is an expression of what Klein (1935) posited as the "manic position," which has become a stable, rigidified, and inflexible structure within the ego, providing a safe if encapsulated haven for the vulnerable infantile self.

Steiner's investigations also led him to highlight the problem of defensive organizations as obstacles to mourning the loss of the analyst during absences (or even after termination of treatment). Along these lines, it might be said that Joel's inability to loosen control over the breaks, his use of marijuana, and perhaps even his acts of "desecration," while functioning to diminish separation anxiety and psychic pain related to an awareness of loss, also impeded the establishment of beneficial experiences that might otherwise have sustained him in my absence.

It would seem that the emphasis, at least in the Kleinian literature, has been on the destructive-persecutory aspects of these defensive organizations, the role which these play in the negative therapeutic reaction, and the control by tyranny and seduction which groups of objects exert upon the naive, dependent, libidinal aspects of the individual. However, from the outset of Kleinian explorations into this area, Riviere (1936) stated that:

> The very great importance of analyzing aggressive tendencies has perhaps carried some analysts off their feet, and in some quarters is defeating its own ends and becoming in itself a resistance to further analytic understanding.
>
> (p. 311)

Riviere went on to warn us that "nothing will lead more surely to a negative therapeutic reaction in the patient than our failure to recognize anything but the aggression in his material" (p. 311). Here I am in full agreement with Riviere, who seems to be alluding to an entanglement and collusion that can develop between the analyst's own defensive organization and that of the patient, in an endeavor driven by the need to establish superiority and righteousness as a base from which the analyst might issue his own authoritative statements, which may serve to stop-up the flow of curiosity and the experience of emotional turbulence in both parties to the process. I will say more about this later on, in relation to my specific experience with Joel.

However, for the time being I would point out that a consideration of yet another aspect of the defensive organization – its original *survival function* (Mitrani 1996) – is facilitated by a model of understanding in which these structures are seen as functioning in much the same way as does a *second skin* (Bick 1968), which I have already elaborated upon in Chapter 2. Perhaps the defensive organization may even be conceptualized as a descendant of these earlier and more primitive autosensual protections. Of course it must be noted that defensive organizations are by far more elaborated in phantasy than either Bick's sensation-dominated "skin" or the shell or barrier of concrete defensive maneuvers, including but not limited to the use of hard "autistic objects" and soft "autistic shapes" (Tustin 1980; 1984). As I have demonstrated in Chapter 3, both autistic shapes and objects serve to provide a *sensation* of impermeability or tranquility. Numerous observable behaviors – for example, the habitual use of drugs such as marijuana and alcohol – can chemically induce such sensations of well-being.

Additionally, the defensive organization, not unlike the "second skin," often takes on not just the perceived sensual characteristics of the mother or other primary caretakers, but also takes on some of the characteristics of inanimate or mechanical objects perceived within and as an integral part of the early caretaking environment, such as glass incubators in cases of premature infants, and perhaps even the closet or iron lung in the case of patients like Joel.

I would propose a model in which such defensive organizations referred to above, as well as the compulsion to repeat, are seen not solely as manifestations of the conservative "death instinct," but paradoxically also as expressions of the infant's hyperbolic striving to preserve life and to protect against unmanageable states of unintegration and disintegration, of non-being and madness equated with the fear of breakdown.

The fear of breakdown

The "fear of the breakdown" is enormous "in some of our patients, but not in others" (Winnicott 1974, p. 173), dependent upon the individual's experiences in early development. Winnicott posited that our capacity to make empathic contact with such fears in our patients suggests that there also exists some universal common denominator in each of us. He went on to say:

> Not all of our patients who have this fear complain of it at the outset of a treatment. Some do; but others have their *defenses so well organized* that it is *only after a treatment has made considerable progress that the fear of breakdown comes to the fore* as a dominating factor. For instance, a patient may have *various phobias and a complex organization for dealing with these phobias*, so that dependence does not come quickly into the transference. At length, dependence becomes a main feature, and then the analyst's mistakes and failures become direct causes of localized phobias and so of the outbreak of fear of breakdown.
>
> (p. 174, my italics)

Here, Winnicott considered "the breakdown" as the failure of *a defensive organization* and he opined that the unthinkable state of affairs that underlies this defensive organization is some universal primitive agony (for example, the agony of unintegration, of falling endlessly, of the loss or failure of psycho-somatic integrity, of the loss of the sense of being, and of the capacity to connect with the object) occurring too near the beginning of the patient's life, and at a moment when the necessary environmental supports were either deficient or altogether missing. He proposed that the *experience* of the primitive agony was *unable to be had by the infant* (see also Mitrani 1995b on "unmentalized experience").

Perhaps one can see this type of primitive agony – experienced by Joel as a bottomless black pit into which he fears falling endlessly – emerging in his dream as he nears the summer holiday break in the analysis. Could this be one expression of that primitive agony originally occurring too near the beginning of his life and insufficiently contained in moments when environmental supports were deficient or altogether missing?

Winnicott (1974) mentioned that the infantile ego's integration is incapable of encompassing this sort of agony and thus it is unable to bring it into the area of what he calls "personal omnipotence" (p. 177). One might hear echoes of Freud's previously cited statements on the compulsion to repeat as Winnicott specifies that the thing feared "*has not happened yet in the experience of the patient because the patient was not there for it to happen to*" (p. 179, my italics).

For Winnicott (1960), the patient (not unlike the baby) can only be said to *come into existence* – that is, he can only be said to *be there* (to the extent that events that happen to him can be experienced by him) – during the phase of relative dependence, which follows a phase of absolute dependence in the analysis. I believe that only after this phase of relative dependence has been reached can we speak of an undifferentiated unit *analyst-patient* (mother-baby).

This differentiation must precede the formation of a clear boundary in the transference between inside and outside, me and not-me, self and other, subject and object. It is only after this boundary has been established, that we can begin to talk about the projective and introjective processes that constitute what Winnicott called the "area of personal omnipotence."

> The patient must go on looking for the past detail which is *not yet experienced*. This search takes the form of a looking for this detail in the future. [In analysis] the way is open for the agony to be experienced in the transference [the area of his or her omnipotence], in reaction to the analyst's failures and mistakes.
>
> (Winnicott 1974, p. 177)

In another paper in which he drew certain parallels between the various stages of infantile development and certain infantile states of mind encountered with analysands, Winnicott (1963) warned that, in the beginning of the treatment and perhaps for a very long time during the phase of absolute dependence, we must not fail in the "infant-care aspects of the treatment," at least until the patient has reached the phase of relative dependence when he makes us fail in ways *determined by his past history*. Winnicott maintained that it is only in this latter phase that the patient can *use* the analyst's failures, now "staged in the transference" (p. 258) and "brought into the area of omnipotent control, and the area managed by projection and introjection mechanisms" (p. 258).

I have found – as I will attempt to illustrate further on in this chapter – that, should our failures lack a certain connection *in the patient's mind* to his own gestures and the area of *normal infantile omnipotence*, we run the risk of driving him back into the safe and secure grip of the defensive organization and *the pathological realm of omnipotence*. I would here point out that, in contrast to the classical Kleinian *metapsychological* view in which the defensive organization is seen as arising from instinctual sources, Winnicott's understanding is *experiential* in nature, thus contributing what I believe to be an additional important dimension to our contemporary understanding of these organizations in terms of their specific dynamics, as outlined in the above sections of this chapter.

In earlier works on the survival function of these organizations, in both their extremely concrete (Mitrani 1992) and their more mentalized forms (Mitrani 1996), I have shown how uncontained fears of the unthinkable (Bion 1962a), of breakdown (Winnicott 1974), and of dissolution (Tustin 1986a) in infancy may initially provoke the creation and may later on justify the perpetuation of the defensive organization. Additionally, I have previously illustrated (Mitrani 1992; 1996) various ways in which the defensive organization goes about producing a sort of *internal propaganda*, perhaps made up of what Bion referred to as "authoritative statements," providing the impetus for actions that work toward sustaining and reinforcing itself when situations beyond control (such as those existing in an analysis) threaten its dispersal along with the annihilation of the self.

At this point, in order to further illustrate the above interaction between the compulsion to repeat, the fear of breakdown, and the ascendance of the defensive organization, I will continue with some additional clinical material from a later period in the analysis of Joel, material which traces the manner in which his fear of breakdown began to emerge "in a big way" (Winnicott 1974, p. 174) in the beginning of the third year of treatment.

The emergence of the fear of breakdown

The emergence of Joel's fear of breakdown took place during one hour in the beginning of a week somewhere midway between my Summer holiday and the four-day Fall break. Several minutes into the hour, Joel's usual Monday "newsreel" – that served explicitly to "fill me in" on his weekend happenings, while implicitly functioning to "fill in" the gap between us created by the weekend – was intruded upon by the cries of another patient in the adjoining office. As the minutes ticked by, I found it increasingly difficult to concentrate on the content of my patient's utterances, which seemed pale by comparison with the agonizing lament permeating our room from next door.

141

As these cries reached a crescendo they took on a painfully disturbing tone, *like those of a baby left too long in extreme distress*, its voice coarsening into a mournful, animal-like wail. It was difficult to be certain in the moment, but I had some sense that *here* was the essence of what lay beneath Joel's routine reporting: the agony of a baby-Joel who had fallen into and was now buried in the abyss of the weekend, covered over by manic activity, and camouflaged by the cries of another.

At that same moment, Joel, unable to ignore these sounds any longer, suddenly shouted at me, terrified and with great anger, "If you think that you're going to get anything like that to come out of me, you're sadly mistaken. There's *nothing* like that in me! And if there is, it's because you put it there! I'm not gonna let you lay that kind of trip on me! Not me! I'll leave before I'll let that happen. There's something wrong there. *That* just shouldn't happen." As he bellowed at me, Joel gripped the couch with tightly clenched fists and hung one leg off the side, as if in conflict over the question of whether hanging onto me or bolting out the door was the best way to survive.

I replied that it seemed he was truly terrified when he felt that I might be filling him with painful, paralyzing, dangerous things during my absences and especially right now: things that threaten to overwhelm and cripple him, leaving him helpless and unprotected. I added that, although there was still a he who was holding onto *the me he had come to trust*, he was also compelled to run for his life, as far from *the dangerous-me* as he could.

In response to this, Joel pulled his leg back on the couch and relaxed his grip, which seemed to reflect his sense of relief when he could realize that I had not denied his negative perceptions of me, nor had I lost contact with his more positive experiences with me. This event ushered in a short period of productive work, before the Fall holiday break, during which Joel spoke about his pet "love birds" who had recently been constructing a nest. He was somewhat concerned that the female might have difficulty laying her eggs and he was fearful that, if he left home for the weekend, the mother-bird might die in the attempt to do so. When he returned after that long holiday weekend, nearly all of his material spoke to his concerns about the next break, now less than a month away.

In the beginning of the following week Joel came in with more news of the birds. He quite enthusiastically announced that there were now four beautiful pink eggs in the nest. I said that he seemed to be expressing his sense that we had created something good, something vital growing between us within the analytic nest we had been able to build prior to the break: the four sessions of the previous week, like the four beautiful pink eggs. However, in the Monday hour of the next week, he reported that one of the eggs had been pushed out to the side of the nest and seemed cracked. He wondered if it was just "a bad egg" and he thought perhaps that this was why the mother-bird had pushed it away, off to one side.

Although I wondered at the time if Joel might be referring to some seed of "bad" feelings about our connection which I may have pushed to the side while attending to the more positive aspects of his communications, I chose to take this up as related to an expression of his feelings about the last hour of the previous weekend, when he had seemed as if he might have felt *himself* to be bad, connecting this sense of his badness with my having pushed him away and out of the center of my life on the weekend.

In retrospect, I believe *I failed to connect the "egg that had been pushed aside" with the event of the auditory intrusion from the room next door,* which had initially primed the fear of breakdown leading up to the holiday break, but which neither one of us had spoken of afterward. It may have been – in the event of the awareness of my helplessness to protect my patient, and myself, from that premature intrusion of primitive agony – that *my own defensive organization became mobilized and joined in collusion with that of the patient,* prompting my "authoritative statements" about the break, which served to stop up the flow of curiosity that might have led me back to the more specific issue of those intrusive sounds coming through the walls and the experience of emotional turbulence to which we were *both* helplessly subjected.

Consequently, in the Tuesday hour, Joel told me that his plans for the Christmas break were to "get out of town." The way in which Joel brought this into the hour led me to understand that this "getaway" was not just a vacation, but some kind of banishment. I said to him that I thought that he seemed to be allying himself with that mother-bird-me who was experienced as always pushing him out of the nest, and how he felt that I was forcing him into exile.

There appeared to be some progress when, one week before the Christmas break, Joel came very poignantly into contact with that part of himself that was aware of how open and vulnerable he had become with me, telling me many things about himself and his behavior with others of which he was anything but proud. For a few moments the patient came painfully face-to-face with the fear that the more he opened himself to me, the more likely it was that he would be rejected and wounded by me.

I was quite touched as Joel concomitantly expressed his worries over the eggs and the baby-birds-to-be that they contained. He said that he thought that the eggs might hatch-out over the holiday. He was apprehensive, considering that something could go amiss, that the mother-bird could cease her nesting and leave the eggs cold, or that both birds might be so upset at his absence that they could go crazy and peck apart the eggs or eat them. He was now determined to find someone to check in on them daily.

During this time, both the terror of and the longing for touch were everywhere in Joel's associations and I told him that I thought that he was torn, wanting some warm contact with me, yet dreading the wounds I might inflict on him if we were to grow too close before the long break. Joel struggled hard with himself, allowing me to remain in contact with him more and more in each session as the end of our time together grew near; however he eventually succumbed to his customary means of buffering the break. By this I mean that he encased the break in a self-imposed absence – one missed hour, fore and aft

143

– as if to steel himself against the unbearable pain of awareness of separation by cauterizing the wounds inevitably created by my going and coming.

When Joel returned after the new year, he seemed thoroughly numbed and our contact was superficial at first. I felt coldly and cruelly rejected in my every effort to reach him. Try as I might, I was unable to penetrate his hardened crust. It seemed at the time that this might be his way of putting me in the proper state of mind for what was to come. As his defensiveness ran its course and my agony was at a peak, Joel finally arrived at the "bad news."

While he had been away, the birds had destroyed the nest and had "viciously pecked apart all but one of the eggs." Joel said that he had "shaken the remaining egg, but it seemed petrified, hardened and dead." Only some bits of shell and a few specks of yolk remained of the others. Indeed bits and pieces seemed to be all that was left of what we had created together in the weeks prior to the holiday break.

When I told him as much, Joel broke down and wept saying that he had never really understood how much his presence had meant to the birds. Without him, he imagined, "they had simply gone crazy." He then added that he thought the same could be said for me. He clarified this by adding that he hated to think that I could be so important to him, but he felt it nonetheless. I said that he seemed to be letting me know how he felt: that he had not been able to get through to me, that I had not understood how much he had needed me to watch over that fragile baby-he that was about to hatch-out, before the holiday break, into the analytic nest we had built together. I added that he felt I had destroyed the nest with my neglect and that this awareness of my unreliability had panicked him, fragmenting that baby, or perhaps hardening and deadening his beautiful pink baby-feelings.

Joel was quite noticeably moved by what I had said to him at first. However, much to my surprise, on the last day of that week he came in saying that he wanted to stop the analysis. He suddenly did not know what he was still doing in analysis, did not know what we had been doing or what we hoped to do in the future, and he thought that we should end it now. The remainder of that hour was one long declaration: *never before and never again!*

It seemed to me that Joel had, in that moment, given himself over to the iron grip of a defensive organization more powerful than anything I or the analysis had to offer: some mighty force that called into question and rendered meaningless all of our work together; some seductive siren offering sanctuary from pain and terror that I had failed to protect him from. Thus, when the fear of breakdown became too great – coinciding as it did, at first, with Joel's (auditory) exposure to the "primitive agony" that violently intruded into our "nest" from the next room, and followed by the breaks in the treatment – my failure may have been experienced as premature, and may "have joined up with the unpredictable variables of [the patient's] infancy and childhood, so I may have truly made [him] ill now, as indeed the unpredictable external factors did make [him] ill in [his] infancy" (Winnicott 1963, p. 259) before he could reach that later stage when he could "*make me fail* in ways determined by [his] past history" (Winnicott 1963, pp. 258–9, my italics).

I believe that it is precisely this *premature failure of the necessary environmental supports* – such as is apparent in Joel's history – that originally necessitated and underlay the creation of his *defensive organization*: that which was originally intended to protect the baby-Joel against the awareness of some *primitive agony* occurring too near the beginning of his life, and later emerging to protect the patient from such primitive agonies reproduced – *out of the area of Joel's personal omnipotence* – in the analytic setting.

Concluding thoughts

It seemed, at least for the time being, that my patient Joel was convinced that he was making "the best of a bad job" by returning to the psychic retreat (Steiner 1993) provided by his former and now reconstituted defensive organization, perhaps wiping out all signs of trauma, past and present. Such experiences remind us that, even in analysis, contact with infantile experiences can be unbearably terrifying, provoking extremes of emotional turbulence and precipitating fears of breakdown, *particularly when this occurs prematurely and outside the realm of the patient's personal omnipotence.*

Indeed, patients like Joel may feel they have no choice but to abandon what may have once been felt to be the safety of the therapeutic womb, especially when untimely failures are felt to transform that womb into a noxious place; when the failure of the analyst to preserve the security of the setting or when the terror and pain of separation imposed by the breaks are felt to penetrate and destroy its delicate environment. Some patients – in panic, rage, and despair – may abort the analysis and the analytic baby. They may resort to their old obsessional means of survival. They may find that the authority of the ever-available defensive organization offers more enduring comfort and safer haven, even though it works to extinguish the spark of human curiosity that ignites ongoing exploration of the mind and of experience. Some patients may harden themselves while rallying hatred to the cause; they may use anger as a shield against vulnerability, and thus may "forget" that they cannot really live without other people.[27]

Regretfully, in the course of any analysis, we are inevitably confronted with much that is beyond our ability to control. We are faced with the limitations in our capacity to "watch over" and protect that fragile, absolutely-dependent baby-part of the patient (previously encapsulated) as it attempts to hatch-out into the analytic nest of relative dependence that we and our analysands have worked to create.

Our absences of body and mind and our errors of tact and timing can be felt to destroy that nest, precipitating a premature awareness of separateness, creating panic, fragmenting the baby, and perhaps provoking a defensive hardening of an otherwise thin "psychic skin" and a deadening of those fragile feelings of dependency and longing that may subsequently be still-born as "the analyst's mistakes and failures become direct causes of . . . the outbreak of fear of breakdown" (Winnicott 1974, p. 174). In the wake of this fear, patients like Joel often leave us – at least for a time – with their own unbearable sense of helplessness. Perhaps, when they do, we would hope to be able to sustain such discomforting feelings, to weather the "emotional storm" created in the wake of abandonment without caving in under the temptation to declare "never before and never again!"

As analysts, we need to be able to find a way to "turn the adverse circumstance . . . to good account. The patient is not obliged to do that; he may not be willing or able to turn it to good account; his aim may be quite different" (Bion 1979a, p. 247). I believe we need to be able to recognize our limitations, to sort out and examine our failures, to account for our losses as best we can, and to keep going forward in our work to help our patients to re-experience some portion of their forgotten lives.

8

Changes of mind: on thinking things through in the countertransference[28]

> When beliefs need some modification,
> We make it with much trepidation,
> For our world is then new,
> And things seem all askew,
> 'til we're used to the new formulation.
>
> Prof. Arnold Tustin

Throughout each of the chapters in this book, I have reported numerous occurrences of my countertransference and have demonstrated my use of these wherever possible. This chapter is devoted to a more thorough-going discussion of this omnipresent aspect of the analytic experience. Having already emphasized the importance of the infantile transference in Chapter 1, it seems only fitting to end this volume with a discussion of its companion in the therapeutic relationship.

Countertransference and the analysand as supervisor to the analyst

The phenomenon of the countertransference has been recognized for several decades (von Hann-Kende 1933; Isakower 1939) to be a crucial tool in the psychoanalytic work, provided its derivatives (that is, feelings, thoughts, and phantasies) are detected by the analyst, transformed and articulated interpretively in the clinical situation. This may be thought of as a significant aspect of what Bion called the "containing function" of the analyst.

Heimann (1950) was probably among the first to address in great detail the use of the countertransference in the formulation of interpretations that aim at a deeper understanding of our patients' material. She stated that:

> The analyst's emotional response to his patient within the analytic situation represents one of the most important tools of his work. The analyst's counter-transference is an instrument of research into the patient's unconscious.
>
> (p. 81)

This approach stood in marked contrast to Freud's (1910; 1937) view of the countertransference as essentially a shortcoming of the analyst, which acts as an impediment to the treatment and requires further analysis in order to restore clear receptivity to and understanding of the patient's dilemma. It was also frowned upon by Klein (Hinshelwood 1989) who had detected the tendency in some of her supervisees to hold the patient accountable for their own state of mind.

Nevertheless, with the further development of the Kleinian and British object relations (Independent) view, countertransference came to be considered as a "total situation" (Racker 1972, pp. 181, 189), echoing the understanding of the transference as a total situation (Klein 1952a; Joseph 1985). Further refinement of Racker's notion that the countertransference is "an expression of the analyst's identification with the internal objects of the analysand" (1968, p. 129) was offered by Grinberg (1979) with the introduction of his concept of *projective counter-identification*. Grinberg coined this term to represent a specific response, on the part of the analyst, to the patient's projective identification:

> which is not consciously perceived by the analyst, who is consequently "led" passively to carry out the role that, actively though unconsciously, the analysand has forced upon him. When this happens – although it may be only for a short space of time, but sometimes dangerously prolonged – the analyst will resort to every kind of rationalization to justify his attitude or his disturbance.
>
> (p. 88)

Money-Kyrle's (1956) conceptualization of *introjective identification* as an essential component of listening to the patient, while re-projection is involved in the interpretive function, preceded Grinberg's formulations and adds credence to the consideration that many of our patients had been massively projected into by their parents in infancy.

In 1915, Freud had noted that "It is a very remarkable thing that the Ucs. of one human being can react on that of the other without passing through the Cs." (p. 194). I believe that our countertransference experience – as a means of connecting with dimensions of our patients' personalities and of their experience that they may be unable to express verbally, and as a way of furthering our understanding of the patient's experience in childhood as well as in the transference – is of fundamental importance in the psychoanalytic process, especially in our work with borderline and schizoid patients.

Money-Kyrle (1956) was one of the first to suggest that when we effectively use those feelings provoked in us by our patients, rather than defensively evading them, we may not only further our understanding of the patient, but we "can make 'post-graduate' progress in his own analysis" (p. 341). Of course such progress is indicative of "normal countertransference" at its best.

In Chapter 5, I have discussed some of the ways in which my patient Chloe "raised me" to a new level of consciousness regarding myself, which in turn furthered my ability to understand her. Perhaps when we can experience the patient as an ally rather than as an adversary to the process of analytic exploration, we may come to consider any and all communications coming from the patient as a useful "second opinion."

In recognizing the "gift" of experience his patients had bestowed upon him, Winnicott (1971) dedicated his book *Playing and Reality* to those patients "who paid to teach" him. The contemporary British independent, Patrick Casement (1985a), based his book about psychoanalytic technique *On Learning From the Patient*. Appropriately titled, this work centered on his years of open-minded observation of the therapeutic inter-play between analyst and analysand, and highlighted the patient's role as supervisor.

Further linking the use of the countertransference with the notion of the patient-as-supervisor, Jacobs (1991) not only vividly demonstrated the ways in which the analyst's experience could be utilized to promote the therapeutic process, but he gave full credit to his patients' capacity to help him to learn something new about himself, which furthered his understanding of them.

Quite early on, Ferenczi (1933) advised us that our "Patients have an exceedingly refined sensitivity for the wishes, tendencies, whims, sympathies and antipathies of their analyst, even if the analyst is completely unaware of this sympathy" (p. 158). Surely each one of us can acknowledge our patients' capacity to stimulate our imagination, to challenge us to construct increasingly articulate models, and to motivate us to seek new metaphors, to tell better "stories" or to construct more evocative interpretations (Mitrani 1996).

In this chapter, I wish to expand on these themes through the presentation of a single clinical hour that may serve to lay bare one analyst's process of thinking through and learning from the countertransference and therefore from the patient. This "thinking through" is a necessary if not sufficient task in our everyday analytic work. It is one that needs to be successfully undertaken in order for the analyst to clear the pathways of receptivity to that which the patient has to offer and to "teach" the analyst about the analyst's as well as the patient's experiences. I will also demonstrate how, when we are able to "keep things in mind" (Britton 1992) *long enough* to adequately transform them into something meaningful *for the patient*, we may be able to achieve a change, not only in our own mental state and attitude, but also in our patients'.

The sphere of this chapter is limited in an effort to present, to focus in on, and to magnify one patient's communications and one analyst's inner thoughts about the material, both during the session and afterward, in the hope of making some additional contribution to the study of the dynamics of "containment" of the patient's and analyst's experience alike. Although I advisedly refrain – mainly in the interest of confidentiality – from discussing the history of this patient, the history of her treatment, and aspects of the vignette that are unrelated to the specific focal point of this chapter, the reader is invited to use this material to speculate about what I *might* have said, and what the outcome might have been if I had said other than I did. This can be a most rewarding exercise indeed, for, as Bion (1965) once wrote, it is the sort of "analytic game" that serves to build mental muscle.

The session

The material I shall present comes from the analysis of a female patient whom I call Marie. While Marie had openly expressed gratitude for her previous analytic experience, she sought additional analysis with me due to a vague feeling of something untouched, and a more well-delineated sense that certain needed "information" had not been obtained through an earlier analytic encounter.

On this occasion, midway into the second year of the analysis, Marie arrived on time and embarked on her final hour of the week, quite agitated and complaining of feelings of "disorganization." She said that she did not know whether to go away for the weekend or to stay at home. If she stayed, she could "do some shopping, buy some new clothes, perhaps a new dress." She then added (it seemed to me reluctantly) that she realized that she was "a little bit ahead financially this month, and could probably buy a new pair of support shoes." The initial impression I had of this was that, in anticipation of the impending weekend interruption in our contact, Marie felt in need of some *thing* or some *place* that would provide her with an experience of being held together, an experience of organization.

After a pause, Marie seemed more relaxed and quite casually said that she could go or not, she knew the choice was hers. At first I thought that this was Marie's way of denying her need for contact with me when I failed to respond to her in a reassuring way, especially when I noticed that her tone had shifted and she now seemed to be reassuring herself that *going or not going* was a simple choice of very little significance, and perhaps also that *ending the week or not* was of little consequence and entirely up to her.

With her anxiety now at least temporarily in abeyance, Marie was able to continue, saying that she had arrived early to her appointment and had remained in her car for some time before coming in to see me. When she left the car, locking the door with one hand, she experienced a moment of panic, thinking that she had locked her keys in the car. This panic lasted briefly until, in the next moment, she realized that she was holding the car keys in her other hand. I thought, but did not say, that she had just locked me out, sealing her anxiety up inside where it was now inaccessible. Perhaps while feeling shut away from me she panicked, although she also seemed to have some awareness that *she* held the keys to her mind, a way to let me in.

There was another few moments' pause before Marie went on as if associating to a dream. She said that "keys get you into places and cars get you around." She said that she was aware that it was "once again the end of the week." She paused once more and I became conscious of feeling pressured to make some all-too-pat interpretation about her feeling of being locked out, without a place to be over the weekend: about her sense of falling apart, and of how she protects herself against any awareness of these unbearable feelings by running away from them or covering them over with a false sense that she is in control.

However, although I felt I had sufficient evidence for this interpretation, I held my breath and waited, in part because I had made such interpretations to her on many other occasions, often with little effect. Additionally, I felt something was still locked up inside her: something fresh and immediate that was lacking in the relaxed tone and tenor of her communications.

Seemingly resigned to my silence, Marie said that she thought, since this was the end of the week, that she was feeling worried about not having access to me and to the "information" I give her, which helps her to get herself going. After another very brief interlude of silence, in which I felt she wished me to confirm her own interpretation, Marie went on to say that she wanted to tell me about a new patient she'd seen for the first time on the previous afternoon. She explained that this man had reminded her of her first love. He was tall and handsome – a high-powered executive – and had phoned her up in a panic to ask for a consultation at the beginning of the week. She further reported that he had recently suffered quite a shock when the woman in his life had left him abruptly. He said that he had thought that he would be settled down with a wife and children by now, but instead he found that he was suddenly all alone.

Marie went on to tell me that, at first, she had felt extremely attracted to this man. This feeling was accompanied by an experience of intense disorganization, which left her unsure that she could help him. She said that, in the past, she might be unable to think, feeling intimidated in the presence of such an attractive single man, and so would either lose such a patient or feel compelled to refer him on. Then she had begun to think about how like herself he was, since she too was disappointed on finding herself in a personal situation that stood contrary to her desires and expectations.

Now seemingly in touch with her patient's loneliness, neediness, and panic – in connection with her own like feelings – Marie said that she had felt gradually less disturbed by her attraction to him. She explained that she had begun to feel more solid – more able to think about the material being presented to her – as she "imagined [me] in the room with" her. She further explained, "It was as if I were *pretending* to be you, thinking about what this patient was communicating, and responding in the way I thought you would have." She added, "I thought, *this is good!* Maybe I'm beginning to introject you. Or is it incorporation?"

Marie then said that she was now attempting to recall the distinction between "introjection" and "incorporation." She said that she thought that one was "taking in the object in such a way that it becomes part of you, like when you eat an apple, it becomes part of you, but you don't become the apple." Then she said, "I'm flashing right now on an image of a boa constrictor who has just eaten a mouse whole. You can still see the form of the mouse inside, before it has been digested. Maybe that's the other."

After some moments of hesitant silence, the patient went on to say that she had always felt that I was "fully identified as an analyst." But she also suspected that I could still feel "somewhat insecure, not really sure of myself, not thoroughly self-confident," and so I could not quite bring myself "to shed some of the non-essential aspects of being an analyst, perhaps [my] reserve." Marie qualified this statement by adding that this had been her impression more frequently at the beginning of our work together, but she was "certain that this impression [of me] had changed over time with our work together."

At first I was surprised, put-off by my patient's statement. I then realized that I was uncomfortable with this view of myself as "mousy" or as having a "reserve" skin that needed shedding, a view that was being reflected back to me by my patient. Consequently I observed myself reaching a bit too hastily, I thought, for *some* understanding of this material. I considered the possibility that when Marie had mentioned that she had more money than she needed and would go away for the weekend or shopping, and later when she talked of her new patient (the handsome executive), she had been attempting to project her feelings of envy and the feelings of despair underlying it into my mind in order to obtain relief from her experience of the weekend break.

I also considered that Marie's seeming reluctance in mentioning to me that she was financially ahead this month might be a sign of her fear of the consequences of her provocation. I wondered, was she attempting to get me to engage in a sado-masochistic connection with her? Was I being nudged (Joseph 1989) to collude with some part of her that attacks her whenever she gets ahead?

I also thought that, to top it off, she might now be subjecting me to an attack on my sense of self in order to "*weak*-end" me; in other words, in order to communicate something of how *she* feels — *weak* and disorganized — as the break in the treatment approaches. Or perhaps she was attempting to bring the two of us closer together to avoid the gap of the weekend by placing us in the same "weak"-end boat, as she may have done with her new patient in order that the difference between them might not seem so intimidating or exciting and therefore "disorganizing," stirring up anxieties of both abandonment and castration.

However, although I sensed that this way of thinking about Marie's material and the feelings this brought up in me *would certainly have gone a long way to diminish my discomfort*, I was not so sure that it would help the patient with hers. My formulations suddenly felt a bit too convenient for me. They seemed defensive and simply did not ring true in the moment.

As I held all of this uncomfortably in mind, and gave myself time to recover from the initial "narcissistic" blow, I began to consider the possibility that the "attack" I had experienced might be coming from within: not an attack coming from the patient, *per se*, but *from my own archaic super-ego*. I wondered, was I attacking myself for being too weak, unsure of myself, and in need of some protective covering? Was I reprimanding myself for the insufficiency of that protection, which this analysand could apparently see right through?

This latter formulation seemed to fit. As I chewed on it for a moment, I was more and more struck by the possibility of the accuracy of Marie's assessment of me, and I was finally convinced that she had indeed given me something new to consider, both about *her* ability to have an impact on my mental functioning and my state of mind, and also regarding my evaluation of the nature and function of – as well as the motivations for – her projective and introjective processes. I wondered, could it be that, by giving me this new understanding, Marie was attempting to help me to be a better analyst so that I might be able to relinquish those "unessential aspects" of my analytic identity – my reserve, my mousiness, or my tough boa-skin – so that I might be even more accessible to her?

Now feeling much less "mousy," my attitude toward my patient markedly improved and I told Marie that I thought that she was trying to help me to understand that, when she finds me too reserved, she is not so sure that I am really solidly rooted and organized within myself, and thus she dares only to try me on, like a new dress in which she can feel good about herself, or a shadow in which she can take shelter. In this state of mind, she can only "pretend" to be me, but cannot take me in – "introject me" – quite yet, and that leaves her feeling unsafe without my physical presence to get inside of, to organize and to hold her over the weekend.

Marie replied, with surprise and relief, that she felt that this was true. She poignantly added that she had considered that my insecurity was what was hidden behind my reserve and it had troubled her. She then said that she felt that what I had just said was helpful to her, although she still had this problem with her new patient. He would be coming back that day, and she was thinking that she would offer to see him twice weekly.

Marie continued to say that she knew that he needed more, and that he spoke openly of his desire to come every day. However, she was afraid that his desire to come with such frequency was merely a sign of a "very thin and tenacious borderline transference." She was concerned that he would break off the treatment as soon as he had gained some immediate relief if she were not cautious. Marie then added that she was not at all comfortable with offering a greater frequency of sessions to this man, since she was not so sure he could or would wish to sustain such intense contact, let alone the financial obligation, and she had never really learned how to ask for this with conviction.

Feeling once again that my patient had added a new dimension to my understanding of her dilemma, I acknowledged that these were most certainly realistic concerns with such a patient, and of course they were worthy of serious consideration. However, perhaps on another level, she was also helping me to understand that when she swallows me whole – incorporates me – what she feels to be an undigested "mousy" bit of me still remains, rendering her uncertain of herself as a therapist, and she is unsure if she can ask her new patient to come five times per week, uncertain that he will stay if she does. Additionally, that "mousy bit" leaves her fearful that I cannot sustain her and, as her patient seems to be troubled with problems similar to her own, she is not so sure that she can sustain him either.

Finally, we came to understand that the dilemma with this new patient – panicked, disorganized, and alone – resonated with Marie's experience of her "first love," her depressed and insecure mother, as it did with her experience of me in the transference, as "mousy" and unsure of myself. Although she was moved to pretend that she could organize both herself and her patient, just as she felt that she could mother herself and heal her frail and depressed parents, in the end she was overcome with terrors of being dropped and lost.

Marie seemed to feel relieved by this understanding, and left the hour hopeful that she "might be able to rely" on her supervisor's assistance with this new patient. This was a distinct change from her usual presentation of herself as not needing help from anyone. I took this as evidence that she was feeling more confident that I might be able to sustain her and less threatened by the feelings aroused in her by an awareness of her own dependence upon me and others.

Afterthoughts

In concluding this chapter, I wish to add that I believe there are times when patients like Marie (and, of course, Chloe in Chapter 5) can and will make important and accurate assessments of our mental states, and that we need to be aware that the outcome of such assessments unconsciously affects their decisions about how to make use of us as analysts. It seems to me that it is important to appreciate that patients who dare to tell us what they think of us *directly*, expose themselves to great dangers since they are thus more vulnerable to our defensive reactions. It would seem that, if we prove ourselves to be trustworthy as well as open to knowing more about ourselves, we may be able to foster such directness in the patient from which the treatment may benefit.

My patient Marie seemed to have an uncanny capacity to be in contact with my mental state and "chose" to projectively rather than introjectively identify with me – not merely in order to control or to harm me, and not simply for communication either, but in order to make the best use of me at the time, in order to insure her survival in a world full of uncertainty.

It would seem that we as analysts must work to overcome our need to deny our deficiencies – our need to be self-sufficient and to survive in the clinical situation that is full of uncertainty – if we expect our patients to do likewise. As I have tried to demonstrate here, these needs are often perpetuated by the ever-lurking threat of attack from our own primitive super-ego. When we become aware of the origins of these needs, we may become more accessible to receiving help from our patients in gaining some new and increasingly meaningful comprehension of ourselves, and consequently of them.

Tustin once wrote that she had "come to realize that, from earliest infancy, there are fluctuating states of consciousness, which are the basis for states of mind throughout life" (1990, p. 217). Similarly, I have come to realize – through my work with Marie and the other analysands whom I have had the opportunity to work with and to write about in this book – that such fluctuating states of consciousness exist in the analyst as well as in the infant: states of alert awareness when we are in touch with the distinction between our experience and the patient's experience, as well as states of confusion and extremes of identification – projective, introjective, and adhesive – wherein separation and therefore the capacity for discrimination is diminished.

Of course, while maintaining awareness of the differences between analysts and analysands, we need to keep in mind the fact that we too are ordinary people capable of erecting some of the most extra-ordinary protections. If we attempt to forcibly, prematurely, and defensively extricate ourselves from the patient and the patient's view of us, we run the risk of creating an agony of awareness (Tustin 1990), which may provoke the patient to further develop a reactive and often manipulative defensiveness in order to protect his or her most vulnerable self. Thus, thinking things through in the countertransference, achieving new discriminations and transformations, is often a painstakingly slow process. However, I am encouraged by the words of the French poet, Paul Valéry (1959a), who wrote in his poem "Palme" (Palm-trees):

> Patience, patience,
> Patience in the blue sky!
> > Each atom of silence
> > Is the opportunity of a ripe fruit![29]

As ordinary analysts, we hopefully strive to gain new levels of awareness, and need – as Bion (1967a) recommended – to *eschew memory and desire*. This includes our ability to consciously and temporarily "let go" of our expectations for ourselves, of our sense of who we generally experience ourselves as, of our ego ideal as well as our theories. Although we may need to *use* our theories as a guide for our work, let us hope that as our defensiveness decreases we need not be held hostage by these theories nor by that early primitive super-ego with which our theories may come to be linked throughout our training and beyond.

9

Concluding thoughts

> Theory may be necessary to represent the similarity between people separated by race, religion, language and distance, measured in terms of or by physical time and space. Our concern is how this "domain," usually left to be "dealt" with by geniuses, is to be managed by ordinary human beings.
>
> W.R. Bion

In writing this book, I have sought to demonstrate one analyst's way of working with certain "ordinary" people who utilize "extra-ordinary" protections – somatic, autistic, and psychotic – for purposes of psychic survival. In the face of unbearable happenings occurring before birth and beyond, certain experiences are never had by the infant, and mental and emotional growth is subsequently truncated. However, such happenings do remain alive-if-encapsulated. Maintained in a kind of stasis, these are often reactivated by ordinary and extra-ordinary life events and, in the course of the psychoanalytic process, the opportunity arises for them to actually be experienced in the transference. Subsequently, development may once more be set in train.

From the moment we respond to the patient's first phone call, the nature of the transference, and therefore the patient's development, is influenced by the quality of our response to his communications. We discover that each patient is a unique individual, the product of one particular permutation of genetics and experience, and we are given the chance to continually learn anew, no matter how many patients we have met before.

Like my patient Chloe, who gathered up her baby's tiny limbs to provide for her a sense of physical security during feeding, right from the start we gather up aspects of the patient's experience in order to furnish him with a safe and "holding" mentality within which to digest and create new meaning. Our analysands may be able to survive being "fed" at arm's length, but they will truly thrive when we provide a close emotional connection in the ambience of the transference relationship, which is the hallmark of psychoanalytic therapy.

157

Our capacity to imagine the experience of the infant in the patient constitutes what Bion called "alpha function," and our ability to communicate our "imaginative conjectures" to the patient – in a timely way, with feeling – promotes the construction of a supportive scaffolding within which a mind may grow, while self-generated bodily sensations and other omnipotent protections are gradually out-grown and relinquished voluntarily.

Throughout the preceding chapters, I have endeavored to describe some important aspects of the evolution of the analytic process, from the first meeting with patients like Anthony, Cora, and Lily in Chapter 1, to the terminal sessions with patients like Hendrick in Chapter 4 and Joel in Chapter 7. The points selected for discussion and the therapeutic situations depicted do not purport to offer a comprehensive view of all aspects of the therapeutic encounter. Neither do they pretend to present clinicians with a norm for clinical practice. However they do address several of the happenings provoked by – and many of the questions that can arise out of – this intense emotional relationship between ordinary patient and analyst as they strive toward a better understanding of some of the features common to this extra-ordinary connection.

It is paradoxical that becoming an analyst – not only in the beginning of training, but with each and every new patient as well – occurs overnight, yet takes years of experience and learning through a process of making many "mistakes." Throughout these pages I have tried to present some of my own mistakes as candidly as possible.

Our experiences with our own analysts provide the basic medium out of which our personal technique unconsciously and consciously grows. However – as I believe I have demonstrated in the cases of Chloe in Chapter 5, Carla in Chapter 6, Joel in Chapter 7, and Marie in Chapter 8 – our patients may also be a significant source of guidance in our professional development, as they let us know when we are helping them to thrive and also when we are obstructing their way. Of course patients vary enormously in their capacity to communicate, to love and to enjoy life, to appreciate us and what we give them, as well as in their tolerance for frustration and deprivation and in their own reactions to these experiences.

In consideration of their individual qualities, we must be willing and able to learn with every new patient how to understand him, how to interpret his needs and desires, and how to detect his responsiveness and to comprehend his lack of responsiveness to our ministrations. To achieve some measure of success in this endeavor takes time and space, attentiveness and sensitivity, forbearance and humility.

To be able to assist in a person's development is one of the greatest pleasures an analyst can experience. However, it is rarely achieved without conflict and struggle. As Tustin said:

> Errors and strife are good things. In a way, they are the growth points. If we're always right, well attuned and wonderfully insightful, there won't ever be any

growing points for the patient. In gardening, the new shoots sprout from the wound where we cut off the leaves, and new roots always grow where we've made a wound at the bottom. As Winnicott once said, if all is going well and we don't interfere, the patient will inevitably make us fail him in just the way he needs us to do so. This is the essence of the transference. The difference between then and now will be in how we are aware of and respond to the fact of our failures.

(1988)

Perhaps the experience of such "failures" on the part of the analyst, and the struggles with various reactions to these, may be of use to the patient as he attempts to face his own inevitable failures, as well as the failures of those important people in his world outside of analysis. The confidence he gains in surviving his internal struggles and the conflicting feelings evoked by the analyst's failures may serve him to live life in full. Nonetheless, when conflict and painful feelings are felt to be too much, the stress may be too great to bear and defensiveness will inevitably increase. At times like these, we need to be especially mindful of our own attitudes and emotions and of the effect these may be having on the patient, so that we might be able to address – with maximal understanding – what he is going through.

We also need to be cautious and cognizant of our own tendency toward arrogance, pride, and omnipotence, as well as our proclivity for undue guilt, shame, and "feelings of failure" when our ideals are not realized. At all times, it is important to keep in mind that we are dealing with distinctly separate individuals with potentials we can appreciate and may gradually help them to fulfill, not possessions of our creation who can be molded at will. The help we may afford our patients depends largely upon our own resources, our limitations, and our personalities, all of which we can strive to be increasingly aware of.

Perhaps, after parenthood, there may be nothing more difficult than "analyst-hood." The role of the analyst is one of responsibility – responsibility for the infant and the child and the adolescent, as well as the adult in the patient – for his mental, emotional, and sometimes even his physical well-being. The weight of this responsibility, especially in the infantile transference, may be so great at times that the analyst might unwittingly harden herself and become insensitive, especially when what the infant-in-the-patient communicates threatens to resonate too strongly with what the infant-in-the-analyst has experienced, evoking a variety of countertransference reactions rooted in happenings from our own infancies. In presenting material from the analysis of my patients, I have tried to be as open as possible about my own countertransference experiences, the ways in which I have detected these in myself, and how I have attempted to put these to good use on behalf of the patient as well as myself.

We all appreciate that it truly takes an enduring effort to receive and to tolerate the patient's unbearable feelings and thoughts, and realize that it requires an active

159

capacity for imagination to transform these into that communicable model of understanding that we call interpretation. Furthermore, in order to understand the infantile aspects of the patient, one has to be willing and able to feel like a baby.

Of course, one might think that, since we have all been babies, this experience would be well within our emotional grasp. However, the vulnerability and sensitivity of the infant and young child are something that we are often tempted to use our adult experience and competence, our training and our theories, to avoid feeling whenever we can. Moreover, this may lead to mis-understanding the patient through interpretations that lack contact on all but an intellectual level. Perhaps the elemental terrors – so vividly brought to light in the work of Bick, Tustin, and Winnicott, and which I have attempted to illustrate in the cases discussed – are amongst those we would often rather overlook.

Consequently, at times it may be far less distressing for us to address the current situation of the patient's life outside the immediate transference happening, his childhood history, or the dynamics of his internal world. However, I have tried to convey how, in turning our interpretive attention to current events in the outside world or toward the historical past, we may be (often accurately) perceived as pushing certain infantile aspects of our patients' experiences away from us, just as we may be felt to be altogether abandoning the infant-in-the-analysand when we choose to discuss intellectually – with an often adaptively/compliantly/precociously adultified patient – his internal conflicts.

Although it can be disconcerting when a patient is not ready to accept whatever he is given, at such times the analyst needs to consider the possibility that what the patient cannot or will not take in may simply be indigestible for him. We may even need to be able to conceive of a situation in which a mouth through which to feed or a stomach in which to hold food has not yet formed in the patient. At such times we must take great pains to understand this, while refraining from accusations and explanations that may only serve to heighten the domination of an archaic super-ego in the patient. We must really stretch to encompass what is immediate for the patient at any given moment.

I hope that what has been written here may serve to assist clinicians in their efforts to reach and to maintain contact with those elements of the patient that are most in need of help: those vulnerable, very early embryonic, fetal, and infantile aspects that have yet to have the experience of being "conceived" in the mind of another and which are not yet fully formed. For without such an experience, primordial happenings that have been necessarily foreclosed from awareness will remain unmitigated, unable to be borne in the mind of the patient, which itself has not had sufficient opportunities for development.

One key to such development of "mind" is what Bion referred to as the "containing function" of the analyst, which must be experienced by the patient consistently over a lengthy period of time. Technically speaking, the gradual introjection of the containing analyst – in the act of receiving, processing, and making meaning of the raw sensory experiences of the patient – may best be achieved through direct, immediate, and clear interpretation of the transference as it is experienced from the vertex of the patient. I am convinced that contact made in this way offers the patient a sense of being in touch with an emotionally and mentally available and a firm–but–not–rigid bounding presence capable of introjective identification. This sense of "being in touch" approximates what Bick (1968) called the "psychic skin" and requires a way of working that is consistent with what Steiner (1993) referred to as the "analyst–centered interpretation."

This mode of interpretation leads to an experience of "being understood" (Joseph 1983; Steiner 1993) and provides an "object lesson" (Tustin 1994b) for introjection rather than for projection, eventuating in a build–up rather than a depletion of the internal world. In other words, along with an experience of being understood, an object capable of tolerance and understanding is established through this kind of interpretive work. The installation of such "understanding objects" lays the foundation for more sophisticated capabilities such as the desire and empathy necessary in order for the patient to understand himself and others.

After this point in mental development has been reached, both genetic reconstructions and intrapsychic formulations of a more "patient–centered" variety (Steiner 1993) may have a truly productive place in analysis. They can and will be received – more often than not – with interest and even appreciation. Additionally, once the patient has developed some presence of mind, these more advanced lines of thinking – when stemming from a benign self– and other–consciousness – will likely be brought into play in a non–defensive and heartfelt manner by the patient himself, where previously it was only possible to "play" these constellations out in relation to the analyst or to articulate them in a manner that resembles echolalia without shared meaning.

The most common lacunae I have found in the analytic work brought to me for comment by students and colleagues lie in the area of "taking" the transference, which – as I have earlier stated – refers not merely to a cognitive understanding of or an empathic attunement with what the patient is feeling toward and experiencing with the analyst in a given moment. It also entails *an unconscious introjection on the part of the analyst of certain aspects of the patient's inner world, and a resonance with those elements of the analyst's inner world, such that the latter is able to feel herself to be that unwanted part of the patient's self or that unbearable object that had previously been introjectively identified with by the patient.* I have touched upon this problem in the case of Hendrick in Chapter 4.

I believe that many of us are drawn to the work of analysis, at least in part, by the desire to do some good. However, this can be the greatest obstacle to actually doing good analytic work. If unbridled, it may prove to be the most obstructive "desire" – in Bion's (1967a) sense of the word – since our patients may need to transform us, in the transference, into the "bad" object: that which does harm.

In terms of technique, this calls for the wherewithal to see, hear, smell, feel, and taste things from the vantage point of the patient. In my work, I have found it is of little use to give the patient the impression, in one way or another, that what he made of what I said or did was neither what I intended nor what I actually did or said. This tactic misses the point and only reinforces the patient's sense that his experiences are unbearable.

Our patients' need to project their "bad" objects and unendurable experiences into us is primary. Within us these objects, and the experiences which have created them, may find an opportunity for rehabilitation and transformation. In this manner, for example, the experience of the "abandoning object" that we become – during weekend breaks, silences, or even absence of understanding in the analytic hour – may have the chance to become an experience of an abandoning object who takes responsibility for having abandoned the patient and who, at the same time, is able to keep the patient in mind sufficiently to be able to think about how he might feel about being abandoned.

Most importantly, that same object may also be experienced by the patient as able to bear being "bad," which is "good"! When re-introjected by the patient in this modified form, the "bad" object is not so "bad" at all: it is human, ordinary, with all the human frailties imaginable, but it is bearable. In this transformed state, the "bad" object (now the contained) is enhanced with a "container" (the analytic object), and the patient is on his way toward acquiring a "psychic skin," and can perhaps begin to bear "being ordinary" or "ordinary being," in the sense that Tustin used the term.

Once again I am suggesting that, if we utilize the patient's "vertex" from which to derive our interpretive observations, we may be able to compose what one might call an *introjective interpretation*, that is, one based upon an act of *introjective identification* on the part of the analyst and which may culminate in an experience of "being understood." In contrast to this, when we formulate interpretations based upon our vertex (that is, what we experience, our sense of the patient, and what we believe he is "doing" to us in phantasy via his defensive maneuvers) this constitutes a *projective interpretation,* wherein *the analyst returns that which had been projected into her by the patient.* This is, in and of itself, an act of projection aimed toward helping the patient to "get understanding" or to gain insight into himself. However this assumes adequate mental space in which to house self-awareness and sufficient ego strength to contend with separateness.

Arguably, interpretations that address the patient's projections may sometimes be helpful to the patient in the beginning of the analysis (that is, when the inception of a containing object and a space for thinking is tenuous and rudimentary) if such projections can be sincerely perceived and identified by the analyst as a part of the patient's attempts to communicate. In other words, the earliest insight or "core" insight – like the "good" object at the core of the ego – must be some "good" aspect of the Self. This subset of projective interpretation serves to acknowledge, touch, and support what Rosenfeld (1964; 1971) referred to as the benign and healthy libidinal aspects of the patient. Such interpretive work strengthens these positive tendencies and fosters the patient's faith in his inner

162

goodness. It also increases his experience of the analyst's goodness – our capacity to receive and to make sense of his communications – and he can thus begin to take us in as an object capable of understanding in relation to a subject who is capable of communicating and being understood.

Toward concluding, I wish to express my gratitude to Frances Tustin who, for over a decade before her death, discussed with me my work with patients. To her credit, and my benefit, she never gave me specific interpretations, convinced that I needed to find my own way of expressing my observations to patients. She thought that the important thing was to be flowing, spontaneous, real, and natural with patients and felt that, if I could grasp her scheme of understanding without being overshadowed by her style, my own formulations would spring up in my mind like seedlings in the sunshine.

Tustin (1986c) thought of our discussions as the soil in which my own individual understanding could grow up and blossom, and she imagined that my interpretations would germinate like plants: that I would be able to say things in an organic way that would prove meaningful to each one of my patients. It is my hope that this book will add the water and fertilize the seeds sown in that soil provided by Tustin and the many others cited in this volume, helping other analytic therapists to bloom and their patients to flourish in their own work and relationships.

Finally, I will leave the reader with another quotation from Paul Valéry (1959b) who wrote:

> Your footsteps, children of my silence, sacredly and slowly placed,
> go mute and icy towards my watchfulness's bed.
>
> Pure being, divine shadow, how sweet they are, your steps withheld!
> Gods! . . . All the gifts I guess at come to me on those bare feet!
>
> If, with your proffered lips, you prepare the nourishment of a kiss
> for the inhabitant of my thoughts, in order to soothe him,
>
> Hasten not that tender action, the sweetness of being and of being not,
> for I have lived waiting for you, and my heart was but your footsteps.[30]

This poem "Les pas" (Footsteps), freely translated and recited in the context of the analytic hour, was one ordinary patient's extra-ordinary way of reminding me that the analytic process is indeed a "tender action" that cannot be hurried; each interpretation is as vital to and as vulnerable in a given clinical moment as a bare footstep on the path of life.

Notes

1 This chapter derives from a paper presented on December 6, 1996 at the 40th Winter Meeting of the American Academy of Psychoanalysis, a version of which was published in 1997 in *The Journal of the American Academy of Psychoanalysis*, 25(1): 1–14.

2 Throughout this book I will be using Bion's term "vertex," rather than the more commonly used "viewpoint" or "point-of-view," which he borrowed from geometry in order to "eliminate the bias in favor of visual criteria" (Meltzer 1978, p. 79) and to allow us to consider the use and expression of other sensual criteria, such as the olfactory, tactile, auditory, and gustatory. Additionally, the term "vertex" was also used to refer to various "value systems" or "world views" such as the value system of the analyst or the value system of the patient (which may often diverge from one another, only gradually finding a point of intersection).

3 After 1980, Grotstein preferred the term "background *presence* of primary identification" in deference to its ineffable quality, not that of an object of the senses, but as an experience of the baby (personal communication, 2000).

4 Freud (1930) – referring to a letter from Rolland regarding the notion of the "oceanic" feeling – stated that, at first "an infant at the breast does not as yet distinguish his ego from the external world as the source of the sensations flowing in upon him. He gradually learns to do so, in response to various promptings" (p. 67). Further on, Freud elaborates on what he means by "promptings" as "sensations of pain and unpleasure" (p. 67) leading to the awareness of the object. He concludes that "originally the ego includes everything, later it separates-off an external world from itself. Our present ego feeling is, therefore, only a shrunken residue of a much more inclusive – indeed, an all-embracing – feeling which corresponded to a more intimate bond between the ego and the world about it. If we may assume that there are many people in whose mental life this primary ego-feeling has persisted to a greater or lesser degree, it would exist in them side by side with the narrower and more sharply demarcated ego-feeling of maturity . . . the ideational contents appropriate to it would be precisely those of a bond with the universe – the same ideas with which [Rolland] elucidated the 'oceanic' feeling" (p. 68). Freud goes on to ask, "have we the right to assume the survival of something that was originally there, alongside of what was later derived from it? Undoubtedly!" (p. 68). Here Freud seems to be suggesting that the persistence of the "oceanic" feeling in later development constitutes a state of being that exists alongside those more discriminative mentalized states which have evolved out of it, "an attitude or

instinctual impulse has remained unaltered, while another portion has undergone further development" (p. 69). He refers to the "oceanic" feeling as a "memory-trace" which is preserved and "in suitable circumstances . . . can once more be brought to light" (p. 69).

5 Freud (1930) stated that "In the realm of the mind . . . what is primitive is so commonly preserved alongside of the transformed version which has arisen from it . . . when this happens it is usually in consequence of divergence of development . . . in mental life nothing which has once been formed can perish" (pp. 68–9).

6 I have earlier coined the term "unmentalized experience" (Mitrani 1993b; 1995b) to denote elemental sense data, internal or external, which have failed to be transformed into symbols (mental representations, organized and integrated) or signal affects (anxiety which serves as a signal of impending danger, requiring thoughtful action), but which are instead perceived as concrete objects in the psyche or as bodily states which are reacted to in corporeal fashion (for example, somatic symptoms or actions). Such experiences are merely "accretions of stimuli" which can neither be used as food for thought nor stored as memories in the mind. Bianchedi (1991) calls these "the 'unthoughts' . . . perceptions and sensations, not yet subjected to 'alpha function' (Bion 1962) . . . " (p. 11). I believe Freud's notion of the "anxiety equivalent" (1895, p. 94) in the actual neurosis was the first attempt to characterize this phenomenon in psychoanalysis.

7 This chapter is a revised version of a paper published in 1999 in *The International Journal of Psycho-Analysis*, 80(1): 47–71.

8 In my understanding of Bion's model of the maternal container or the analyst-as-container, (s)he for the most part demonstrates the capacity to receive and take-in (introject) projected parts, feelings, and unprocessed sensory experiences of the infant; to experience the full effect of these on the psyche-soma and to bear those effects; and to think about and understand these projections (transformation), gradually returning them to the infant in due time and in decontaminated form (publication/interpretation). This assumes a mother/analyst who has her own boundaries, internal space, a capacity to bear pain, to contemplate, to think and to reflect back. A mother/analyst who is herself separate, intact, receptive, capable of "reverie," and appropriately giving is suitable for introjection as a good containing object. Identification with and assimilation of such an object leads to the development of a capacity to make meaning (alpha-function), increased mental space, and the development of a mind which can think for itself. Bion coined the term "reverie" for the attentive, receptive, introjective and experiencing aspect of the container and I believe that this function of the maternal environment is analogous to the mental/emotional aspect of what Winnicott (1941) referred to as "holding," which may be analogous to "taking the transference."

9 Although I am aware that it is the practice of many analysts – perhaps after a medical tradition – to solicit a detailed history from a patient before agreeing to commence an analysis, I find it suits my *personal style* to allow the "history" of a patient to unfold within the context of the transference or in associations freely given, in much the same way as I handle a dream wherein I refrain from soliciting associations to one or another element or indeed to the dream as a whole. Instead I consider that whatever is brought either before or after the presentation of a dream is contextually associated to that dream. In this way I feel more confident that what is offered comes more directly as a *communication from the unconscious* of the patient and is not so much reactive to my bidding.

10 With time I came to understand that Hendrick did not see himself as a misfit in the common sense of the word. Rather he was attempting to connote his feeling of

"mis-fit" with his family. In other words, Hendrick's sense of there being no place for him and his painful awareness of missing such a place (perhaps having to do with a preconception of a baby who fits into his mother's arms and is welcomed in her thoughts) were often transformed into fits of fiery, self-righteous rage that protected him from succumbing to an icy despair of aloneness.

11 Alongside possible environmental failures, various constitutional deficiencies must also be considered in Hendrick's case. Freud described the child's experience of loving and hating, of being loved and hated in the triad. He identified the epistemophilic instinct – a component of the libido – expressed in the desire to "know" about the parents' sexuality (the primal scene). Klein thought that the desire to "know" was an expression of anxiety related to phantasies of destroying the object, and an attempt to quell those anxieties by testing reality in hope of finding the loved parents still alive and loving and thus available for introjection necessary to shore up a precarious internal world. However Bion, extending Freud's (late) and Klein's (early) Oedipus models, observed that anxieties about the state of the internal world are often dealt with by interrupting awareness of one's own feelings and mind. He posited that learning and knowing require the capacity to bring things together in the mind (linking thoughts with feelings, phantasy with reality, one idea with another), which is not unlike tolerating the parents coming together in the sexual act. Bion's oedipal situation – a precursor of both Freud's and Klein's oedipal situations – has important implications for patients like Hendrick who exhibit difficulties in symbolic thinking as well as sexual disturbances: disturbances in the mind as well as in the body.

12 Since my husband and I share a waiting room in our office suite, we stagger our session times by a quarter of an hour to avoid "traffic jams" in doorways and to preserve, as best we can, the privacy of the patients. Of course these "best laid plans," like any other feature of the analyst or her set-up, may be utilized by the patient in the service of enactment and hopefully communication. I find that it is always fruitful to observe the various ways patients have of using whatever is at hand, rather than to prematurely interrupt what is being "played out" by articulating interpretations aimed at resistance or destructiveness. In any case, there is always time for the latter.

13 I think it worth saying that, although there is here a direct reference to my husband by the patient, the way in which he tells the story and the feelings conveyed by him, lay emphasis on his experience of myself in the transference. In other words, I believe there was sufficient evidence that, at this juncture, my husband was being "symbolically equated" with me (Segal 1957).

14 An abbreviated version of this chapter was presented at a meeting of the Center for Object Relations in Seattle, Washington, on May 21, 1999, and at the Frances Tustin Memorial Lecture at the Tavistock Clinic in London, England, on October 19, 1999.

15 The fact that even a "good" container has its limitations has certainly not escaped any of us. However, the fact that *our patients may often perceive these limitations* and will quite *unconsciously* adjust their behaviors accordingly is rarely acknowledged in the literature. I have often suspected that some patients wait until they perceive that we are "in the mood" to handle some new bit of their experience before presenting it and often prove to be fine judges of character. Not unlike the analyst who waits until she "feels" that the patient can hear a given interpretation and may be able to put it to good use, our patients will also "wait," contending with their experiences in any way they can until they sense the time is right for the analyst to take these on.

16 I further address this important concept of Winnicott's in the context of the case of "Joel" in Chapter 7.

17 A version of this chapter was published in 1998 in *The Psychoanalytic Quarterly*, 67(1): 102–27. An earlier draft was included as a part of J. Mitrani and T. Mitrani (eds.) *Encounters With Autistic States: A Memorial Tribute to Frances Tustin* (published by Jason Aronson in 1997).

18 It is well known that Tustin was analyzed by Bion for over fourteen years and was supervised by Meltzer while training at the Tavistock Centre. Her work on autism dovetailed with Meltzer's and they were both deeply influenced by Esther Bick's notion of adhesive identification and the concept of the psychic skin, which is closely associated with Bion's model "container-contained." Additionally, both Meltzer and Tustin were profoundly affected by Bion's thinking and each in their own way utilized, extended, and expanded upon his concepts throughout their own writings.

19 Piontelli's extensive pre-natal ultra-sound, infant-observational, and psychoanalytic longitudinal studies have provided copious behavioral evidence of the continuity of intra- and extra-uterine life, the concordance between parental pre-natal conscious and unconscious fantasies and anxieties and fetal/neonatal behavior and psychology, and the impact of the mother's physical and mental state on the fetal mind/body. Mancia (1981) has unearthed evidence, both analytical and bio-medical, for the beginnings of mental life and the development *in utero* of what Bick (1968) called the "psychic skin," and Osterweil's (1990) excellent study of the beginnings of fetal mental life presented a comprehensive review of the bio-medical data regarding fetal perceptual capacities. What these researchers are finding seems to be concordant with clinical inferences derived from analytic work in the primitive *infantile transference* with adult and child patients. For example, near the end of his life, Rosenfeld (1987) dared consider the occurrence of "maternal projective identification" and the impotence of the fetus under the sway of the presence of what he termed "the osmotic pressure of the mother's mental states." Also, Tustin (1991) posited that certain auto-immune reactions as well as autistic defensive maneuvers may be rooted in fetal life. Most recently, Maiello (1995) explored one particular aspect of pre-natal experience, presenting convincing clinical material suggesting that the sound of the mother's voice, alternating with silence, may give the child a proto-experience of presence and absence, which not only gives rise to primitive defensive reactions but may also be said to form the basis of a pre-natal sensual-object. As I have already pointed out in Chapter 2, she suggested that this "sound-object" is connected with a preconception of the breast and may be one of the many precursors of the post-natal maternal inner object. I have previously offered a model whereby the baby's earliest – even pre-natal – experiences of the (m)other might be stored at a somatic or sensation-based level as body memories, without presuming a degree of mental capacity on the part of the fetus or neonate that would stretch our credibility (Mitrani 1996).

20 Over the weekend prior to this hour the management of the building in which my office is situated installed locks on the public restroom doors on each floor to discourage transients. The keys for the restrooms were readily displayed in my waiting room, although I had not had the opportunity to inform patients of this change.

21 Kohut (1971) also discussed mirroring and mirroring transferences as "the therapeutic reinstatement of that normal phase of the grandiose self in which the gleam in the mother's eye, which mirrors the child's exhibitionistic displays, and other forms of maternal participation in and response to the child's narcissistic-exhibitionistic enjoyment confirm the child's self esteem and, by gradually increasing selectivity of these responses, begin to channel it into realistic directions" (p. 116). However, I believe that Winnicott and Kohut were not directly addressing the conflict between the infant's pre- and post-natal experiences of the mother's mental/emotional and

physical presence, and its attempts to sort out and derive some meaning from these as they affect its developing sense of self. Nor were they directly addressing the issue of the mother's self-esteem and how this affects not only the infant's self-esteem, but also the build-up of its internal world of object and self-representations, along with the emotional links between them. Although aesthetic issues were not mentioned, Winnicott (1948) addressed related matters with regard to the depressed mother's impact on the formation of the baby's internal world, which I have also addressed in Chapters 4 and 5 in the cases of both Hendrick and Chloe.

22 Fairbairn's (1952) model of the "schizoid dilemma" may be apposite here as well, since he maintains that the establishment of the baby's sense that its love is good depends upon how this love is received and responded to by the mother. Furthermore, Winnicott (1956) suggests that the baby's view of itself is initially incumbent upon how it sees itself reflected in the eyes of the mother. He states that "The important thing is that the analyst is not depressed and the patient finds himself because the analyst is not needing the patient to be good or clean or compliant and is not even needing to be able to teach the patient anything" (p. 94).

23 Bion coined the term "Super" ego to denote an internal organization lacking the usual characteristics of the super-ego we commonly understand in psychoanalysis. This "Super" ego is "an envious assertion of moral superiority without any morals . . . the resultant of the envious stripping or denudation of all good and is itself destined to continue the process of stripping" (Bion 1962a, p. 97) concomitant with what Bion called the "minus K" condition associated with negative narcissism, and he described this condition as follows: "In −K the breast is felt to remove the good or valuable element in the fear of dying and force the worthless residue back into the infant. The infant who started with a fear of dying ends up by containing a nameless dread. . . . The seriousness [of this situation] is best conveyed by saying that the will to live, that is necessary before there can be a fear of dying, is a part of the goodness that the envious breast has removed" (p. 96).

24 This chapter is a revised version of a paper published in 1998 in *The International Journal of Psycho-Analysis*, 79(2): 301–16.

25 Casement (1985b) discussed the unconscious search for new solutions and the repetition compulsion as an expression of unconscious hope. He suggested that, once a genuine solution to a previously unresolved conflict is found, the compulsion to repeat will be discontinued.

26 I wish to thank Dr. Judith Broder for calling my attention to a paper by Dr. Bernard Brandschaft (1993) in which he addresses the phenomenon of the pathological defensive organization (from a Kohutian perspective, with which I am admittedly largely unfamiliar) as "the enslaving tie to the self-annihilating self-object" (p. 225).

27 Subsequent to the writing of this chapter, Joel resumed the analytic work with me when his defensive organization once again began to crumble. As his defensiveness weakened, he gradually became "curious" as to why he had left and, as he could find no sensible reason for breaking off the treatment, he reinstated his analytic hours.

28 An abbreviated version of this chapter was published in 1997 in an issue of *The Journal of Melanie Klein and Object Relations*, 15(2): 317–28, dedicated to the memory of Wilfred Bion.

29 *Patience, patience,*
Patience dans l'azur!
    Chaque atome de silence
    Est la chance d'un fruit mûr!

30 *Tes pas, enfants de mon silence,*
    Saintement, lentement placés,
    Vers le lit de ma vigilance
    Procèdent muets et glacés.

    Personne pure, ombre divine,
    Qu'ils sont doux, tes pas retenus!
    Dieux! . . . tous les dons que je devine
    Viennent à moi sur ces pieds nus!

    Si, de tes lèvres avancées,
    Tu prépares pour l'apaiser,
    A l'habitant de mes pensées
    La nourriture d'un baiser,

    Ne hâte pas cet acte tendre,
    Douceur d'être et de n'être pas,
    Car j'ai vécu de vous attendre,
    et mon coeur n'était que vos pas.

Bibliography

Anzieu, D. (1989). *The Skin Ego*. New Haven: Yale University Press.

Balint, M. (1968). *The Basic Fault*. London: Tavistock.

Benedek, T. (1952). *Psychosexual Functions in Women*. New York: Ronald Press.

—— (1959). Parenthood as a developmental phase. *Journal of the American Psychoanalytic Association*, 7: 389–417.

Bianchedi, E. (1991). Psychic change: The "becoming" of an inquiry. *International Journal of Psycho-Analysis*, 72(1): 6–15.

Bibring, G. (1961). The study of the psychological processes in pregnancy and of the earliest mother–child relationship. *Psychoanalytic Study of the Child*, 16(9): 9–24.

Bick, E. (1964). Notes on infant observation in psychoanalytic training. *International Journal of Psycho-Analysis*, 45: 448–66.

—— (1968). The experience of the skin in early object-relations. *International Journal of Psycho-Analysis*, 49: 484–6.

—— (1986). Further considerations on the function of the skin in early object relations. *British Journal of Psychotherapy*, 2(4): 292–301.

Bion, W.R. (1957). Differentiation of the psychotic from the non-psychotic part of the personality. *International Journal of Psycho-Analysis*, 38: 266–75.

—— (1959). Attacks on linking. *International Journal of Psycho-Analysis*, 40: 308–15.

—— (1962a). *Learning From Experience*. London: Heinemann. (London: Maresfield Reprints, 1984.)

—— (1962b). A theory of thinking. *International Journal of Psycho-Analysis*, 43: 306–10.

—— (1965). Transformations. In *Seven Servants*. New York: Jason Aronson.

—— (1967a). Notes on memory and desire. *Psychoanalytic Forum*, 2(3): 272–3.

—— (1967b). *Second Thoughts*. London: Heinemann.

—— (1975a). Caesura. In *Two Papers: The Grid and Caesura*. Rio de Janeiro, Brazil: Imago Editora.

—— (1975b). *Brazilian Lectures, II*. Rio de Janeiro: Imago Editora.

—— (1976a). On a quotation from Freud. In *Clinical Seminars and Four Papers*, ed. F. Bion. Abingdon: Fleetwood Press, 1987.

—— (1976b). Evidence. In *Clinical Seminars and Four Papers*, ed. F. Bion. Abingdon: Fleetwood Press, 1987, pp. 239–46.

—— (1977a). *Two Papers: The Grid and Caesura*. Rio de Janeiro: Imago Editora.

—— (1977b). *Seven Servants*. New York: Jason Aronson.

—— (1979a). Making the best of a bad job. In *Clinical Seminars and Four Papers*, ed. F. Bion. Abingdon: Fleetwood Press, 1987, pp. 247–57.

—— (1979b). *The Dawn of Oblivion: Book III of A Memoir of the Future*. London: Karnac, 1991, pp. 427–579.

—— (1992). *Cogitations*. London: Karnac.

Blum, H. (1981). The maternal ego-ideal and the regulation of maternal qualities. In S. Greenspan and G. Pollock (eds.) *The Course of Life*, Vol. III. Washington, DC: NIMH, pp. 91–114.

Brandschaft, B. (1993). To free the spirit from itself. In A. Goldberg (ed.) *The Widening Scope of Self Psychology: Progress in Self Psychology*, Vol. 9. New York: Analytic Press, pp. 209–30.

Britton, R. (1992). Keeping things in mind. In R. Anderson (ed.) *Clinical Lectures On Klein and Bion*. London: Routledge, pp. 102–13.

Casement, P. (1985a). *Learning From the Patient*. New York: Guilford Press.

—— (1985b). Unconscious hope. In *Learning From the Patient*. New York: Guilford Press, pp. 293–307.

Chodorow, N. (1978). *The Reproduction of Mothering*. Berkeley: University of California Press.

Coolidge, T. (1999). Personal communication. Seattle, WA.

Costello, E. (1996). *All This Useless Beauty*. London: Plangent Visions Music.

Deutsch, H. (1942). Some forms of emotional disturbance and their relationship to schizophrenia. *Psychoanalytic Quarterly*, 40: 301–21.

—— (1944). *Psychology of Women*. New York: Grune and Stratton.

Erickson, E. (1965). Inner and outer space: reflection on womanhood. *Daedalus*, 93: 582–603.

Etchegoyen, H. (1991). *Fundamentals of Psychoanalytic Technique*. London: Karnac.

Fairbairn, W.D. (1952). *Psychoanalytic Studies of the Personality*. London: Tavistock.

Ferenczi, S. (1933). Confusion of tongues between adults and the child. In *Final Contributions to the Problems and Methods of Psycho-Analysis*. pp. 156–67. (London: Maresfield Reprints, 1988 first published 1955).

Freud, S. (1895). On the grounds for detaching a particular syndrome from neurasthenia under the description "anxiety neurosis." In *Standard Edition of the Complete Works of Sigmund Freud*, 3: 85–120. London: Hogarth Press, 1957.

—— (1910). The future prospects of psychoanalytic therapy. In *Standard Edition of the Complete Works of Sigmund Freud*, 9: 141–51.

—— (1912). The dynamics of transference. In *Standard Edition of the Complete Works of Sigmund Freud*, 12: 99–108.

—— (1913). On the beginning of treatment. In *Standard Edition of the Complete Works of Sigmund Freud*, 12: 123–44.

—— (1914). Remembering, repeating and working through. In *Standard Edition of the Complete Works of Sigmund Freud*, 12: 147–56.

—— (1915). The unconscious. In *Standard Edition of the Complete Works of Sigmund Freud*, 14: 166–204.

—— (1917). Introductory lectures on psycho-analysis. In *Standard Edition of the Complete Works of Sigmund Freud*, 16: 3–182.

—— (1920). Beyond the pleasure principle. In *Standard Edition of the Complete Works of Sigmund Freud*, 18: 1–64.

—— (1923). The ego and the id. In *Standard Edition of the Complete Works of Sigmund Freud*, 19: 3–68.

—— (1925). An autobiographical study. In *Standard Edition of the Complete Works of Sigmund Freud*, 20: 3–76.

—— (1926). Inhibitions, symptoms and anxiety. In *Standard Edition of the Complete Works of Sigmund Freud*, 20: 75–175.

—— (1930). Civilization and its discontents. In *Standard Edition of the Complete Works of Sigmund Freud*, 21: 59–148.

—— (1937). Analysis terminable and interminable. In *Standard Edition of the Complete Works of Sigmund Freud*, 23: 209–53.

—— (1940). An outline of psycho-analysis. In *Standard Edition of the Complete Works of Sigmund Freud* 23: 141–208.

Fuller, P. (1980). *Art and Psychoanalysis*. London: Writers and Readers.

Gaddini, E. (1969). On imitation. *International Journal of Psycho-Analysis*, 50(4): 475–84.

Gibran, K. (1923). *The Prophet*. New York: Alfred Knopf, 1976.

Gill, M. (1979). The analysis of the transference. In R. Langs (ed.) *Classics in Psychoanalytic Technique*. New York: Jason Aronson, 1981. pp. 69–82.

Gomberoff, M.J., *et al.* (1990). The autistic object: its relationship with narcissism in the transference and countertransference of neurotic and borderline patients. *International Journal of Psycho-Analysis*, 71: 249–59.

Gooch, S. (1991). Infantile sexuality revisited: the agony and the ecstasy of the mother–child couple. *Journal of the American Academy of Psychoanalysis*, 19(2): 254–70.

Grinberg, L. (1979). Projective counteridentification and countertransference. *Contemporary Psychoanalysis*, 15(1): 84–106.

Grotstein, J. (1980). Primitive mental states. *Contemporary Psychoanalysis*, 16: 479–546.

—— (1986). The dual track theorem. Unpublished paper.

—— (1990). Nothingness, meaninglessness, chaos and the black hole. *Contemporary Psychoanalysis*, 26(2): 257–90.

—— (2000). Personal communication. Los Angeles, CA.

Hansen, Y. (1994). The importance of the birth experience in early integrations. Paper presented at the conference, June 25, 1996, for the Psychoanalytic Center of California on *The Detection and Understanding of Primitive Mental States*.

Heimann, P. (1950). On countertransference. *International Journal of Psycho-Analysis*, 31: 81–4.

Hinshelwood, R. (1989). *The Dictionary of Kleinian Thought*. London: Free Association Books.

Innes-Smith, J. (1987). Pre-oedipal identification and the cathexis of autistic objects in the aetiology of adult psychopathology. *International Journal of Psycho-Analysis*, 68: 405–14.

Isaacs, S. (1952). The nature and function of phantasy. In J. Riviere (ed.) *Developments in Psychoanalysis*. London: Hogarth Press, pp. 67–121.

Isakower, O. (1939). A contribution to the pathopsychology of phenomena associated with falling asleep. *International Journal of Psycho-Analysis*, 19: 129–38.

Jacobs, T. (1991). *The Use of the Self*. Madison, CT: IUP.

Joseph, B. (1975). The patient who is difficult to reach. In P. Giovacchini (ed.) *Tactics and Techniques in Psychoanalytic Therapy*, Vol. 2. New York: Jason Aronson, pp. 205–16.

—— (1983). On understanding and not understanding: some technical issues. *International Journal of Psycho-Analysis*, 64: 291–8.

—— (1985). Transference: the total situation. *International Journal of Psycho-Analysis*, 66: 447–54.

—— (1989). *Psychic Equilibrium and Psychic Change*. London: Routledge.

Keats, J. (1820). Ode on a Grecian urn. In *Keats: Poetical Works*, ed. H. W. Garrod. London: Oxford University Press, 1970, pp. 209–10.

Khayyám, O. (1923). *The Rubáiyát*.

King, P. and Steiner, R. (1991). *The Freud–Klein Controversies 1941–1945*. London: Routledge.

Klein, M. (1935). Contribution to the psychogenesis of manic depressive states. *International Journal of Psycho-Analysis*, 16: 145–74.

—— (1946). Notes on some schizoid mechanisms. In *Envy and Gratitude and Other Works 1946–1963*. London: Hogarth Press, 1975, pp. 1–24.

—— (1952a). On observing the behavior of young infants. In *Envy and Gratitude and Other Works 1946–1963*. London: Hogarth Press, 1975, pp. 94–121.

—— (1952b). The origins of transference. In *Envy and Gratitude and Other Works 1946–1963*. London: Hogarth Press, 1975, pp. 48–56.

—— (1957). Envy and gratitude. In *Envy and Gratitude and Other Works 1946–1963*. London: Hogarth Press.

—— (1963). On the sense of loneliness. In *Envy and Gratitude and Other Works 1946–1963*. London: Hogarth Press.

Klein, S. (1980). Autistic phenomena in neurotic patients. *International Journal of Psycho-Analysis*, 61(3): 395–401.

Kohut, H. (1971). *Analysis of the Self*. New York: International Universities Press.

—— (1977). *The Restoration of the Self*. New York: International Universities Press.

Kristeva, J. (1982). *The Powers of Horror: An Essay on Abjection*. New York: Columbia University Press.

Lacan, J. (1949). Le stade du miroir. In *Ecrits*. Paris: Editions du Seuil, 1966.

Lechevalier, B. (1997). Expressions of annihilation anxiety and birth of the subject. In J. Mitrani and T. Mitrani (eds.) *Encounters with Autistic States*. Northvale, NJ: Jason Aronson, pp. 327–40.

Leifer, M. (1977) Psychological changes accompanying pregnancy and motherhood. *Genetic Psychology Monograph*, 95: 55–96.

Lewin, A. (1951). *Pandora and the Flying Dutchman*. London: Romulus Films.

McDougall, J. (1980). A child is being eaten. *Contemporary Psychoanalysis*, 16(3): 417–43.

Mahler, M. (1958). Autism and psychosis: two extreme disturbances of identity. *International Journal of Psycho-Analysis*, 39(1): 77–83.

Mahler, M., Bergman, A., and Pine, F. (1975). *The Psychological Birth of the Human Infant*. New York: Basic Books.

Maiello, S. (1995). The sound object. *Journal of Child Psychotherapy*, 21(1): 23–42.

Mancia, M. (1981). On the beginning of mental life in the fetus. *International Journal of Psycho-Analysis*, 62: 351–7.

Meltzer, D. (1975). Adhesive identification. *Contemporary Psychoanalysis*, 11(3): 289–310.

—— (1978). *The Kleinian Development, Part III*. Perthshire: Clunie Press.

—— (1988). The aesthetic conflict: its place in the developmental process. In D. Meltzer and M.H. Williams (eds.) *The Apprehension of Beauty: The Role of Aesthetic Conflict in Development, Art and Violence*. Perthshire: Clunie Press, pp. 7–33.

Meltzer, D. and Williams, M.H. (1988). *The Apprehension of Beauty: The Role of Aesthetic Conflict in Development, Art and Violence*. Perthshire: Clunie Press.

Meltzer, D., Bremner, J., Hoxter, S., Weddell, D., and Wittenberg, I. (1975). *Explorations in Autism*. Perthshire: Clunie Press.

Mitrani, J.L. (1992). On the survival function of autistic maneuvers in adult patients. *International Journal of Psycho-Analysis*, 73(2): 549–60.

—— (1993a). Deficiency and envy: some factors impacting the analytic mind from listening to interpretation. *International Journal of Psycho-Analysis*, 74(4): 689–704.

—— (1993b). Unmentalized experience in the etiology and treatment of psychosomatic asthma. *Contemporary Psychoanalysis*, 29(2): 314–42.

—— (1994a). On adhesive-pseudo-object relations: part I – theory. *Contemporary Psychoanalysis*, 30(2): 348–66.

—— (1994b). Unintegration, adhesive identification, and the psychic skin: variations on some themes by Esther Bick. *Journal of Melanie Klein and Object Relations*, 11(2): 65–88.

—— (1995a). On adhesive-pseudo-object relations: part II – illustration. *Contemporary Psychoanalysis*, 31(1): 140–65.

—— (1995b). Toward an understanding of unmentalized experience. *Psychoanalytic Quarterly*, 64: 68–112.

—— (1996). *A Framework for the Imaginary: Clinical Explorations in Primitive States of Being*. Northvale, NJ: Jason Aronson.

—— (1997a). Analytic listening, transference interpretation, and the emergence of infantile dependency: do we really need to educate patients about analysis? *Journal of the American Academy of Psychoanalysis*, 25(1): 1–14.

—— (1997b). Changes of mind: working things through in the countertransference. *Journal of Melanie Klein and Object Relations*, 15(2): 317–28.

—— (1997c). Further notes on an embryonic state of mind. In S. Alhanati and K. Kostoulos (eds.) *Primitive Mental States. Across the Lifespan*. Northvale, NJ: Jason Aronson.

—— (1998a). Never before and never again: the compulsion to repeat, the fear of breakdown, and the defensive organization. *International Journal of Psycho-Analysis*, 79(2): 301–16.

—— (1998b). Unbearable ecstasy, reverence and awe, and the perpetuation of an "aesthetic conflict." *Psychoanalytic Quarterly*, 67(1): 102–27.

—— (1999). The case of the "flying Dutchman" and the search for the containing object. *International Journal of Psycho-Analysis*, 80(1): 47–71.

Mitrani, T. (1992). Personal communication. Los Angeles, CA.

Money-Kyrle, R. (1956). Normal countertransference and some of its deviations. *International Journal of Psycho-Analysis*, 37: 360–6.

—— (1969). On the fear of insanity. *The Collected Papers of Roger Money-Kyrle*. Perthshire: Clunie Press, pp. 434–41.

Ogden, T. (1989). The autistic-contiguous position. *International Journal of Psycho-Analysis*, 70(1): 127–46.

O'Shaughnessy, E. (1964). The absent object. *Journal of Child Psychotherapy*, 1: 134–43.

—— (1981). A clinical study of a defensive organization. *International Journal of Psycho-Analysis*, 62: 359–69.

Osterweil, E. (1990). *A Psychoanalytic Exploration of Fetal Mental Development and Its Role in the Origin of Object Relations*. Unpublished Doctoral Dissertation.

Paul, M.I. (1981). A mental atlas of the process of psychological birth. In J. Grotstein (ed.) *Do I Dare Disturb the Universe*. London: Karnac, pp. 551–70.

—— (1989). Notes on the primordial development of a penitential transference. *Journal of Melanie Klein and Object Relations*, 5(2): 43–69.

—— (1990). Studies on the phenomenology of mental pressure. *Melanie Klein and Object Relations*, 8(2): 7–29.

Pines, D. (1972). Pregnancy and motherhood: interaction between fantasy and reality. *British Journal of Medical Psychology*, 45: 333–43.

—— (1982). The relevance of early psychic development to pregnancy and abortion. *International Journal of Psycho-Analysis*, 63: 311–19.

Piontelli, A. (1985). *Backwards In Time*. Perthshire: Clunie Press.

—— (1987). Infant observation from before birth. *International Journal of Psycho-Analysis*, 68: 453–63.

—— (1988). Pre-natal life and birth as reflected in the analysis of a two-year-old psychotic girl. *International Review of Psycho-Analysis*, 15: 73–81.

—— (1992a). On the continuity between pre-natal and post-natal life: a case illustration. Paper presented to the Psychoanalytic Center of California, Los Angeles.

—— (1992b) *From Fetus to Child: An Observational and Psychoanalytic Study*. London: Routledge.

Racker, H. (1953). Contribution to the problem of countertransference. *International Journal of Psycho-Analysis*, 34: 313–24.

—— (1968). *Transference and Countertransference*. London: Karnac.

—— (1972). The meanings and uses of countertransference. In R. Langs (ed.) *Classics In Psychoanalytic Technique*. New York: Jason Aronson, 1981, pp. 177–200.

Raphael-Leff, J. (1991). *Psychological Processes of Childbearing*. London: Chapman and Hall.

—— (1993). *Pregnancy: The Inside Story*. London: Sheldon Press.

Reid, S. (1990). The importance of beauty in the psychoanalytic experience. *Journal of Child Psychotherapy*, 16: 29–52.

Riviere, J. (1936). A contribution to the analysis of a negative therapeutic reaction. *International Journal of Psycho-Analysis*, 17: 304–20.

Rolland, R. (1930). *Prophets of the New India*. New York: Boni.

Rosenfeld, D. (1992). *The Psychotic Aspects of the Personality*. London: Karnac.

—— (1997). Understanding varieties of autistic encapsulation. In J. Mitrani and T. Mitrani (eds.) *Encounters with Autistic States*. Northvale, NJ: Jason Aronson, pp. 163–78.

Rosenfeld, H.A. (1947). Analysis of a schizophrenic state of depersonalization. In *Psychotic States*. New York: IUP, 1966, pp. 13–33.

—— (1964). On the psychopathology of narcissism. *International Journal of Psycho-Analysis*, 45: 332–7.

—— (1971). A clinical approach to the psychoanalytic theory of the life and death instincts: an investigation into the aggressive aspects of narcissism. *International Journal of Psycho-Analysis*, 52: 169–78.

—— (1987). *Impasse and Interpretation: Therapeutic and Anti-Therapeutic Factors in Psycho-analytic Treatment of Psychotic, Borderline, and Neurotic Patients.* London: Routledge.

Searles, H. (1975). The patient as therapist to his analyst. In R. Langs (ed.) *Classics in Psychoanalytic Technique.* New York: Jason Aronson, 1981, pp. 103–38.

Segal, H. (1957). Notes on symbol formation. *International Journal of Psycho-Analysis*, 38: 391–7.

—— (1981). *The Work of Hanna Segal.* New York: Jason Aronson.

Share, L. (1994). *When I Hear a Voice, It Gets Lighter.* New York: Analytic Press.

Spillius, E. (1993). Varieties of envious experience. *International Journal of Psycho-Analysis*, 74(6): 1199–212.

Steiner, J. (1982). Perverse relationships between parts of the self. *International Journal of Psycho-Analysis*, 63: 241–51.

—— (1987). The interplay between pathological organizations and the paranoid-schizoid and depressive positions. *International Journal of Psycho-Analysis*, 68: 69–80.

—— (1990). Pathological organizations as obstacle to mourning. *International Journal of Psycho-Analysis*, 71: 87–94.

—— (1993). *Psychic Retreats.* London: Routledge.

Sterne, Laurence (1860). *Tristram Shandy.* As quoted in *The Oxford Dictionary of Quotations*, 3rd edn. Oxford: Oxford University Press, 1980.

Stoller, R. (1976). Primary femininity. *Journal of the American Psychoanalytic Association*, 24: 59–78.

Symington, J. (1985). The survival function of primitive omnipotence. *International Journal of Psycho-Analysis*, 66: 481–8.

Tustin, A. (1984). From unpublished limericks. Personal communication. Amersham, England.

Tustin, F. (1972). *Autism and Childhood Psychosis.* London: Hogarth Press.

—— (1980). Autistic objects. *International Review of Psycho-Analysis*, 7: 27–38.

—— (1981). Psychological birth and psychological catastrophe. In J. Grotstein (ed.) *Do I Dare Disturb the Universe?* London: Karnac, pp. 181–96.

—— (1984). Autistic shapes. *International Review of Psycho-Analysis*, 11(3): 279–90.

—— (1986a). *Autistic Barriers in Neurotic Patients.* London: Karnac.

—— (1986b). The rhythm of safety. In *Autistic Barriers in Neurotic Patients.* London: Karnac, pp. 268–85.

—— (1986c). Personal communication. Amersham, England.

—— (1987). Personal communication. Amersham, England.

—— (1988). Personal communication. Amersham, England.

—— (1990). *The Protective Shell in Children and Adults.* London: Karnac.

—— (1991). Revised understanding of psychogenic autism. *International Journal of Psycho-Analysis*, 72(4): 585–92.

—— (1992a). *Autistic States in Children.* London: Routledge (revised edition, first published in 1981).

—— (1992b). Personal communication. Amersham, England.

—— (1994a). The perpetuation of an error. *Journal of Child Psychotherapy*, 20: 3–23.

—— (1994b). Personal communication. Hyde Heath, England.

Tyler, A. (1974). *Celestial Navigations.* New York: Berkeley Books.

Valéry, P. (1959a). Palme. In *The Penguin Book of French Verse*, ed. A. Hartley. Baltimore: Penguin, pp. 72–6.

—— (1959b). Les pas. In *The Penguin Book of French Verse*, ed. A. Hartley. Baltimore: Penguin, p. 51.

von Hann-Kende, H. (1933). On the role of transference and countertransference in psychoanalysis. In G. Devereux (ed.) *Psychoanalysis and the Occult*. New York: IUP, pp. 158–67.

Winnicott, D.W. (1941). The observation of infants in a set situation. In *Collected Papers: Through Pediatrics to Psycho-Analysis*. New York: Basic Books, 1958, pp. 72–6.

—— (1945). Primitive emotional development. In *Collected Papers: Through Pediatrics to Psycho-Analysis*. New York: Basic Books, 1958, pp. 145–56.

—— (1948). Reparation in respect to mother's organized defense against depression. In *Collected Papers: Through Pediatrics to Psycho-Analysis*. New York: Basic Books, 1958, pp. 91–6.

—— (1949). Mind and its relation to the psyche-soma. In *Collected Papers: Through Pediatrics to Psycho-Analysis*. New York: Basic Books, 1958, pp. 243–54.

—— (1951). Transitional objects and transitional phenomena. In *Collected Papers: Through Pediatrics to Psycho-Analysis*. New York: Basic Books, 1958: pp. 229–43.

—— (1956). Primary maternal preoccupation. In *Collected Papers: Through Pediatrics to Psycho-Analysis*. New York: Basic Books, 1958, pp. 300–5.

—— (1958). The capacity to be alone. In *The Maturational Process and the Facilitating Environment*. New York: International Universities Press, 1965, pp. 29–36.

—— (1960). The theory of the parent–infant relationship. In *The Maturational Process and the Facilitating Environment*. New York: International Universities Press, 1965, pp. 37–55.

—— (1962). Ego integration in child development. In *The Maturational Process and the Facilitating Environment*. New York: International Universities Press, 1965, pp. 56–63.

—— (1963). Dependence in the infant-care, in child care, and in the psycho-analytic setting. In *The Maturational Process and the Facilitating Environment*. New York: International Universities Press, 1965, pp. 149–59.

—— (1967). Mirror-role of mother and family development. In *Playing and Reality*. London: Tavistock, 1985, pp. 111–18.

—— (1971). *Playing and Reality*. London: Tavistock.

—— (1974). Fear of breakdown. In G. Kohon (ed.) *The British School of Object Relations*. London: Free Association Books, 1986, pp. 173–82. (Originally published in the *International Review of Psycho-Analysis*, 1: 103–6.)

Wittenberg, I. (1997). Autism as a defense against hopelessness. In J. Mitrani and T. Mitrani (eds.) *Encounters with Autistic States*. Northvale, NJ: Jason Aronson, pp. 125–42.

Index

abandonment: clinical examples 69–70, 74, 75, 83–4, 131, 137, *see also* loss; separation
abject, jettisoned object 40
acting in 7
acting out 6
adhesive equation, Tustin on 32
adhesive identification 19–40; and adhesive equation 32; failure of mirroring, clinical example 119–22; reverence and awe 123–4
adhesive identity, autistic children 32
adhesive pseudo-object-relations 37–40
aesthetic conflict 113–14, 117–18, 125–7; clinical examples 114–16, 119–22, 122–3; containment 113–28; Frances Tustin on 124–5; giver-receiver relationship 127–8; and state of anesthesia 121
aggression, defensive organization 138
alone, capacity to be alone 26, 116
alpha elements 80; REM sleep 30
alpha function 158; reversal of 27
alpha membrane, development 29
analyst-analysand relationship 7–8; analysand's concerns for needs of analyst, clinical example 87, 89–90, 100, 101, 105; analysand's will to survive analysis 23; analyst's failure and infant-in-the-analyst 159–60; analyst's fluctuating states of consciousness 155; analyst's need to be without needs 8; collusion to transform relationship into autistic object 36; communicating imaginative conjectures 158–63; countertransference and containment 150–4; dissolution, lonely state over weekend break 44–6; errors and their role 93–4; as "gentle straitjacket" 52; giver-receiver relationship 127–8; inappropriate interpretation, clinical example 86–92; likeness to parent-child relationship 92–3; omnipotent need for analyst's failure 93–4, 141, 144–5, 159; patient's perception of analyst's limitations 166n; transference and introjection of aspects of patient's inner world 57–8, 161; withdrawal 41–2, *see also* clinical examples; countertransference; "taking the transference"
"analytic game" 150
anesthesia, premature loss of at-one-ment 121
anxieties: adhesive pseudo-object-relations 38–9; new mother, clinical example 109–10
Anzieu, D., skin ego 23–5
"as-if personality", autism 33
at-one-ment: premature loss and anesthesia 121; and two-ness 113; unbearable ecstasy 124–5, *see also* one-ness; separation; two-ness
"authoritative statements": and curiosity 135–6, 143; internal propaganda 141

interpretations 162; lack of impact and catastrophic anxiety 28; transference interpretations 6–7
introjection: analyst's, transference relationship 57–8, 161; internal object capable of bearing feelings of ecstasy 124; introjective interpretation 162; and projection 24; psychic skin 20
introjective identification 80, 148, 149, 162
introjective interpretation 162

Jacobs, Theodore J. 149
jealousy, husband during pregnancy, clinical example 100
jettisoned objects 40
Joseph, Betty: acting in 7; defensive organization 137
Jung, Carl G., persona 42

-K 168n
Kafka, Franz 118
Keats, John 113
Klein, Melanie 24, 39; countertransference 148; envy 126; fantasy and transference 5; good breast 118; idealization and separation 20; integration 103; manic position 138; mother-infant relationship, unconscious processes 85; projective identification 20; splitting and transference 5–6
Klein, Sidney, troubled separation 35
knowledge 2; oedipal situation 166n
Kohut, Heinz: idealizing transference 113; mirroring 167n
Kristeva, Julia, abject 40

Lacan, Jacques 121; idealizing transference 113
learning, and knowing 166n
Learning From the Patient (Casement) 149
Lechevalier, B., non-verbal transmission 37
Lewin, Albert 56–7
libidinal baby-self, and the mind 136
linking, attacks on 16
loss: clinical example 72–3; reaction to of normal and adhesive individual

compared 39, *see also* abandonment; separation

McDougall, J. 102
Mahler, Margaret S. 31
Maiello, S.: *in utero* "sound-object" 36; pre-natal sensual-object 167n
Mancia, Mauro: active sleep 29; development of psychic skin *in utero* 29–30; *in utero* mental life 167n
manic position 138
masculinity: clinical example 74–5, *see also* father
maternal container 165n
maternal projective identification 167n
maternal transference: clinical example 14–15, *see also* mother-infant relationship
me-ness, and otherness 104
meaning: collapse of in adhesive pseudo-object-relationship 39; infant's knowledge of mother's "inside" world 117–18, *see also* mind; thinking
Meltzer, Donald 125; aesthetic conflict 117–18, 125; unintegration 27–9
mind: and libidinal baby-self 136; of ones own 16, *see also* ego; meaning; thinking
mirroring object 116, 167–8n; failure of 121
Money-Kyrle, R. E., introjective identification 148, 149
mother-infant relationship: aesthetic conflict 117–18; autistic defences against depressive anxiety 36; containment and detoxification 80; good-enough mothering 26; likeness to analyst-analysand relationship 92–3; maternal container 165n; maternal preoccupation 16; maternal projective identification 165n; mirroring 167–8n; and mother's inadequate support 34; over-protection 34; unconscious processes 85; voice and silence *in utero* 36; withdrawal 41, *see also in utero*; infant; maternal transference; pregnancy
mourning, clinical example 72–3